Our New Social Life

Our New Social Life

*Science-Backed Strategies for Creating
Meaningful Connection*

Natalie Kerr and Jaime Kurtz

OXFORD
UNIVERSITY PRESS

Oxford University Press is a department of the University of Oxford. It furthers
the University's objective of excellence in research, scholarship, and education
by publishing worldwide. Oxford is a registered trade mark of Oxford University
Press in the UK and certain other countries.

Published in the United States of America by Oxford University Press
198 Madison Avenue, New York, NY 10016, United States of America.

Library of Congress Cataloging-in-Publication Data
Names: Kerr, Natalie, 1973– author. | Kurtz, Jaime, author.
Title: Our new social life : science-backed strategies for creating meaningful connection /
Natalie Kerr and Jaime Kurtz.
Description: New York, NY : Oxford University Press, [2025] |
Includes bibliographical references and index.
Identifiers: LCCN 2024021268 (print) | LCCN 2024021269 (ebook) |
ISBN 9780197749951 (hardback) | ISBN 9780197749975 (epub)
Subjects: LCSH: Interpersonal relations. | Loneliness.
Classification: LCC HM1106 .L395 2025 (print) | LCC HM1106 (ebook) |
DDC 302—dc23/eng/20240725
LC record available at https://lccn.loc.gov/2024021268
LC ebook record available at https://lccn.loc.gov/2024021269

DOI: 10.1093/oso/9780197749951.001.0001

Printed by Marquis Book Printing, Canada

Contents

Contents

Preface

We have a confession to make.

We are two social psychologists who have spent decades exploring the complexities of social life. We've shared our knowledge with thousands of students, as well as with audiences of teachers, health care providers, retirees, and conference attendees. From what we've learned and from what we've lived, we know that one of the biggest contributors to a happy and healthy life is the quality of our social connections. It is this core belief that got us here, writing this book, to share what we have learned with you.

And yet, we have both struggled to find meaningful social connection at certain times in our own lives. We're just like countless others around the world who've discovered that the road to connection isn't always easy to navigate; it's often full of speedbumps, roadblocks, and detours, especially in the modern world where so many people are overscheduled and overwhelmed. Of course, rocky roads aren't always bad. Sometimes, an unexpected detour leads to a breathtaking vista that you never could have imagined. But, other times, you find yourself stranded on the side of the road, feeling alone and wondering whether you'll ever reach your destination.

For Natalie, a significant detour occurred when she accepted a faculty position at James Madison University (JMU), which required her to move away from Richmond, Virginia, where she had deep roots, to Harrisonburg, Virginia, where she didn't know a soul. Here's the story in her own words:

After completing my Ph.D., I wanted to find an academic position close to Richmond, but the closest opportunity was a visiting (temporary) position at JMU in Harrisonburg, about two hours away. I took the job thinking that I'd stay for one year. As fate would have it, two important things happened during that year: I was offered a permanent position at JMU, and I met and fell in love with someone who lived in the area. Because the job opportunity was so incredible—and I wanted to see where the relationship would lead—I decided to stay. And I'm still here, 21 years later.

In those early days, I didn't like Harrisonburg—and secretly hoped that I would be able to move back to Richmond one day—but I slowly began to settle down. I made a few close friends, married the man I fell in love with, and got involved in some local organizations. My social life wasn't exactly vibrant, but it was good enough.

Things changed once I started a family. I discovered firsthand why they say "it takes a village to raise a child" and I had to admit: I didn't have much of a village. Like me, my husband had relocated to this area, and our families and closest friends were several hours away. We loved hanging out with our local friends, but we naturally spent less time with them as we became parents and they chose not to. Also, in the beginning, we had trouble making friends with other parents, for a few different reasons. One reason was that we were slightly older than the other parents we crossed paths with (though, in hindsight, I realize that the problem was not the age difference as much as our limiting beliefs about it). Another reason was that I developed a chronic illness that depleted my energy. After taking care of professional and family obligations, I simply had no energy left for socializing. So, after a while, I started to feel lonely. As the loneliness grew, I started to feel anxious in social settings, especially around women who had "mom friend" potential. I wasn't normally an anxious person, but I became increasingly anxious pursuing the thing I wanted most: connection.

One night, I awoke in the middle of the night in a panic. My heart was pounding. I had a single terrifying thought: *Other than my husband and me, no one in this town loves my kid like family.* The thought didn't just make me feel sad and alone; it made me feel unsafe. I didn't understand why until, a short while later, I came across the book *Loneliness: Human Nature and the Need for Social Connection.*[1] I learned the theory that loneliness evolved as a biological warning system to alert humans to the dangers of being alone and to motivate them to reconnect with others. And, because the brain interprets perceived social isolation as a threat to survival, loneliness is often accompanied by anxiety. I suddenly understood what was happening to me. It was a comfort to realize that there was nothing wrong with me! In fact, everything was working as it should: My brain was just trying to signal that my social life needed attention.

After reading Cacioppo's book, I began to devour the scientific literature on loneliness (which we'll highlight in Chapter 3). I learned that overcoming loneliness isn't always as simple as making new friends. Sometimes, the biological warning system of loneliness goes a little haywire and you have to consciously work to correct the malfunction. With this new understanding, I began the work needed to overcome my own loneliness, using a number of different strategies that we'll share later in the book. After several months of applying the strategies and reaching out to others in new ways, I was able to emerge from that season of loneliness and make some of the best friends I've ever had. Today, I still miss having family nearby, and I still feel lonely on occasion, but I'm incredibly grateful for the village I've built. Harrisonburg now feels like *home*.

If Natalie's story resonates with you—if you haven't found your village or you've moved far away from it—know that you're not alone. As we'll see in the pages ahead, there are millions of people around the world who feel isolated and alone. And there are countless others who simply want more from their relationships, including Jaime. Here's her story:

Like many people pursuing an academic career, my 20s and 30s required some pretty dramatic residential moves—from Pennsylvania to Virginia to California to Oregon and then, finally, back to Virginia. During this time, I learned that I was totally fine with picking up and moving to a place where I knew no one, certain I'd quickly connect with people over a shared passion for outdoor adventures, wineries, local theatre, or—if we ran out of more fun topics—the stress of the academic job market during a recession. Armed with this confidence, I happily hopscotched from one part of the country to another, eager to soak up all that a new place had to offer. After all, I was young and free and I figured I could always just settle down and find long-term, deep connections later.

When I finally landed a permanent faculty job and was able to set down roots in Virginia, I was forced to look at my social life in a new way. And I realized that my previous presumption—that I'd just create deeper connections later—was a bit naïve. Yes, I was pretty good at forming quick, casual acquaintanceships. I was adept at small talk and was (and still am) eager for what I now call "activity partners"—people who are open to exploring new places and having adventures. But I realized that I wasn't sure how to convert these relationships into the sorts of close friendships that I craved in this new, stable adult life. How do people go from "hiking buddies" or "karaoke friends" to something deeper and long-lasting? How do people nurture and maintain relationships over the course of years, not just months? I was learning first-hand that I wasn't sure. This was a humbling realization . . . and a lonely one.

I also realized that, while my high school and college friends were sharing social media posts highlighting their enduring friendships, I hadn't maintained close contact with almost anyone from this part of my past. Nor had they with me. Same for all of the cool people I had met in my short-term stints in California and Oregon. Sure, we occasionally "liked" each other's Facebook posts and wished each other a happy birthday, but there were no lengthy phone chats or plans to get together in the future.

Why did these relationships fade? Was it because I had moved around a lot? Did our lives just take different paths? Did we not put in the work? Or was there more to it? I started to think that maybe I just didn't know how to cultivate deep and lasting friendships and I worried about what this meant for my life in Virginia.

At this new stage in life, one where I had finally achieved so many markers of stability—a permanent address, a permanent job—I also wanted to cultivate permanent relationships. I started to read up on how to do this thing that other people seem to do so naturally. Some of what I learned felt risky and scary: it turns out that short-term acquaintanceships, focused on shared interests and activities, are easy! You make small talk, you laugh, you explore, and you can easily avoid the tougher topics. Short-term acquaintances don't call you in tears late at night. They don't reveal their deepest fears and insecurities. But this might just be what gives them the depth to endure over the years. Researcher Brené Brown's work on vulnerability really opened my eyes to the importance of letting your guard down and sharing vulnerabilities to develop deeper friendships. It's hard for me to avoid couching these things in humor and self-deprecation (or packaging vulnerability, as psychologist Marisa Franco calls it). But I'm trying!

I also realized that relationships require an investment of time and energy. I really try to make my favorite people a priority, trying to never fall back on "I'm too busy" (after all, doesn't that often just mean "you're not a priority?"). Investing in community has also really helped me feel more rooted in where I live, rather than being someone who's just passing through. I try to check in on friends who are having a tough time. I work harder at listening. I've started volunteering in our local theater and running communities. I recently became the volunteer race director of a beloved community four-mile run/walk and breast cancer fundraiser. I still relish making casual acquaintanceships over shared interests (not every relationship can be deep, right?), but I'm enjoying flexing this new social muscle as well.

It's not easy for us to confess these things. To say, "This is hard for us, too." Yet the truth is that it's difficult for many people to create and sustain meaningful social connection in the modern world, despite how much we want it. But there is good news! We wrote this book because, while we've discovered that there are some predictable rough patches on the road to connection, we also know that the science of connection offers a useful roadmap for navigating around them. This map has been tremendously helpful in our own lives. We hope it's helpful in yours, too.

Introduction

If you could change one thing about your social life, what, if anything, would you change?

Would you want more casual friends to hang out with on Saturday nights? Or more *close* friends—the ones who bring over chicken noodle soup when you're sick? Do you want a best friend who prioritizes spending time with you? A romantic partner who loves and appreciates you? Or do you simply want more time to socialize?

We recently asked the "if you could change one thing" question in an anonymous online survey and heard things like:

- I'd want fewer, but closer friends.
- I'd be more extraverted.
- I'd be more comfortable talking to new people.
- I'd have less anxiety about social situations.
- I'd have a life partner.
- I'd put in more effort to see my old friends.
- I'd want to see friends more often, outside of playdates that are focused on my kids.
- I'd live in a tight-knit community where everyone knows and cares about their neighbors.
- I'd change the way I communicate with people—less superficial small talk at the expense of real connection.
- I'd have friends from different backgrounds and cultures.
- I'd close the geographical distance between me and my friends (or get a pilot's license!).

Respondents also indicated their wish that:

- People would be more open to informal and spontaneous hangouts (like dropping by someone's house).
- There were more human-to-human interactions and fewer digital ones.
- There was less pressure to have social media.

These responses highlight the fact that many of us are craving more—and more meaningful—social connection. More systematic research tells a similar story. In a 2023 survey of people from 142 countries, only 35% said they felt "very connected" to others. Half of respondents admitted that they felt some degree of loneliness.[1] How is it that, on a planet with more than 8 billion people, so many of us feel alone? It certainly seems like we're in the midst of what experts call a "crisis of connection" or an "epidemic of loneliness."[2]

Many people are reluctant to admit to feeling lonely, but loneliness is not a personal failing. It is simply the negative feeling that arises when we perceive a *discrepancy between what we want from our relationships and what we're getting.* And, in modern life, it's becoming increasingly difficult to get what we want, socially speaking. The truth is that many people—lonely or not—feel like something's missing in their relationships. Why is that? What's making it so hard? In the online survey we mentioned earlier, we asked the question: "What prevents you from having a more satisfying social life?" Respondents frequently noted their busy lives, and the fact that people are "always on their phones." Other common responses were:

- I'm exhausted.
- My social anxiety gets in the way.
- The people I most want to see either live far away or have different daily and weekly rhythms than I do.
- I don't have anyone to watch my kids, and babysitters are too expensive.
- My life seems to revolve around my child's travel soccer schedule.
- I had to relocate because of my job, and I haven't made any new friends in this town.
- It's hard to make friends as an adult.
- I tend to be awkward at times.
- I worry that people won't like me.
- I can't find "my people."
- I don't know how to connect.

These responses reveal that there are many different barriers to social connection in the modern world. As scientists who study social behavior, and as people with social lives of our own, we often think, *Connection shouldn't be this hard!* But it *is* hard for many of us living in the 21st century.

This complicated social landscape is what we call *our new social life.* In the new social life, it's becoming increasingly difficult to create and sustain meaningful social connection. In our view, socializing today is a bit like eating a modern "Western" diet that's full of ultra-processed foods—or "edible food-like substances," as journalist Michael Pollan calls them.[3] These junk foods tend to satisfy us in the moment, but they also leave us deeply hungry for more. Similarly, there's plenty of "junk" in our social diet that leaves us wanting more. For example, passively scrolling through social media might feel good in the moment, but it can ultimately leave us feeling dissatisfied and disconnected. There's also a parallel between the way we eat and the way we socialize, especially in the Western world. In both domains, we like things *fast*. We might pull into the drive-thru instead of making a healthier meal at home, just like we might choose to send a quick text message to a friend instead of calling. We end up sacrificing quality for convenience. And, when we're especially exhausted, stressed, or busy, we might choose to forgo the meal—or the connection—altogether.

Another parallel is that both eating and socializing in the modern world can be downright confusing. With food, it's hard to know when, what, and how much to eat. *Should I eat breakfast? Can I snack in between meals? Do I have to cut back on carbs? And what's so bad about gluten?* Just like healthy eating has become complicated, connecting with other people has become unnecessarily complicated, too. Many of us are apprehensive about—or simply don't know—the most effective ways to connect. How do you make new friends when you move to a new city, or you're newly divorced? How do you have a meaningful conversation without making things awkward?

The purpose of *Our New Social Life* is to help make social life a little less complicated and a lot more satisfying. We will identify some key barriers to social connection and provide evidence-based strategies for overcoming them. Despite the sometimes difficult terrain, we firmly believe that everyone can learn to navigate the modern social world in a way that satisfies their deepest cravings.

Removing the Barriers to Connection in the Modern World

If you ask Google how to find social connection, you might come across advice like "join a club," "meet new people," or "visit places where you can be around other people, like a park." This common-sense advice implies that the way to create connection is simply to reach out to other people. Reaching out *is* important, as we'll explain in later chapters, but it's often not enough. It might even backfire for people who view the social world as a risky or hostile place. That's why we believe that the *first* step toward greater connection is to identify and remove the obstacles that stand in the way of it.

In his musings about love, the 13th-century mystic Rumi wrote: "Your task is not to seek for love, but merely to seek and find all the barriers within yourself that you have built against it." Rumi believed that when you remove the barriers, you can feel the love that's always available to you. Similarly, if you're looking for more *connection*, your primary task is not to simply meet new people. It's to find and remove the barriers that stand in the way of greater connection. When you remove the barriers—even just one or two of them— you might discover that connection happens more easily, and more naturally.

In this book, we will shed light on seven key barriers to social connection— each corresponding to a different chapter—and offer research-based strategies for removing them. Some of these strategies might seem obvious (although we suspect that they are often easier to understand than they are to execute), but others might surprise you. (For example, did you know that meditating can help you feel more socially connected, even when you're doing it alone?) The strategies in the book can help you live a more connected life, and they might also help you live a *longer* life. As we'll see, research shows that your feelings of connection are a significant predictor of how long you'll live![4]

So, what are the barriers to connection? There are dozens—maybe hundreds— of beliefs, behaviors, and social forces that make it harder for us to connect with others, and we've organized them around seven key barriers. Some of the barriers are clearly a function of modern life, while others are more timeless. In the chapters that follow, we'll explain each barrier, explore why it exists, and offer practical, research-based advice for how to overcome it. Here's an overview:

Barrier #1: We View Social Connection as a Luxury Rather Than an Essential Human Need

As humans, we have a fundamental need for social connection. We live happier, healthier, and longer lives when we have enough of it. And yet, in the modern world, we often view socializing as a luxury we can afford to live without. It feels more like an *indulgence* than an essential health behavior. When we feel pressed for time, and want to cut back on something, happy hours, date nights, and brunches with friends are often the first things to go. This mindset is a barrier to connection we'll explore in Chapter 1.

Barrier #2: We're Influenced by Social Norms That Foster Disconnection

Social norms, the unwritten rules for typical and desirable behavior, have a subtle yet powerful influence on us. From the way we interact with strangers on a train to the way we date, these unwritten rules prescribe what is "normal" or acceptable behavior in a given context. Many of us feel pressure to align our behavior with the norms of modern life, but doing so can ultimately leave us feeling adrift. For example, research has shown that:

- We are spending less and less time hanging out with family and friends, and more time on our devices.
- The size of our social networks has decreased.
- We view busyness as a status symbol—and pack our schedules so full that there's little room left for spontaneous connection.
- Many of today's parents are, as one psychologist put it, "sacrificing their social lives on the altar of intensive parenting."[5]

If we want to improve our social lives, we need to recognize the often subtle but powerful influence social norms have on us—and be willing to push back against them at times. We'll take a closer look at these social forces in Chapter 2.

Barrier #3: Our Thoughts Distort Our Perception of the Social World

Countless self-help books offer some variation of this advice: change your mind, change your life. It's good advice! Decades of research show that our thoughts can have a huge impact on our health and well-being, as well as on the success of our relationships.

When it comes to thinking about our social world, we have a few common biases and blind spots that prevent us from seeing things clearly. For example, most of us think we're better-than-average in a number of domains (like driving ability), but we're overly pessimistic about our social life. We inaccurately think that other people attend more parties, have more friends, and enjoy a larger social circle than we do ourselves. It's a blind spot that leaves us dissatisfied for no good reason. In Chapter 3, we'll point out some of the common biases in social thinking and help you develop a more accurate—or even a rosier—perspective, one that can make it easier to connect with others.

Barrier #4: We Have Miscalibrated Expectations of Social Interaction

Research shows that we also have mistaken (or "miscalibrated") expectations about reaching out and connecting with others. We tend to underestimate how much we'll enjoy socializing and how much others will appreciate our efforts to connect. This keeps us from doing things like striking up conversations with strangers (who might eventually become friends), expressing gratitude to those we've never properly thanked, and offering social support to friends in need. The gap between our expectations and other people's experiences creates a barrier to social connection but, as we'll explain in Chapter 4, the gap *can* successfully be bridged.

Barrier #5: We Overlook the Simple Factors That Create Connection

What determines whether you like a new person, or have chemistry with a potential romantic partner? You might think that the process of interpersonal liking is mysterious, or determined by a person's unique attributes—like a great sense of humor or good looks, for example. These factors *do* matter, but research in social psychology suggests that liking is also triggered by simple, mundane factors—like how often you cross paths with someone, or how much you have in common. Overlooking these simple factors can cause you to miss out on opportunities for connection that are right in front of you. We'll discuss this barrier and ways to sidestep it in Chapter 5.

Barrier #6: We're Reluctant to Do What It Takes to Create Deeper Connection

Many of us crave deep, meaningful connection, but we're often reluctant to engage in the behaviors that help foster this type of connection—things like having deep conversations, disclosing personal information, and showing vulnerability. In Chapter 6, we'll show you why opening up might seem emotionally risky, and why it's a risk worth taking. We'll offer suggestions on how to dive deeper into your relationships and reemerge with a stronger, more satisfying sense of connection to others.

Barrier #7: We Miss Opportunities to Create Connection on Demand

When we think about improving our social lives, we tend to think about changing our circumstances, often in dramatic ways (*I'd have more friends if*

I moved to a more progressive city). Or we wait for other people to show up (*I'll be happy once I get married*). But research shows that we don't have to wait for our circumstances to change. Perhaps even more surprisingly, we don't need to be in the presence of other people in order to feel connected! We can create connection on demand, by engaging in practices that boost our inner, subjective sense of connection. In the final chapter, we'll discuss strategies that help us increase this inner sense of connection—including being a better friend to ourselves, practicing meditation, experiencing gratitude, spending time in nature, and getting in touch with our spiritual side.

Making This Book Work for You

We realize that everyone who picks up this book has their own unique motivations for doing so. Maybe you just moved to a new town and—because you haven't had to make new friends in ages—you aren't sure how to connect with the strangers all around you. Maybe you already have a wide range of acquaintances and casual friends, but you're not sure how to convert them into deep, lasting friendships. You might feel that nagging sense of loneliness that plagues so many of us—or you're hoping to help a child, parent, or friend cope with their own social struggles. Or maybe you're just interested in the science of social connection!

Regardless of the reason, we know that no two readers are the same. Having said that, though, we do want to lay out a few general principles that have guided our thinking and writing.

This Book Is for *Everyone*

Just as everyone has their own reason for reading this book, everyone faces unique barriers on the path to connection, depending on their relationship history, social aptitude, social identity, and a host of other factors. We can't include all of these factors in the book, but we tried to write in a way that reflects the full spectrum of experiences. This *is* a book for *everyone*, including:

- Extraverts, introverts, and those who fall in between.
- Females, males, and nonbinary people.
- People from racial and sexual minority groups.
- Those who are socially anxious.
- Those who are neurodivergent.

- People struggling with their mental health.
- People living with a physical disability or chronic illness.
- People across the lifespan—from late adolescence to late adulthood.

Not Every Piece of Advice Will Suit Every Reader

Of course, writing a book that we hope is useful to everyone means that not every piece of advice will suit every reader. As you progress through the various chapters, some ideas may make you think, *I already do that!* or *That absolutely does not suit my personality* or even *That sounds dreadful.* This is to be expected. In the same way that a personal fitness trainer wouldn't suggest the exact same exercise plan for every person, we would be naïve if we thought that everyone needs to work on their social fitness in the exact same way. To give just a few examples, someone with social anxiety might feel overwhelmed at the idea of striking up a conversation with a stranger. A person whose trust has been violated in the past might balk at the idea of opening up and being vulnerable with a new friend. Certain physical limitations or living in a dense urban environment might make a nature walk inaccessible. And being neurodivergent could make many of our strategies seem out-of-reach.

It's important to point out that—as is often the case with social-psychological research—much of the work we'll be describing here relies on college students as research participants. This is often out of convenience: because so much academic research takes place in universities, students are an easily accessible population. We do include research from other populations when available, but we don't want to assume that the findings generalize to all people. You are the best judge of what does and does not seem to fit you and your unique circumstances.

Moreover, while the strategies we'll be telling you about are all backed by research, it's important to realize that the results are based on *averages*. Some people may have benefited from a strategy, others less so. People are different! So, if in your gut something truly just doesn't seem right for you, move on! That said, we *are* confident that there is something in here for everyone. Some strategies might immediately seem interesting and manageable. With these, we encourage you to jump right in. Others might seem intimidating at first, but they might just seem more accessible as your confidence grows. We encourage you to reconsider these later, because you might feel differently at another time, or with another person.

There Are No Guarantees

You might love the idea of a specific strategy we explain here, but know that, if you try it out, the person on the receiving end might not respond exactly as you wish. For example, let's say you try out the simple strategy of giving a genuine compliment. You approach someone, say something nice to them, and they don't respond in the way you'd hoped. That's disappointing. But, really, you just never know: a person might be busy, distracted, anxious, unusually averse to compliments, or any number of other things. It doesn't mean the strategy is bad, and we encourage you to keep trying.

More Isn't Always Better

Throughout the book, we'll suggest strategies such as simply being physically present, making eye contact, pointing out similarities, smiling, asking questions, and expressing gratitude. We don't suggest a specific "dosage" of a given strategy (meaning, how intensely or how much to do it)—it depends on the context, the person you're interacting with, the chemistry between the two of you, and many other factors. But we hesitate to have you "max out" on a given strategy. Small doses, while paying attention to the feedback you're receiving, can take you quite far.

It Takes Time

Some of the strategies in the book will help you feel more connected almost instantly, but forming and strengthening genuine, enduring relationships takes time. Researcher Jeffrey Hall found that it takes about 40–60 hours for someone to transition from an acquaintance to a casual friend and more than 200 hours for them to become a good or best friend.[6] Try to be patient with the process.

Some Issues Cut Deeper

While neither of us are clinical psychologists, we know that many of the issues underlying social disconnection and loneliness have deep roots, including adverse childhood experiences, harsh rejection, betrayal, or abuse.

We also know that, for many people with these past experiences, the thought of reaching out to others can be accompanied by crippling anxiety. There are successful treatments for these sorts of issues. If you need help overcoming trauma or dealing with other mental health challenges, we encourage you to seek professional treatment—or check out a self-help workbook.

And keep reading this book. It's not a substitute for psychotherapy, but we think it could be a useful supplement. After all, learning strategies for more and better connection can help to ease the burden of life's struggles, providing healthy distractions, new perspectives on problems, a sense that we're not alone, and the opportunity to laugh. Plus, many of the strategies in the book can improve your psychological well-being alongside your social life.

A Better Social Life

Our new social life can be challenging—and, if we're being honest, sometimes lonely. But the things you'll learn in this book can help you overcome the challenges of modern social life and create deep, meaningful, lasting connection.

We won't promise it will always be easy. Some of the strategies you'll learn will require you to challenge well-worn habits, intuitions, and social norms. Some will push you outside of your comfort zone. But, if you're willing to make some changes and accept a little discomfort, you'll likely be rewarded with a better social life.

As you learn more about the barriers to connection and begin to implement some of the strategies to overcome them, remember that you're not alone. We're all in this together. We're all trying to find our bearings in this busy, distracted, and divided world.

Together, let's get started.

1
Social by Nature

Why Connection Is an Essential Need

Man is by nature a social animal.

—Aristotle

In the reality television show *Alone*, ten contestants—all trained survival experts—are dropped off in a remote wilderness area where they must survive in total isolation. They carry cameras to document their experiences, which revolve around finding food, water, and warmth, and avoiding unfriendly encounters with grizzly bears and other predators. The ultimate goal is to be the "last person standing" who wins up to a million dollars.[1]

What's striking about this show is that many of the contestants struggle more with being alone than with the hunger pangs and freezing temperatures. Many of those who drop out of the competition do so because they can't deal with the misery of extreme social isolation. As one of the contestants from Season 1 said, "The real challenge is the psychology of being here alone . . . I don't have any interaction whatsoever, except for me and this camera, and it's freaking me out." Just before dropping out, he added, "The isolation . . . completely broke my spirit. It broke my will."

In dramatic fashion, the show *Alone* highlights the reality that humans are social animals. We're made to be in relationships with one another. We're not meant to be completely alone. Research confirms this, too.[2] All of us—male or female, young or old, introverted or extraverted—share in the funda-mental need:

To belong.
To be loved and accepted.
To feel deeply connected to the people in our lives.

While we might experience this in different ways and to different degrees, our need for social connection is as essential as our need for food, water, and shelter.[3] We simply can't survive—let alone thrive—without the support of other people. Our need for people is so fundamental that we have built-in biological mechanisms to motivate us to seek out social connection, just as we have mechanisms to ensure that we eat and drink when necessary. When we are socially isolated, our brain triggers cravings for human contact that are similar to the ones evoked by hunger.[4] We *literally* crave connection!

Looking Ahead

In this chapter, we'll make the case that humans have an essential need for social connection, and that we live happier, healthier, and longer lives with enough of it. We'll also discuss the first of seven key barriers to social connection in today's world: viewing social connection as a luxury we can afford to live without. By the end of the chapter, we hope to convince you that you're a social animal with a hard-wired need for connection—and to motivate you to socialize like *your life depends on it.*

Before we start addressing the barriers, let's make sure we're all thinking about social connection in the same way. What *is* social connection? What are the different types of social connection? And why should we care about it?

What Is Social Connection?

Researchers use *social connection* as an umbrella term that encompasses the structure, function, and quality of social relationships. The structural component of social connection involves the number of your social relationships and the frequency of your social interactions. The functional component involves the degree to which you can rely on others for support. And the quality component involves the degree to which your relationships are personally satisfying. All three of these components—structure, function, and quality—are important predictors of health and well-being.[5]

Social connection exists on a continuum ranging from highly connected to highly disconnected. And, importantly, social connection involves both objective elements (like the number of friends you have) and subjective ones (like your perception of how supportive those friends are). You can have a lot of friends but still feel disconnected if you feel like they don't support you, understand you, or prioritize spending time with you. Perception is reality, as they say. In the same vein, social disconnection can involve objective social isolation or loneliness (which can be thought of as a subjective sense of isolation). Social isolation involves being physically alone whereas loneliness involves *feeling* alone, even while surrounded by other people.

We have written this book to help you improve the objective markers of connection—like the breadth and depth of your social ties. But we also want to help you increase your inner, subjective sense of connection. Both of these things are important for a healthy social life. Improving the objective aspects of connection will require the cooperation of other people, and may take a little time. But you can strengthen your inner sense of connection on your own. You don't have to wait for your social circle to grow, or for your social calendar to fill. You can feel more connected by simply changing your thoughts or engaging in some of the practices described later in the book. This source of inner connection is helpful to draw upon when you're physically alone (an idea we'll explore in more depth in Chapter 7). It also provides a solid foundation on which meaningful relationships can be built.

Three Sources of Social Connection

Social psychologists have identified three primary sources of (objective) social connection: intimate connection, relational connection, and collective connection. *Intimate* connection is the feeling of connection to a "significant someone." This is the person you can rely on for emotional support during crises. The one who will show up for you, no matter the inconvenience. The one who most affirms your value as a person.[6] In the film *Shall We Dance?*, Susan Sarandon's character describes an intimate connection as one in which you serve as a witness to the other person's life: "you're promising to care about everything: the good things, the bad things, the terrible things, the mundane things, all of it . . . You're saying, 'your life will not go unnoticed because I will notice it. Your life will not go unwitnessed because *I will be your witness*.'"[7]

People who are married or living with a romantic partner tend to feel more intimately connected than others, but, of course, not everyone in a romantic relationship feels close to their partner. And you can find intimate connection outside of a romantic relationship, too. In the television show *Grey's Anatomy*, Cristina Yang (Sandra Oh) and Meredith Grey (Ellen Pompeo) are friends who develop an intimate connection. Before a frightening medical procedure, the normally stoic Cristina tells Meredith that she put her name down as an emergency contact: "The clinic has a policy. They wouldn't let me confirm my appointment unless I designated an emergency contact person, someone to be there just in case and to help me home . . . Anyway, I put your name down. You're my person."

Cristina's declaration ("you're my person") has become a catchphrase in popular American culture.[8] It has appeared in thousands of Instagram posts, which feature many different types of intimate connection—spouses, best friends, siblings, parents, grandparents, even pets. Clearly, there is no standard formula for intimate connection. And some people have more than one "person" who helps them feel intimately connected.

The second type—*relational* connection—is the feeling of connection to a group of supportive friends and family members. These are the people you hang out with regularly. The ones who show up for your kid's performance in the school musical. The ones who are willing to help you move large pieces of furniture. People with a large circle of supportive friends and family members tend to feel more relationally connected than those with a smaller circle; however, there's no magic number here. The size of the ideal circle will be different for everyone. Plus, the quality of your relationships is more important than the quantity. What matters is feeling supported and cared about.[9]

The third type of connection—*collective* connection—is the feeling of belonging to meaningful groups such as a church choir, volleyball club, alumni association, political party, or even the Harry Potter fandom. Not surprisingly, you can gauge this by simply assessing the number of voluntary groups you belong to. Of course, quality matters here, too. It's best to belong to groups in which people personally know and care about you. One of the reasons why people love going to group fitness studios is that many of them intentionally cultivate a sense of belonging. One of our friends calls Orangetheory Fitness her "home away from home." She shows up for classes 4 to 6 days a week, not just for fitness, but also for the sense of community the space provides.

Psychologist John Cacioppo, one of the pioneers of research on loneliness, likened the three sources of connection—intimate, relational, and collective—to a three-legged stool. He argued that we need all three types and "when events knock one of the three legs of the stool out from under you . . . the safe and comforting feeling of stability falls away, and even someone who has always felt intensely connected can begin to feel lonely."[10] As we'll see in later chapters, it's not enough to find "the one." People are better off when they get their connection from multiple sources—intimate partners, friends, immediate and extended family members, coworkers, neighbors, and acquaintances. Even minimal social interactions with strangers can leave you feeling happier and more connected than you might think.[11] To be sure, opportunities for greater connection are all around you, and they might look different than you expect.

Social Connection as an Essential Need

Some of you may be thinking: *sure, social connection makes me happy, but is it really an essential need?* There's strong evidence suggesting that it is. In fact, social neuroscientist Matthew Lieberman argues that our need for social connection is just as essential as our need for food, water, and shelter.[12] Consider infants, who are born into a state of complete dependency: they need food to survive, but they also need someone to feed them. They won't survive without someone who's committed to caring for them until they're old enough to care for themselves. And while it will manifest in different ways throughout our lives, this fundamental social need remains paramount. We need other people to care about us throughout our entire lives.

Lieberman and his colleagues—including his wife, Naomi Eisenberger—have conducted numerous studies that support the idea that social connection is an essential need. Their research examines what happens in the brain when we experience *social pain*—the pain we feel when we're picked last in a game of dodge ball, when we experience a breakup, or when we're grieving the loss of a loved one. In one study, they asked participants to get into an fMRI scanner and play an online video game called *Cyberball*. During the game, participants threw a digital ball around with what they believed to be two other players, also in fMRI scanners. In reality, the other "players" were characters controlled by a computer program that stopped throwing the ball to the participant after a few minutes. The game was designed to mimic the experience of being socially excluded (while also respecting the constraints of the fMRI machine, in which a person must lie very still and refrain from talking). Once the game ended, participants climbed out of the scanner and filled out a survey about their experience. It might surprise you to learn that being left out of a virtual game of catch hurts people's feelings, but that's what happened: participants reported feeling ignored and excluded.[13]

What's really fascinating about this study is the neurological data. When the researchers analyzed the results of the brain scans, they found that the experience of exclusion (a type of social pain) was processed in the same part of the brain that processes physical pain (the dorsal anterior cingulate cortex). The results of this study—and several others—show that social and physical pain share a common neural mechanism, and that social pain is every bit as "real" as physical pain. We might use statements like "it hurt me when you said that" or "you broke my heart" as metaphors for pain, but it's far more than that. Rejection literally hurts.

Surprising as they initially seem, the results of this research make sense when you think about the purpose of pain. As much as we wish to avoid it, pain helps ensure that we take care of our essential needs. When we need water, the aversive state of thirst motivates us to find something to drink. When we need food, the pain of hunger motivates us to open the fridge or call out for pizza. If social connection is truly an essential need, we would expect to experience some type of pain when we're low on it. And we do: we feel the strong signals of rejection, loneliness, and other forms of social distress. These painful experiences often motivate us to repair or replace our social bonds. As Lieberman concludes: "the neural overlap between social and physical pain . . . ensures that we will spend our entire lives motivated by social connection."[14]

Neuroscientist Kay Tye and her collaborators have explored the neural underpinnings of this motivation. They proposed that social animals, including humans, have neural circuits dedicated to maintaining "social homeostasis." In general, homeostasis refers to any process organisms use to maintain stable conditions necessary for survival. For example, the homeostatic system of thermoregulation detects the body's temperature, compares it to an established set point (98.6°F) and triggers a response to cool or warm the body as needed. *Social* homeostasis is the ability of individuals to detect the quantity and quality of social contact, compare this information to an established set point (one's desired level of social contact), and make changes to seek the optimal level of social contact.[15]

Tye and her colleagues have tested the idea of social homeostasis by isolating mice, highly social animals who prefer the company of other mice. When a mouse is left alone for 24 hours, neurons deep within the brain create a "loneliness-like state" that increases their motivation to engage in social contact. When the mouse is brought back to the group cage, it experiences a rebound of social interaction. For a time, the mouse is even more social than usual, which helps correct the social deficit and maintain homeostasis.

Does the same thing happen in humans? To find out, Tye partnered with Livia Tomova and a group of other researchers. They asked 40 socially active volunteers to come to their lab and spend 10 hours alone—with no social interaction and no other social stimulation (like scrolling through social media, checking email, or even reading fiction). After 10 hours of isolation, the participants had their brains scanned while they looked at pictures of their favorite social activities. For comparison, the researchers asked the same participants to undergo 10 hours of fasting (on a different day) and have their brains scanned while looking at pictures of their favorite foods.[16]

Tye, Tomova, and their colleagues confirmed that isolation had the intended effect: it resulted in greater loneliness and an increased motivation to seek out social interaction. Then, they compared the brain scans for the two states of deprivation. They found that the brain's responses to viewing social images after isolation were very similar to the brain's responses to viewing food images after fasting. In both cases, the brain triggered a craving response. The authors concluded that people who are forced to be isolated crave social interaction in much the same way that a hungry person craves food. (No wonder so many of us felt starved for connection during the COVID-19 lockdowns!)

This study adds to the accumulating evidence that social contact is regulated in a homeostatic manner and that social connection is an essential need. When we experience a social deficit—during a global pandemic, after a breakup, or when a demanding work schedule crowds out time for socializing—our brain responds in ways that motivate us to correct the deficit. Social hunger may be nature's way of helping us meet one of our most basic needs.

Social Connection and Physical Health

If you want additional evidence that connection is an essential need, consider the research on social relationships and health. In 1938, researchers began following two groups of men from adolescence to old age, hoping to uncover the secrets of a well-lived life. The first group of men attended Harvard University, and the second grew up in some of the poorest neighborhoods in Boston. This study—known as the Harvard Study of Adult Development—has become one of the world's longest studies of adult life. When the study's current director, Robert Waldinger, analyzed the most recent results, he found that it wasn't wealth or fame—or even cholesterol levels—that predicted the men's well-being in later life. It was their *relationships*. He concluded, "The people who were the most satisfied in their relationships at age 50 were the healthiest at age 80."[17]

Many other studies confirm the fact that people with strong social connections enjoy greater health than those with weaker connections. Note that many of these studies are correlational by necessity. To definitively say that strong social connections *cause* long-term health outcomes, researchers would need to deprive some people of rewarding connection while allowing others to enjoy it, while also holding constant every other aspect of their lives. It's just not possible, or ethical. Still, scores of correlational studies provide convincing evidence for the link between strong social connections and good health. For example, those with supportive social relationships are less likely to catch the common cold, have a stroke, or get heart disease. And women who have a large circle of supportive friends and family members are more likely to survive breast cancer. As psychologist Susan Pinker notes, social relationships seem to create a "biological force field against disease."[18]

Social connection also predicts how long we'll live. Psychologist Julianne Holt-Lunstad and her colleagues found that people with strong social relationships are 50% less likely to die prematurely than those with weaker connections. And, on the flip side, both social isolation and loneliness (which, remember, is *perceived* social isolation) increase the risk of early death as much as obesity, excessive alcohol consumption, and smoking. After sharing this research in her 2022 TED talk, Holt-Lunstad concluded: "It's time to prioritize our relationships like our life depends on it, because it does."[19]

Social Connection and Psychological Well-Being

Social connection doesn't just add years to our lives; it also adds life to our years. Here's how:

- *It makes us happy.* People routinely say that socializing is one of the highlights of daily life, and most of us—extraverts and introverts alike—tend to be happier on days that contain more moments of social interaction. What's more, research shows that satisfying social relationships are one of the key elements of a happy life. Good relationships don't guarantee happiness, but true happiness doesn't occur without them.[20]
- *It makes the good times even better.* Research shows that pleasant experiences are more intense when they're shared with another person.[21] That's one reason why most of us want company when we're eating a delicious meal or watching a beautiful sunset. As many of us have learned, sharing these experiences amplifies the joy and appreciation they bring us. On a related note, studies show that we also laugh more when we're in the presence of others. And that makes for more than just a fun time. Laughter has clear benefits for our physical health, reducing elevated heart rate and blood pressure and releasing natural opioids that combat physical pain.[22]
- *It makes the hard times easier.* Our close social ties help us navigate life's difficulties by providing social support. And, whether it comes in the form of advice, empathy, or a ride to the airport, social support helps us buffer the damaging effects of stress. Even the mere presence of a loved one can help us feel safe and supported in hard times. One study found that if you quietly hold the hand of a supportive partner when in a stressful situation, your brain will show a diminished response to stress. Given the toxic effects of chronic stress on the body, it's easy to see how

this kind of social support is related to greater physical health and longevity over the long term.[23]

- *It makes our lives more meaningful.* Relationships that promote a strong sense of belonging make our life seem more meaningful. When we belong somewhere—whether it's a family, a group of friends, a school, a church, or a club—we get the sense that we matter. We feel like we are making contributions to the world and leaving a legacy for the future. Meanwhile, feeling like we haven't found "our people" or like we're not understood or accepted can make life seem empty and far less meaningful.[24]

The First Barrier to Social Connection

The research we've reviewed so far suggests that we have a hard-wired need for social connection—and that we live happier, healthier, and longer lives when we feel closely connected to others. The problem is that millions of people around the world feel deprived of the nourishing, life-giving relationships they need and desire. Why? Why is it so hard for us to connect in the way nature intended?

For one thing, we're living in an environment that's vastly different from the one our ancestors lived in. Hunter-gatherers lived in small groups ranging from 50 to 150 people, surrounded by familiar others on whom they depended for their very survival. Today, many of us live in cities and we're surrounded by thousands or even millions of people we don't know. Many of us live alone or in isolated nuclear families, with no grandparents, aunts, uncles, or cousins nearby (no wonder it's so hard to find a babysitter!). Additionally, in ancestral environments, there were only a few dozen potential mates to choose from. Now, today's singles have a seemingly unlimited number of potential partners—and the search to find "the one" among the multitude is often exhausting.[25]

Clearly, the social world has changed dramatically since we hunted and gathered our food. It has also changed dramatically in just *the last few years*. Before we became tethered to our smartphones, we talked to our friends on a landline phone—if they happened to be home when we called. Kids spent more time hanging out with their friends in person. And people expressed romantic interest with eye contact, body language, and words—not a careless swipe to the right.

Though the social world has changed dramatically over the years, humans actually haven't changed all that much. We're still social animals who evolved to be in relationships with one another. We still have a fundamental need for social connection. Yet, many of us view social connection as a *want* rather than a *need*. We tend to forget—or deny—our inherently social nature. More and more, we think of ourselves as isolated individuals rather than members of a family, group, neighborhood, or community.[26] In the words of Mother Teresa, "we have forgotten that we belong to one another."

It's easy to forget this truth in the modern world. Many of us can meet our basic biological needs without relying heavily on others (thanks to grocery delivery and other modern conveniences). We can survive the weather without huddling together. We don't need help fending off predators. And, thanks to modern technology, we can work, shop, join a yoga class, and learn how to play the ukulele without leaving the comfort of our own homes—and without ever having to talk to another human being. In this modern environment, it's easy to forget that we were made to depend on each other.

This creates an obvious barrier to connection. When we view social connection as a luxury rather than an essential need, we tend to relegate it to the bottom of the priority list. We tend to squeeze it in after work, after meeting family obligations, and after the chores are done. This may help explain why the average American socializes for a mere 34 minutes a day.[27]

Even Vivek Murthy, the US Surgeon General and author of the book *Together: The Healing Power of Human Connection in a Sometimes Lonely World*, failed to prioritize social connection during his first term as Surgeon General. He later reflected:

> I . . . made a critical mistake. I . . . largely neglected my friendships during my tenure, convincing myself that I had to focus on work and I couldn't do both. Even when I was physically with the people I loved, I wasn't present—I was often checking the news and responding to messages in my inbox. After my job ended, I felt ashamed to reach out to friends I had ignored. I found myself increasingly lonely and isolated, and it felt as if I was the only one who felt that way.

Murthy's struggle with isolation led him to rethink his priorities. Now in his second term as Surgeon General, he says: "I am a making a much bigger effort to build and maintain my relationships. I am a better father, husband, friend, and surgeon general as a result."[28]

As Murthy discovered, the solution to overcoming the first barrier to connection is simple, although not necessarily easy. We need to remember that we have a fundamental need to be a "we." We need to view socializing as an essential health behavior—as important as sleeping, exercising, and eating healthy meals. And we need to prioritize it accordingly.

If we want to have a healthier, more satisfying social life, we need to invest time, energy, and other resources into creating and strengthening our relationships. Imagine what would happen if we spent more time laughing with friends. If we knew our neighbors' names. If we smiled at strangers. If we weren't so lost in the virtual world. If we defined success not in terms of our wealth or productivity, but in the strength of our connections. Of course, recognizing the need to connect and knowing how to do it are two different things. Many of us want connection badly, and yet we're not sure exactly how to get it. The good news is, once we acknowledge some of the additional barriers to connection, which we lay out for you in the book, the path becomes more clear.

Let's check in with *you*. Are you sold on the idea that you have a hard-wired need for connection? Are you willing to prioritize your social life? Are you willing to invest your limited resources into growing social connection? If so:

- What are some specific ways you can incorporate more social interaction into your daily routine?
- What can you scale back on or give up in order to make more room for connection in your life? (If you're feeling stressed about a busy schedule, we'll offer some research-based suggestions for feeling more "time affluent" in the next chapter.)

Meeting *Your* Need for Connection

To overcome the first barrier to connection, we need to realize that, not only is social connection an essential need, but the need is felt differently based on some key individual differences. Indeed, each of us has been shaped by nature and nurture to have our own preferences for social interaction. In the next section, we'll explore a few of the most important differences.

Extraverts, Introverts, and Everyone In Between

You don't need a degree in psychology to know that some people are naturally more talkative and outgoing than others, and you probably know that this difference is largely due to one's level of extraversion. According to contemporary personality psychologists, extraversion reflects our level of sociability, energy, dominance, and positivity. Those who score high on extraversion (extraverts) tend to be outgoing, talkative, energetic, assertive, and joyful, while those who score low on extraversion (introverts) tend to exhibit these characteristics less often. It's important to note that introverts tend be more quiet and reserved than extraverts, but they're not necessarily shy, as many people believe. They're also not necessarily more thoughtful, reflective, or "turned inward."[29]

A key point is, both extraverts and introverts have an essential need for connection, but they satisfy that need in different ways. For example, extraverts prefer higher levels of social stimulation and activity than introverts. They engage in more conversations, say more words, and speak in a louder voice than introverts—and, online, they talk about themselves more. Extraverts also spend less time alone than introverts. Additionally, extraverts seem to get more from the social world: they tend to have larger social networks, are more satisfied with their relationships, feel more socially connected, and are generally happier than introverts.[30]

That said, much of the conversation about this personality dimension overlooks a critical point: *introversion-extraversion falls on a continuum*. Researchers use the words "introvert" and "extravert" for convenience (and so do we), but they actually view introversion-extraversion as a continuous dimension, with the majority of people landing somewhere near the middle. Very extreme extraverts and introverts are rarer than you might think. Although many people are fascinated with labels such as introverts, extraverts, and ambiverts (those who fall in the middle of the spectrum), using these categories can be problematic. Research shows that our social behavior varies greatly from situation to situation, and that personality can change over time.[31] So don't cling too tightly to labels.

It might also be useful to think of extraversion as a *state* as well as a trait.[32] An extraverted state is simply one in which you're acting like an extravert (by being talkative and sociable, for example). Extraverted states are associated with greater momentary happiness, and extraverts tend to enact these states more often, which helps explain why extraverts are generally happier than introverts. So, can introverts reap the benefits of being an extravert—just by acting like one?

In a 2020 study, researchers Seth Margolis and Sonja Lyubomirsky asked participants to engage in both extraverted and introverted behavior, each for a week at a time. The specific instructions for the "extraverted week" were: "Try to act as talkative, assertive, and spontaneous as you can." For the "introverted week," participants were told to act as "deliberate, quiet, and reserved" as possible. The results showed that extraverted behavior led to an increase in positive emotions and social connectedness while introverted behavior led to a decrease in these measures. Most importantly, this pattern of results was evident for both extraverts and introverts.[33] These results are consistent with other studies showing that there are benefits to both being and *acting* extraverted.[34]

When introverts think about "acting extraverted," they worry that it will be exhausting, or that they'll feel inauthentic, but that's often not the case, at least not in the short term.[35] So, if you're more introverted, consider acting extraverted a little more often. You're probably doing it to some degree already. Many situations in modern life require you to push yourself to be a little more social than you're naturally inclined to be—like when you have to take a job candidate to lunch or make small talk at a party. Of course, we're not suggesting that introverts should change their personality, or be someone they're not. All we're saying is that introverts can benefit from engaging in extraverted behaviors (like being talkative and sociable) a little more often. Just don't push too hard; if you act "out of character" for too long, you might lose the benefits of this practice. The key is finding the right balance for you.

Another key to well-being for introverts is *self-acceptance*. Although many cultures prize extraversion, and we've spent the past few paragraphs convincing introverts to act a bit more extraverted, the truth is that there's nothing wrong with being introverted. In fact, there are many unique benefits to being more introverted, aptly described in Susan Cain's book *Quiet: The Power of Introverts in a World That Can't Stop Talking*.[36] So, if you're more on the introverted end of the spectrum—even if you're on the extreme end—we encourage you to embrace your personality. Research shows that introverts who are comfortable with their introversion enjoy greater well-being than those who wish they were more extraverted.[37] The goal might be to accept yourself as you are—while also engaging in behaviors that increase your well-being.

What advice do we have for extraverts? Well, you might not need a nudge to prioritize socializing, but you may need a reminder that there are many situational factors that can make it difficult to get the social contact you crave. If you recently moved to a new city, are homebound with a chronic illness, or are just too busy to socialize, know that there are plenty of solitary activities that can help maintain your sense of connection in a social dry spell—things like meditating and walking in nature (which we'll discuss in Chapter 7). Sometimes, there are benefits to acting more like an introvert!

Those Who Are Secure in Their Relationships . . . And the Rest of Us

According to attachment theory, the experiences we've had with our close relationship partners, beginning in infancy, contribute to our attachment style.

If we learn through experience that people are available to us and responsive to our needs, we tend to develop a *secure attachment style*. If, on the other hand, we learn that people aren't there when we need them, we're likely to develop an *insecure attachment style*. Research shows that people who feel securely attached are more likely to initiate new relationships, and experience more closeness in their relationships, than those who feel insecurely attached.[38]

In her book *Platonic: How the Science of Attachment Can Help You Make— and Keep—Friends*, psychologist Marisa Franco says that people who have a secure attachment style are naturals at making friends. She calls them "super friends," noting:

> Secure people assume they are worthy of love, and others can be trusted to give it to them. This belief becomes an unconscious template that trickles into all their relationships, leading them to give others the benefit of the doubt, open up, ask for what they need, support others, assume others like them, and achieve intimacy.[39]

So, people who feel secure in their relationships probably have an easier time meeting their need for connection than those who don't believe in their self-worth or in others' supportiveness. The relationally rich seem to get richer here. But there is good news for those who don't feel secure in their relationships: attachment styles *can* change over time. One way to increase your sense of security is to simply have more positive relationship experiences, and the advice in this book can help with that![40]

Those At Higher Risk of Isolation and Loneliness

In 2023, the US Surgeon General released an *Advisory on Our Epidemic of Loneliness and Isolation*. In it, he noted that "access and barriers to social opportunities are often not the same for everyone and often reinforce long-standing and historical inequities."[41] As a result, some groups are at a higher risk of isolation and loneliness—including people from underrepresented racial groups, sexual minorities, immigrants, people with disabilities or hearing loss, and those with autism spectrum disorder, just to name a few. There's also evidence that men are struggling more than women and, contrary to popular belief, young adults tend to be lonelier than older adults.[42]

We also want to acknowledge that your unique life circumstances might create additional barriers to connection. If you have to work two jobs to pay the bills or you're a single parent of a child with special needs, you might not have much leisure time. If you're living in a city where you don't speak the native language, you might have trouble connecting with the people around you. This was true for a Korean-speaking woman interviewed by *Humans of New York* who admitted that she was lonely because she couldn't communicate clearly. She said, "I think a lot about everything . . . but since I can't express these . . . deep thoughts well enough in English, I feel like I don't come across authentically."[43]

We know that there are many other circumstances that might make connection more difficult for you. If you're struggling to find the connection you crave—like so many others in the modern age—don't be discouraged. There are steps you can take to enjoy a more satisfying social life regardless of your personality, relational history, social identity, or life circumstances. Your path might look very different than other people's. You might have to fight harder to get—and keep—connection. But this book offers many evidence-based strategies that can help.

In this chapter, we've highlighted the first barrier to social connection in the modern world: viewing connection as a luxury we can afford to live without. We hope we've convinced you that it's an essential need and inspired you to make it more of a priority, in the way that suits you best. In the next chapter, we'll explore the social forces that can create additional barriers to connection and how to overcome them.

Takeaways

- Don't forget that you're a social animal. Social connection is an essential need, not a luxury you can afford to live without.
- Prioritize social connection like *your life depends on it*. Identify some specific ways you can incorporate more social interaction into your daily life.
- Remember that everyone travels a different path to connection. Have faith that you can find your way, even if your way looks a little different than other people's. If you notice yourself feeling more connected, more understood and valued, and less alone as you proceed on your journey, you are probably doing something right!

2
Recipe for Disconnection

How the Norms of Modern Life Are Pulling Us Apart

Know the rules well, so you can break them effectively.
—The Dalai Lama

In our social psychology courses, we ask students to break an everyday social norm and then write a paper about their experiences. One of our former students walked into a crowded elevator and, instead of turning around to face the doors like people usually do, stood "backwards," facing the crowd. Another approached a stranger in the dining hall and asked if he could join them for lunch, when he could have easily found a spot elsewhere. Still another student brought a meal to class (complete with ceramic plate and silverware), arranged it on his desk, and then enjoyed it like he was having a nice dinner at home. One of our favorite students refused to do the assignment and turned in a paper about how his refusal was a violation of the norms governing academic life (he got an A).

In all the years we've given this assignment, we've noticed a consistent theme: students tend to be anxious about breaking the norm they've chosen. They worry that they'll be perceived negatively by others, even if the onlookers are merely strangers. After breaking the norm, many students immediately feel compelled to explain *why* they were acting strangely ("My psychology professor made me do it!"). But, despite the discomfort they feel, most students later credit the assignment with helping them appreciate the power of the pressure to conform to social norms.

This pressure isn't just felt by students; it's felt by people of all ages, in all cultures. The pressure—like a magnetic pull back to the "normal" behavior in the situation—is incredibly powerful and, yet, often invisible. In many cases, we're not even consciously aware of it until we make the choice to break a norm. We're like fish in the ocean who don't realize that we're surrounded by water. And yet this social pressure has a huge impact on the way we relate to others, how much time we spend with our friends, and how much we enjoy being with them.

Looking Ahead

In this chapter, we'll discuss several norms of modern life that can negatively impact our social lives. These include living alone and moving frequently, a heavy reliance on technology and social media, and the pervasive beliefs that men should be "manly," children should be busy, and busyness is sign of value. These social forces are often subtle, steering our thoughts, feelings, and behavior in a way that we fail to realize. We hope that, by reading this chapter, you'll become more aware of the invisible forces at play in your social circles and in the wider social world—and learn how to push back against them if needed.

Life's Unspoken Rules

Social norms are the often-unspoken rules about what is considered typical or desirable behavior in a given context or culture. For example, in many cultures, there is a *norm of reciprocity*. If someone does something kind for you (a friend treats you to dinner, for example), you feel compelled to return the kindness at some point in the future. There are also unspoken rules regarding the distance we keep between ourselves and other people (*norms of personal space*) and they vary widely by culture.

Traveling to other countries can make you more cognizant of the norms operating in your own culture. Jaime recently observed that, in Denmark, asking new people what they do for work early in a conversation is a bit odd ("That *is what you want to know about me? Of all the things we could talk about?*") whereas in the United States, we do that all of the time. And in Italy, she noticed that getting coffee to-go was unusual; people were more likely to linger and enjoy it than to rush off like we tend to do in the United States. Not only are these things interesting to casually observe, but they also offer lessons on deeper cultural differences (in these examples, we might get a glimpse into Americans' joint obsession with work and busyness).

Research shows that there are two primary reasons why we conform to social norms, and both are vital to our ability to function in social situations. In many cases, we conform in order to avoid social disapproval or gain social approval. This is true for teenagers who engage in risky behaviors to fit in with their peers. But it also applies to adults' decisions about whether to strike up a conversation with a stranger, whether to sign their child up for travel softball, or whether to pay over $200 for the latest Nike shoes. We're hard-wired to want social approval, so it's not surprising that we'll go along with the crowd to get it.[1]

In other cases, we conform to norms because they provide evidence ("social proof") about the appropriate course of action in a given situation. We think, *If everyone is doing it, it must be the right thing to do.* If everyone is engaging in small talk at the office party, you assume that substantive conversational topics are off the table. If all your parent-friends are signing their kids up for multiple extracurricular activities, you think it's a reasonable thing to do. These two motives—to gain approval and to be right—are not mutually exclusive. We can chase approval and appropriateness simultaneously, of course. For example, we might ask friends what they're wearing to an upcoming wedding because we don't want to incorrectly interpret the dress code, and also because we want others' approval (whether we admit it or not).

Whatever the motivation, going along with, or conforming to, social norms is helpful in many situations, although the word "conformity" has a negative connotation. Following an unwritten social script helps us know what to expect during social interactions. It also keeps us in people's good graces. The problem is that many of the norms of modern times, particularly those in Western cultures, are pulling us apart and fueling the crisis of connection. For example:

- More and more of us live alone.
- We're spending less time socializing in person.
- When we *do* get together, many of us are distracted by our phones.
- Modern parents are investing significantly more time and energy into parenting, potentially at the expense of their social lives.[2]

The truth is that it's starting to feel *normal* to be busy, distracted, and disconnected. And because social norms guide our behavior in a subtle way, we're often unaware of their power. We don't realize how these norms are changing our social lives.

In this chapter, we'll discuss some of the modern norms that can create a barrier to a healthy social life. And we'll encourage you to break some of these norms, even if doing so makes you feel a little anxious at first. Keep in mind: If enough people break the rules, *the rules will eventually change.*

Living Alone and Living Single

Living alone is a practice that's becoming more common around the world. For example, according to census data, 28% of US households were one-person households in 2020, a significant increase from 8% in 1940. One-person households are even more common in Northern European countries like France (36%), the Netherlands (38%), and Germany (42%). Sociologist Eric Klinenberg described this trend in his book *Going Solo: The Extraordinary Rise and Surprising Appeal of Living Alone.* He wrote, "Our species has embarked on a remarkable social experiment. For the first time in human history, great numbers of people . . . have begun settling down as singletons [people who live alone]."[3]

The results of this experiment aren't yet clear, in part because researchers who study people who live alone often combine those who *choose* to live alone and those who do so reluctantly. Another problem is that living alone is often conflated with being socially isolated or feeling lonely. Many people who live alone have incredibly vibrant social lives and feel deeply connected to others. Still, living alone can increase the risk of social isolation and loneliness for some people and in some circumstances. If you live alone, and don't have built-in moments of connection with roommates, friends, or family members, you might want to make a concerted effort to find that connection in other places.

A related trend is the rise in the number of single adults. People who are single are plagued by the cultural myth of being somehow "less than" partnered people. This stigma can keep people from fully embracing the benefits of singlehood and enjoying their lives. One study found that people are reluctant to go into public venues likes restaurants, museums, and movie theaters alone because they think they'll be judged by others. But those who were asked to wander through an art gallery alone enjoyed it more than they expected—and as much as those who had a companion. If you stay home for fear of public scrutiny, you might miss out on fun times—as well as opportunities to make new connections. So, if your friends are busy but you still want to go out, do it! As we'll discuss in Chapter 3, your solo status is probably far less obvious to others than you think it is. And take comfort in the fact that solo experiences—like travel or dining—may be on the rise.[4]

To sum it up, solitary living is becoming more common in the modern world (and the often-solitary practice of working from home is gaining popularity, too). Living alone doesn't guarantee that you'll become isolated or feel lonely. You might absolutely love it. But don't forget that you're a social animal whose well-being is tied to the frequency of your social interactions.[5]

Moving On

Another practice that can impact our social lives is *residential mobility* (meaning the frequency with which people change their residence). Although it is more residentially stable than it was in the past, the United States remains one of the most mobile nations in the world. According to the US Census, 9.8% of the population moved in 2019. That's almost one in ten people. Although most of these moves are local (about 60% of movers stay in the same county), that still means that hundreds of thousands of Americans are making a significant move—and dramatically disrupting their social lives—every year. Residential mobility has become increasingly common in other parts of the world, too.[6]

What effect does this have? How do people pursue social connection when they suspect they might be moving? Or when they live in a residentially mobile community—one that people tend to move in and out of frequently? Social and personality psychologist Shigehiro Oishi has been investigating these questions. He's found that frequent movers tend to compartmentalize their friendships, at least when they consider social support an important part of friendship. They might go to happy hour with one friend and to the gym with another—rather than doing multiple things with the same friend. This helps build a large social network, which is a good strategy if you're worried about losing friends. In fact, one study found that a "broad but shallow" networking strategy is advantageous in mobile communities, while a "narrow but deep" strategy is optimal in more stable communities.[7]

Residential mobility is also linked to the way people connect with groups. In one study, Oishi and colleagues obtained game-attendance records from Major League Baseball teams, as well as mobility data from major US cities. Interestingly, those living in more mobile cities (such as Phoenix, Atlanta, and Dallas) tended to be "fair-weather fans," attending home games primarily when their teams were doing well, but less so when the teams were in a slump. Residents of more stable cities (such as Pittsburgh, New York City, and Cleveland) were less conditional in their fandom, coming out to show their support regardless of how the team was doing.[8]

Though most of the research on residential mobility is correlational, and we must be cautious about drawing causal conclusions, it's possible that mobility creates a barrier to meaningful connection. Mobility may also negatively impact psychological well-being. Some research shows that frequent movers are less happy than those who are residentially stable because they spend less time on activities that boost happiness—such as hanging out with friends. In addition, children who move frequently tend to have less satisfying relationships and lower well-being in adulthood, especially if they're more introverted.

Of course, residential mobility is not a uniformly bad thing. It's a signifier of freedom, of options. Pursuing a job prospect in an exciting new location can be thrilling, as can retiring to one's dream house by the beach. And countless members of marginalized groups have thrived after moving to a more progressive region and finding their "family of choice." But making a significant move—or moving frequently—may impact your social well-being in ways you fail to anticipate. This may be especially true for introverts, who might not be as eager to throw themselves into a new social world following a move.

Buying Disconnection

Another factor that impacts the quality of our social lives is the way we think about *money*. Social psychologist Cassie Holmes asked thousands of people whether they would prefer more money or more time, and the majority chose money. However, if you want more meaningful connection in your life, you might want to choose more *time*. In a field experiment, Holmes invited students entering a café to fill out a questionnaire that primed them to think about either time or money, and then secretly recorded how they spent their time in the café. Participants primed to think about time spent less time working and more time socializing—and left the café happier—than those who were primed to think about money. In other studies, researchers have found that people who routinely value time over money are happier and more likely to invest in daily social interactions. Thinking about money seems to make us less attuned to others, whereas thinking about time makes us more attuned and more open to connection.[9]

The value we place on money has social consequences, but so does the way we spend it. While "self-care culture" encourages us to treat ourselves with indulgences such as manicures, laser treatments, and lattes, research suggests that we might be better off spending some of our discretionary income on *others*. People from around the world—even in countries where people struggle to meet their needs—experience more happiness when they spend their money on others rather than on themselves, likely because this *prosocial spending* enhances feelings of social connection. One study found that spending just five dollars on someone else led to a significant mood boost. Spending money on socially shared experiences (like going to a concert with a friend) also promotes happiness and connection. So, while money alone doesn't guarantee a fulfilling life, we can choose to think about and spend money in ways that might get us there.[10]

Starved for Time?

Mainstream culture's fixation on money is especially interesting when you consider that our real poverty lies elsewhere: we just do not have enough *time*! People around the world report feeling like they have too many things to do and not enough time to do them—a feeling researchers call *time poverty*. Strangely, time poverty has become an aspirational status symbol; being busy makes us feel important somehow. Yet, research suggests that time poverty is associated with high levels of depression, anxiety, and stress. And, when we're feeling short on time, we're less likely to give it to others—further depriving us of the social connection that's so important for our well-being.[11]

Fortunately, research shows that there are specific steps you can take to feel more time affluent—and more socially connected. Here are a few:

- *Buy time.* Spending money to free up time can reduce time poverty and increase happiness. You can pay to outsource an unpleasant chore, get a direct flight instead of a cheaper one with a layover, or pay a toll to drive the fastest route home. Whatever fits your budget. Then, you can invest your windfall of free time in something socially engaging—like calling a friend or hanging out with your kids. Despite the benefits of "buying time," many people are reluctant to use it. Some are reluctant to do so because they see it as an indulgence, or something reserved for the wealthy. But research shows that buying time is a practice that's helpful for people at all income levels. You don't have to spend a fortune. Spending just a few dollars is enough to make a difference.[12]
- *Give time.* Another way to get more time is, surprisingly, to *give it away*. In a study called "Giving Time Gives You Time," researchers asked people to devote part of their Saturday morning to doing something for themselves that they weren't already planning to do—or to doing something for someone else. The people who gave away their time later felt like they had more of it. Doing something for someone else seems to expand our sense of time. Other research shows that helping others—by volunteering in the community, providing social support to a friend, or performing a random act of kindness for a stranger—can also increase our sense of social connectedness and decrease loneliness.[13]

- *Do less.* Perhaps the most obvious solution to reduce time poverty is to stop cramming so many things into the day. We don't have to keep up with the frenzied pace of the modern world. We can make a deliberate effort to say "no" to things that bring us little meaning, enjoyment, or connection. We can choose to slow down—and maybe even do nothing from time to time. Research shows that most of us don't like being idle, but that's probably because we've been conditioned by a culture that's obsessed with productivity, success, and wealth. So, what if we stopped contributing to the culture of busyness? What if we stopped automatically responding "I'm so busy!" when people ask us how we're doing? What if we left more room in our schedules for casual get-togethers . . . and took steps to make them happen?[14]

Ultimately, how you choose to use your time can greatly affect your happiness—and the quality of your social life. Spend it wisely.

Digital (Dis)Connection

Speaking of time, how much time have you spent on your phone today? This week? If you're like us, it might be helpful to honestly consider how your phone—and the time you spend on it—affects your psychological and social well-being.

There is a raging debate among researchers—and in the popular press—around this topic. And the scientific literature is full of conflicting findings. However, when researchers review all the evidence as a whole, the picture becomes clearer: smartphones can either help or hurt our well-being, depending on when and how we use them. When we use our smartphone to schedule a coffee date with a friend, stay in touch with a geographically distant loved one, or meet new, like-minded people, it can improve our well-being—and help meet our social needs.[15]

The problem is that smartphones can all too easily interfere with social life. Nearly 90% of US adults admit to using their phone during their most recent social interaction. You can see this play out at nearly any restaurant, sporting event, wedding reception, or fraternity party. And you've probably had the experience of being *phubbed* (being snubbed by someone who's using their phone). Although it's become the norm, it still feels pretty crummy. Research shows that phubbing (the actual term used in scientific papers) can make us feel rejected and less connected to our social partners. In couples, phubbing is linked to increased relationship conflict and decreased relationship satis-faction. And children who are phubbed by their parents feel socially discon-nected from them—and are at higher risk for behavior problems.[16]

Most of us understand that diverting attention to our phones can have negative social consequences. But we continue to do it anyway. Why is that? One reason, proposed by Elyssa Barrick and her colleagues, is that we have a "phubbing blind spot." We acknowledge that other people's phone use has a significant impact on us, but we underestimate the negative impact of our own phone use on them. We also attribute our phone use to more positive motives than others' phone use. Specifically, we think our phone use enhances the conversation ("Let me look up the name of that book you're talking about.") or is uniquely important ("I really have to respond to this."). Barrick also found that many of us believe that we are more capable of multitasking than others are—although most people are *terrible* at multitasking. These bi-ased attributions and assumptions keep us on our phones, which keep us at a distance from others.[17]

Phone use can also undermine our enjoyment of social interactions. In one study, Ryan Dwyer and his colleagues recruited people to have dinner at a restaurant with their friends or family. Participants were randomly assigned to keep their phones within arm's reach or to put them in a basket in the middle of the table. Participants who had easy access to their phones felt more distracted during the meal and they enjoyed the experience less than those who put their phones away. In another study, Dwyer examined college students' everyday social interactions. When students socialized with (versus without) phones, they reported being more distracted and feeling less socially connected to their friends.[18] These studies—and many others—suggest that our smartphone use can diminish our enjoyment of social interactions and undermine our feelings of connection with friends and family.

Smartphone use can also harm our relationship with our children, as researchers Kostadin Kushlev and Elizabeth Dunn recently discovered. They invited parents who were spending time with their children at a science mu-seum to participate in a study on phone usage. Those who agreed were ran-domly assigned to use their phone as much as they safely could or to refrain from using their phones as much as possible. As expected, parents who were assigned to use their phone frequently felt more distracted and less socially connected during the museum visit. In another study, Kushlev and Dunn tracked parents' phone use in their daily lives. They found that parents who used their phone while spending time with their kids felt more distracted and less connected to their kids than parents who stayed off the phone. Kushlev and Dunn concluded that "the very devices intended to connect us with others can, ironically, undermine our feelings of connection while spending time with the most important people in our lives."[19]

Our devices can also interfere with the everyday exchanges we have with strangers, which provide important moments of connection. Think about the new trend of contactless payment: it allows us to grab dinner, groceries, or coffee without ever interacting with a human being. Or think about what happens in a waiting room or subway car: strangers typically ignore each other while staring at their screens. Kostadin Kushlev and another group of colleagues studied this phenomenon in the lab. They asked people to sit in a waiting room for ten minutes with a stranger, either with or without their smartphones. The participants' behavior was videotaped and later analyzed. Kushlev found that participants who had access to their phones were less likely to initiate conversation with each other—and less likely to smile at each other. Kushlev and his team didn't examine *why* smartphones reduce social interaction, but one likely reason is that phones offer "a familiar, comfortable alternative to engaging in potentially awkward interactions with strangers." This work is consistent with survey research showing that 23% of phone owners say they use their phone to avoid interacting with others, at least occasionally.[20]

The advice here is obvious: limit phone use in social spaces. Of course, we know first-hand that this advice is hard to follow. Our smartphones are intentionally designed to capture our attention, as explained in the compelling documentary *The Social Dilemma*[21] and in Johann Hari's book *Stolen Focus: Why You Can't Pay Attention—and How to Think Deeply Again.*[22] Many of us have become hooked, and we check our phones compulsively (ourselves included!).[23]

Hari offers a great suggestion for combatting digital distractions: *precommitment.* Precommitment involves making decisions in the present that will limit our temptations in the future (like throwing away the last piece of pie so we can't eat it later). After admitting that his phone use was out of control, Hari bought a timed locking container that locks away his phone for as long as he selects. Once locked, the container won't open until the timer reaches zero. We've heard of people who use these locking containers during family dinner night, but you don't have to go that far. Just turn off your phone. Or leave it in the car. Or in another room. For a less extreme strategy, you can also turn off notifications. Or set up your phone so that you receive notifications in predictable intervals (or "batches"), which has the added benefits of lowering your stress and improving your psychological well-being.[24] Again, we know that this advice is easy to comprehend but difficult to execute. Start by scaling back your usage just a little bit and notice how it impacts the quality of your interactions. That lesson alone might be enough to inspire greater change.

When Social Life Goes Virtual

We can't talk about "our new social life" without talking about social media. Sites like Facebook, Twitter, TikTok, and Instagram are used by more than 4 billion people worldwide, and that number is projected to increase to almost 6 billion by 2027. And most people visit these platforms daily. Social media is surely bringing the world closer together, at least in some ways. It's a blessing for people who live far away from loved ones, for those who are homebound with a chronic illness, and for members of marginalized groups who struggle to find a sense of belonging where they live. It's also enabled countless reunions of long-lost friends, high-school sweethearts, and even twins separated at birth.[25]

Does social media use also have negative consequences? It depends on who you ask. The literature is full of seemingly conflicting findings, which leaves lots of room for debate. Part of the trouble is that there are many different things you can do on social media—you can actively engage with friends' posts or just mindlessly scroll through your feed. You can use it to learn more about fitness trends, or you can compare your body to other people's. You can connect with a new neighbor or stalk your ex-boyfriend.

In 2018, researchers synthesized the literature and concluded that "whether behavior on social network sites is good or bad for well-being depends on whether the behavior advances or thwarts innate human desires for acceptance and belonging."[26] If you use social media to make meaningful connections, it's probably going to enhance your well-being. If you use it passively—to look at your friends' photos without commenting, for example—you might experience negative consequences. Passive scrolling triggers social comparison, which is a recipe for dissatisfaction. When you compare the mundane aspects of your daily life with everyone's highlight reel, you're more likely to feel envy and depression.

And then there's finding out that you weren't invited to the party. In a *New York Times* article entitled "They Left Me Out and I Saw It All," Hallie Reed describes having this painful experience during her first year of college. She made friends with a group of women who seemed like "college besties." But, while she was scrolling on Instagram, she discovered that they were spending the weekend in Chattanooga together. Without her. No matter how old you are, that *really* hurts.

Reed writes,
We tend to talk a lot about having FOMO when we scroll through our social media feeds, but *fearing* you're missing out and *knowing* you've been left out are different.

We can let our imaginations fill in the gaps about other people's lives, but sometimes it doesn't take much imagination at all to see that people are doing awesome
things with you. That's the cost of living with social media . . . It's hard not to feel
hurt and betrayed."[27]

Reed's experience is consistent with research showing that young adults who
use social media tend to feel more lonely than those who don't.[28]

There is a lot more research on the topic—and many more nuances to consider. (If you're really interested in the research, you might want to read Brian
Primack's book *You Are What You Click: How Being Selective, Positive, and
Creative Can Transform Your Social Media Experience*.[29]) For now, let's embrace the simple principle that *the effect of social media depends on how you
use it*. We can also assume that the effects of social media are different for
everyone. We encourage you to consider how social media affects *you*. Does it
help you feel more connected, or does it make you feel envious, sad, or left out?
Do some platforms make you feel better than others? Does social media feel
like a waste of your precious time? If you feel badly after using it—or you're
not sure how you feel— consider cutting back on it. Some research shows that
limiting social media use to 30 to 60 minutes a day and minimizing exposure
to strangers' content (like celebrities' Instagram posts) leads to improved well-
being, at least for some people.[30]

When Parenting Gets Intense

So far, we've talked about how our mindsets, values, and habits can create
detours on the road to connection. Now let's zoom out and examine how our
expectations for our social *roles* can impact our social lives, beginning with
the role of parent.

As a parent, it can be hard to know if you're doing the right thing. *Should
I let my baby cry it out? Is my 12-year-old too young for a smartphone? What
should I do when my child is bullied at school?* When you're unsure what to
do, you might seek out expert advice or you might do something a lot easier
and more natural: simply observe the behavior of other parents. What are
they doing?

When you look to the behavior of other parents, you'll see the growing
trend of *intensive parenting*—an approach that requires parents to invest a
significant amount of time, energy, and money in their children, well above
what's necessary, and maybe at a cost to their own social lives. This style of
parenting has become the norm. Indeed, parents across different social classes

believe that intensive parenting practices—like enrolling children in lots of extracurricular activities and participating in children's play at home—are measures of good parenting for both mothers and fathers.[31]

Parents can feel badly when they don't conform to the norm of intensive parenting. "There's this sense that something is wrong with you if you aren't with your children every second when you're not at work," a mom said in a recent *New York Times* article. But research suggests that this time- and energy-intensive style of parenting doesn't necessarily improve children's outcomes. In some cases, it can even be harmful. Consider parental involvement: it's associated with many positive child outcomes, but *more* isn't necessarily better. In fact, children of overly involved parents are more likely to experience mental health problems.[32]

Intensive parenting is also linked to negative outcomes for parents. For example, researchers found that mothers who endorsed the belief that "children's needs should come before their parents' [needs]" were less satisfied with their lives than other mothers. Another study found that mothers who sign their children up for lots of extracurricular activities—and become heavily involved in those activities—are less satisfied with parenting than other mothers. These are correlational studies, so we can't be sure what's causing the negative outcomes. But the weight of the evidence leads psychologists Miriam Liss and Holly Schiffrin to conclude that "parenting, like most things, is best done in moderation."[33]

There are virtually no studies examining the link between intensive parenting and parents' *social* well-being, but we speculate that intensive parenting can get in the way of a satisfying social life. Part of it simply boils down to the time it takes. If you spend hours each week driving your child from violin lessons to soccer games to birthday parties, you'll have less time to nurture your other relationships. As one psychologist bluntly put it: today's parents are "sacrificing their social lives on the altar of intensive parenting." Indeed, the norm of intensive parenting might help explain why parents are more likely to struggle with loneliness than nonparents. And this is significant because parental loneliness is associated with negative outcomes for both parents and children.[34]

So, what can modern parents do? A recent article in *The Atlantic* offered a promising solution: "we need to normalize saying yes to prioritizing adult friendships. . . . We need to reassure one another—explicitly, publicly—that being a whole person *is* being a good parent."[35] Having a satisfying social life is good for parents' health and happiness, and having happy and healthy parents is good for kids. So, our advice to parents is: love your kids fiercely, spend quality time with time, invest in their future, but save a little time and energy for your own extracurricular activities.

Let's Hear It for the Boys

While social connection can be hard for anyone, men in many parts of the world face a unique barrier: the norms of traditional masculinity. The specific norms vary by culture, but people typically expect boys and men to be strong and independent, and to avoid excessively displaying traits or behaviors associated with femininity—like being warm, expressing emotion, and showing vulnerability. In the United States, masculine norms put pressure on men to be self-reliant and tough, control their emotions (except anger), avoid doing anything perceived as "feminine," hold disdain for men who they consider "feminine," and be very, very interested in sex.[36]

Children around the world—from San Francisco to Shanghai—learn gender norms at an early age, and they tend to disapprove of those who don't conform. This socialization process is beautifully depicted in the 2023 film *Close*, an Oscar nominee for Best Foreign Language Film. The film tells the story of two 13-year-old boys named Léo and Rémi (played by Eden Dambrine and Gustav De Waele) who develop a close, affectionate bond. The beginning of the film shows them enjoying their summer vacation together: running and biking through the Belgian countryside, sleeping over at each other's houses, and displaying unabashed affection. When Léo and Rémi start a new school together, other kids notice their affectionate bond and question whether they're "together." Léo quickly denies any romantic attachment but, in the days that follow, he becomes the target of bullying. Rémi seems to take things in stride, but Léo becomes increasingly self-conscious about his actions and determined to follow the unwritten rules for boys his age. He joins the hockey team, makes other friends, and begins to pull away from Rémi. He recoils when Rémi tries to physically lean on him during recess. He expresses disapproval when Rémi shows up to watch one of his hockey practices, like a boyfriend might. In the end, the boys lose the friendship that they once held so dear.[37]

The film *Close* was inspired by developmental psychologist Niobe Way's book *Deep Secrets: Boys' Friendships and the Crisis of Connection*. This book details Way's studies of boys and their friendships throughout adolescence. She found that, in early and middle adolescence, boys "speak about their male friends with abandon, referring to them as people whom they love and can't live without." The boys delight in sharing their secrets and feelings. But by age 15 or 16, the boys are less likely to share their feelings, and they don't typically speak about their friendships with affection. They realize that their close friendships put them at risk of being teased or ostracized, so many of them deny their desire for emotional closeness and distance themselves from their friends.[38]

By adulthood, men report having fewer close friends than women. Men still desire intimate friendship, even with other men, but many find it elusive. A 2021 survey found that most American men are dissatisfied with the size of their friendship group, and 15% of men have no close friends at all. The number of men without close friends is even higher in the U.K. and Australia. Men also report being less emotionally close to the friends they do have. In the American sample, 48% of women said they shared personal feelings or problems with a friend in the past week, whereas only 30% of men did.[39]

According to the American Psychological Association, traditional masculine ideology is the primary reason men tend to have fewer close friends than women. It's hard to be close to others if you're not willing to admit to yourself that you desire intimate friendship, or you're afraid to be vulnerable enough to share your true feelings or ask for help when you need it. Not all men try to adhere to the rules of traditional masculinity, of course, but those who follow the script may face yet another barrier to social connection.[40]

So, what's the solution? You could wait for gender norms to change (and there's some evidence that they *are* changing[41]), but we recommend taking a more active approach. Break the rule that "manly" men don't express emotion and show affection. And encourage the young boys in your life to do the same. Breaking this norm might be a little uncomfortable, but the payoff is closer, more satisfying friendships. In ongoing research, social psychologist Beverly Fehr asked pairs of male friends to engage in one of four activities together: watching an exciting hockey game, playing hockey on the Nintendo Wii, engaging in casual conversation, or engaging in more substantive conversation (which involved answering questions like, "How do you feel about your relationship with your mother?") She then asked all the men to indicate how close they felt to their friends after the activity. Fehr is still analyzing the data, but preliminary results suggest that men felt closest after engaging in the deep conversation. Those who played Wii hockey together were not far behind. What about watching a hockey game? Fehr said the men enjoyed it, "but it doesn't move the dial on their friendships."[42]

This study suggests that men might benefit from doing exciting things together, and perhaps even more, by opening up in conversation (two strategies that we'll discuss in later chapters). The finding that men bonded after playing

Wii hockey together is consistent with earlier research that men tend to connect "side by side" (through shared activity). However, Fehr's preliminary
results—and other research—suggests that men also benefit from connecting
"face to face" (through talking).[43] If the idea of opening up while staring into
someone's eyes makes you uncomfortable, you could do it while you're engaged in an activity—while working out at the gym or restoring an antique
car. One word of caution though: open up *slowly*. Disclosing too much, too
fast, might push people away (see Chapter 6 for more).

A Call to Action

In this chapter, we've discussed just a few of the social norms that can create a
barrier to connection, but there are many others that we *could* have included
but didn't have space for. For example, we're switching jobs more often, potentially making it harder to cultivate meaningful relationships in the place
where we spend the most time (the office). We also feel social pressure to be
happy all the time, and this can make us feel isolated from others when we're
feeling down.[44]

Don't worry about identifying all the relevant social norms that are at play.
The important thing is to realize that there are invisible forces acting upon
you. You're being influenced by other people's behavior and the culture at
large—in ways that are often very subtle. Being aware of this social pressure
makes it easier to resist.

Now, we're going to give you the same assignment we give our students: break
a social norm. If you're feeling feisty, break a few of them. Just remember that
it's normal to feel a little anxious about breaking the rules. It's the anxiety that
keeps us in line, conforming to norms that ultimately hurt our well-being. We
encourage you to push through that anxiety, and see what happens. Just be
sure to do it in a way that feels safe.

Takeaways

- Many of today's norms are getting in the way of a healthy social life.
  Maybe it's time to name them . . . and break them!
- If you live alone, or move away from friends and family, consider the impact this will have on your social life. Make sure you're getting the social
  contact you need.

- Consider spending some of your discretionary income on other people. A gift of a $3 chocolate bar might the highlight of someone's day.
- Feel like there's never enough time in the day? Try out one of the strategies in the chapter to increase your sense of time affluence. You might consider paying someone to do a chore that you dislike. Or, you might help someone else out—essentially, giving time away—to feel more time-affluent.
- Be cognizant of how technology affects your relationships. You might consider a "digital detox" or social-media fast.
- If you're a parent, don't give up your social life. It's essential for your health and happiness, and your kids need you to be healthy and happy.
- Remember that intimate connection shouldn't be gendered; it's a *human* thing.
- When it feels risky, start by simply bending the rules.

3
A Distorted Reality

Seeing the Social World through Our Personal Filter

We don't see things as they are, we see them as we are.

—Anaïs Nin

On November 23, 1951, Princeton played Dartmouth in one of the roughest and dirtiest games in the history of college football. Princeton's star player—fresh off the cover of *Time* magazine—left the field with a broken nose. And one of Dartmouth's players left with a broken leg. The game drew a lot of media attention and also inspired a classic study in social psychology led by Albert Hastorf and Hadley Cantril. These researchers asked students at both universities who they thought was to blame for starting the rough play. Around half of Dartmouth students thought *both* sides were at fault, but 86% of Princeton students thought Dartmouth was to blame. When Hastorf and Cantril showed the students a film of the game and asked them to count the number of infractions of the rules, Princeton students counted more than twice as many as Dartmouth students. Clearly, the Princeton and Dartmouth students "saw" a very different game. Hastorf and Cantril concluded that "the 'game' was actually many different games and that each version of the events that transpired was just as 'real' to a particular person as other versions were to other people."[1]

This study shows that we don't see a football game—or the world—as it actually is. We tend to see it the way we *expect* to see it. This means that our perception of reality—including our social reality—can be wrong. Have you ever thought someone disliked you, only to realize you were mistaken? Ever fretted over a social blunder, only to learn that no one really noticed or cared? Ever felt rejected when a friend didn't return a text, only to find out that they lost their phone?

If you're like us, you've had the experience of getting it wrong. After all, no one interprets the social world perfectly accurately at all times. However, the way we think about ourselves and other people—our *social cognition*—has a massive impact on our sense of connection and our success in relationships. And this complex system operates in a way that we often fail to appreciate.

The fact is, we all have a unique filter through which we see the world. It is created and sustained by our past experiences (for example, one betrayal may make us suspicious in relationships going forward), our personality (optimists might naturally think other people have good intentions), and our goals (an entrepreneur might naturally notice enterprising qualities in others). Whatever the nature of your filter, it's important to realize that it can be become quite distorted. This distorted filter will impact the way you perceive yourself in social situations, how you make sense of others, and how easily you are able to connect with them.

Looking Ahead

In this chapter, we will help you identify exactly *why* your filter on the world is so distorted, by describing common errors and biases in social thinking. This should help you appreciate sources of misunderstandings without ascribing blame (*It's not me! It's my distorted filter!*). We'll also explain how loneliness can change the way you think about yourself and other people, and how these changes can trap you in cycle of loneliness that increases your risk of health problems and early mortality. Throughout the chapter, we will suggest how to develop more accurate ways of thinking about the social world to pave the way for deeper connection.

Before we get into specifics, consider these two basic tenets of social cognition that underlie much of what we will discuss in this chapter. First, *we prioritize efficiency*. We often gather just enough information to make a social judgment, and often don't think beyond that. Taking it a step further, we interpret people's behavior in a way that's consistent with those initial views. This is all more likely to happen when we're tired, distracted, or unmotivated.

Second, *self-protection is key*. In many cases, our unique filter on the world developed to help us feel safe or to make the world seem orderly. (For example, jealousy may help us stay attuned to potential infidelity.) Even after it's no longer serving us well (meaning, when we are in a trusting relationship), these things tend to linger, as habits so often do.

Thinking about Ourselves

Let's start off with a few biases we have about ourselves. Researchers call these *egocentric biases*, not because we're self-centered but because we often can't help but see the world from our own perspectives.[2]

Removing the Spotlight

Imagine you're in a work meeting, sitting around a conference table with about twelve colleagues. At one point, you have the floor. You feel you're making an important point, confident and in control. After the meeting, you head into the restroom and, as you check yourself in the mirror, you realize that you had spilled some coffee down the front of your shirt, and it was clearly visible throughout the entire meeting. You feel the heat rise to your face and wish that the floor would open up and swallow you whole. Surely, everyone saw how sloppy and ridiculous you looked!

Since you can't stay in the restroom all day, you take a few deep breaths and slink back to your desk. You share your humiliation with a trusted colleague and they stare at you blankly. "Huh? You looked fine! By the way, you made a really important point in that meeting!" they say. Wait, did they really *not notice*? How could that be? It was so obvious!

You have just fallen prey to the all-too-common *spotlight effect*, a specific egocentric bias where you believe that others are paying more attention to you than they actually are. Not to say that we're all narcissists, but we *are* at the center of our own worlds. As such, we can't help but view things from a self-focused perspective. And it's hard to imagine that others aren't putting us in the spotlight, too.

In one study, social psychologist Tom Gilovich and colleagues wanted to create a sense of embarrassment in their participants. To do so, they asked them to wear what was predetermined to be a cringe-worthy t-shirt, one emblazoned with the face of pop star Barry Manilow. (Note that this study was done in the late 1990s. If Barry Manilow doesn't trigger embarrassment for you, we encourage you to imagine wearing a t-shirt that does.) Participants were asked to estimate how many of their peers noticed the t-shirt. They guessed around 50%. But when the researchers surveyed the others, it turned out that less than 25% actually noticed.[3]

In another study, Gilovich asked participants to engage in a 20-minute discussion with a group of strangers. Afterward, the participants estimated how the group would rank them on a number of positive and negative dimensions—for example, how much they advanced the discussion, the number of speech errors they made, and the number of offensive things they said. Then, participants ranked everyone on those same dimensions. The results showed that participants thought the group members would rank them *higher* than they actually did—for both positive and negative behaviors. In other words, participants overestimated the salience of their behavior, good or bad. Gilovich concluded that it "appears that the average person's actions command less attention from others than he or she suspects, and that the social spotlight may shine less brightly than he or she believes."[4]

In addition to overestimating the extent to which people will notice us, we also overestimate the extent to which they will *judge* us. When we commit a *faux pas*—like forgetting an acquaintance's name or tripping on the sidewalk—we often think that others will form a negative impression of us. However, research shows that people are usually less critical than we think.[5]

One of the reasons why we overestimate the negativity of others' judgments is that we tend to focus on our mistakes more than others do. If we stumble over a single sentence in a five-minute speech, our thoughts afterward are likely to be focused on the blunder. However, the audience's impression is likely based on the bigger picture—the ideas we shared, the confidence we projected, and so on. So, the next time you have an embarrassing mishap, and you fear that others will think you're awkward or weird, consider that your fears might be overblown.

One corrective for the spotlight effect is to simply acknowledge that it might be operating on you. How would it feel to tell yourself, "A few people probably noticed, but not as many as I think"? And those who *did* notice probably quickly moved on to something else." Remember that everyone is at the center of their own worlds, living life in their own spotlight. This is a comforting realization, especially when you realize you're wearing socks that don't match or have spinach in your teeth.

No One Is Reading Your Mind

Do us a favor. Stop reading for a moment and tap out the rhythm of the song "Happy Birthday." As you do this, you can't help but "hear" the tune and lyrics as you tap, right?

Next time you're in the presence of someone else, do the same thing. Ask the person to guess what song you're tapping. What you'll find is a startling disconnect: to you, the song is obviously "Happy Birthday." How could it possibly be anything else? But the other person will find it virtually impossible to identify the song. After all, they are not privy to the tune and lyrics in your head. All they hear is a meaningless set of beats.[6]

This is a demonstration of the *illusion of transparency*, an egocentric bias where we believe that our internal states—our thoughts and feelings—are more obvious than they are. Researchers found evidence of the illusion of transparency in a study in which participants played a variation of the "two truths and a lie" game. Thinking that others could see right through them, the participants overestimated the extent to which others could detect their lies. In another study, participants were asked to conceal their reactions after drinking either Kool-Aid or a nasty, vinegar-based drink. The participants believed that they wouldn't be able to hide their reactions, and that observers would be able to tell which drink they had consumed. But, in actuality, the observers couldn't tell.[7]

Keep in mind the illusion of transparency when you feel anxious about giving a speech, withholding a secret, or talking to someone new. You might assume that your anxiety is on full display—visible for everyone to see—but you probably hide it better than you think.[8]

Avoid Social Comparison

Are you financially successful? Good looking? Vacationing in the best possible places? And are your children doing all the right things to earn a spot at a competitive college? How can you possibly know?

A very natural tendency is to engage in *social comparison*, seeing how you stack up to the people around you. At best, social comparison can be inspiring. Witnessing someone relatable achieve something incredible can make you feel like—just maybe—you can do it too. More often, though, it leaves you unhappy, feeling less good about yourself and your life.[9] Why?

First, there is a lack of control inherent in the comparison process—you can't dictate or predict what other people are doing. If your self-worth hinges on being "the best" at something, what happens when someone better inevitably comes along? Second, excessive social comparison can distract from your own authentic wishes and values. Do you *really* want that luxury sports car, or are you just trying to one-up the neighbor? Finally, as more and more social comparison takes place over social media, we can find ourselves unknowingly comparing our real, messy lives with other people's carefully curated ones. This can make us feel particularly badly about the nature of our social lives. We inaccurately think other people attend more parties, have more friends, and enjoy a larger social circle than we do ourselves.[10] One likely reason for this is the simple fact that it's those fun, special moments that get shared online. Many people are also sitting home watching TV with the cat, but those moments don't make the highlight reel. Logical as this seems, it's easy to forget this fact as we mindlessly scroll.

Thinking about Others

Our distorted filter doesn't only impact how we see ourselves, though. It also impacts our judgments of others. We aren't just neutral observers of other people's behavior. We're constantly making inferences about their thoughts, feelings, and motivations, often based on very small snippets of information. And, because we can't read their minds, many of these inferences are incorrect. We'll lay out how this affects specific social situations in the next chapter. For now, consider this next section your essential background lesson.

Why You're Pulled to the Negative

We might all fare a bit better socially—or at least have more social confidence— if we interpreted other people's behavior in a way that made us feel good about ourselves. But people tend to focus more on the negative—including past experiences of rejection or betrayal, friendships gone wrong, even small slights, hurts, and criticisms—than on the positive. This "bad is stronger than good"[11] effect has a clear survival function: our attention naturally gets pulled to problems, not because they are fun to think about, but because we want to avoid anything like that happening again! "Once bitten, twice shy," as the saying goes. The result? Positive social experiences, like compliments, laughter, and happy times, get minimized or forgotten, while negative events can take on a life of their own. As neuroscientist Rick Hanson once said, "Our brains are like Velcro for negative information, and Teflon for positive."[12] The negative stuff sticks, while the positive slides right off.

For a simple example, imagine a good friend telling you that you're a bad listener. Does adding, "but you're really trustworthy" negate that initial criticism? No! There's not a one-to-one correspondence here. You're going to mull over that criticism: *Why did they say that? Exactly what did I do wrong?* You might dissect your recent conversations, looking for any sign of bad listening. We are fixers. We want to understand our missteps and try to resolve them, lest we face potential social rejection. A compliment doesn't get that kind of attention. We might take it in, feel good for a moment, and then move on.

There is no easy fix for this negativity bias, as it seems to be part of an innate and important survival mechanism, but one idea is to help consciously stack the deck in favor of positivity by cultivating a sense of gratitude. Doing so can help us notice and appreciate the good things in our daily lives and balance out our inherent tendency toward the negative. We'll come back to gratitude in later chapters.

Mental Shortcuts in the Social World

Imagine this: you overslept the morning after a heated argument with your partner. Those who know you well would say that you're normally an up-beat, outgoing person. But on this particular morning, as you head to the office, your head feels foggy and you're still harboring some resentment about what was said in this argument. And in your distracted state, you realize you left some important paperwork at home. So, on top of everything else, you're now ill-prepared for the workday. Needless to say, you're in a terrible mood.

In an effort to wake up and feel a little more alive, you hurry into a coffeeshop. When the cheerful barista greets you and asks you how your morning is going, you look at her with annoyance, ignore her question, and bark out your order. Running late, eager to caffeinate, and completely uninterested in upbeat small talk, your grab your coffee without saying thank you and rush out the door.

What will the barista think of you? She *could* pause for a moment, consider all that you could possibly have going on, and conclude, "Wow, that lovely person must be having a terrible morning!" It's possible. But there are a few important reasons why reflecting on your backstory wouldn't be natural for her. For one, as a stranger, she simply doesn't know that you're normally not like this! She also has no way of knowing what you've been through: your upsetting argument, your fatigue, your forgotten paperwork. She only sees the grumpy person standing in front of her, angrily demanding coffee. Second, she's got work to do. There are cappuccinos to make, counters to wipe, and other customers to serve. Taking the time to pause and consider your unique situation is a luxury she doesn't have.

Given all of this, what she's likely to do is to commit the *fundamental attribution error*, automatically assuming that your behavior is an accurate reflection of your personality, while downplaying the role of the temporary situation you're in. A person behaving in a rude and grumpy manner is a rude and grumpy person. Period. And sometimes this *is* true! But it's also the easiest and most natural story to tell oneself. As perceivers of the social world, it's something that we tend to do all of the time.

In a classic study, participants were asked to read and evaluate an essay, ostensibly written by another student, on a controversial political topic. Even when the participants were told that the student *had no choice* in the stance they took in their essay, participants still thought the essay reflected the student's true opinion. The error here was that the participants ignored the very important situational factor (the fact that the essay topic was assigned, not chosen) when making their judgment.[13] This error has been demonstrated many times, in a variety of circumstances.

Now, in real life, we sometimes *do* get the chance to learn that we were wrong in our initial judgments of others. Let's say that, a few days after your horrible Monday morning, you return to that coffeeshop as your typical jovial self. The same barista is working, so you smile, ask her how her day is going, and apologize for your previous behavior, explaining that you were having a terrible morning. She now can revise her initial impression of you. But these second chances don't always present themselves. And even if they do, first impressions of people are extremely powerful and enduring.

Why? Imagine that, upon your return to this coffeeshop, the barista sees you coming. She might mutter to a colleague, "Oh brother, here comes *this* one again." Without even realizing it, she is likely to see everything you do through the lens of her initial impression. This pervasive tendency, called the *confirmation bias*, suggests that even your smile and your cheerful greeting will be filtered to fit with her initial story about you. Therefore, your genuine attempt to be warm and friendly could be seen as disingenuous or even manipulative. Does that seem unfair? Sure! But people can't help but see the world in way that makes sense to them. And it doesn't stop there.

When Expectations Become Reality

Complicating matters further, the barista's behavior toward you is going to influence how you behave in return. So, upon seeing you, she'll steel herself for another nasty interaction, her normal smile wiped away, her warmth suppressed. She just wants to get it over with.

Despite your initial goal to be friendly, you can't help but pick up on her chilly energy. Your smile disappears, you don't attempt to engage, and you quickly leave the coffeeshop. The barista's initial impression of you is maintained. However, on this second meeting, she doesn't realize the role *she* played in pulling those unfriendly behaviors out of you.

We can't help but take our initial impressions into a social interaction, and these impressions can dramatically influence how things turn out. In a classic experiment, male college students talked on the phone with a woman they didn't know. The researchers led the men to believe that the woman was either physically attractive or unattractive (by showing them bogus photographs). The results show that the men were more sociable when they believed they were speaking to an attractive woman (no big surprise there). But, more importantly, the women on the other side of the phone—who had no connection to the photographs the men were initially shown—behaved in a more friendly and sociable manner when they were *believed* to be attractive. This occurred because the men's expectations and subsequent treatment of the women pulled out the very qualities that they expected to see. The women heard the voice of a man who sounded very interested—or very uninterested—in talking to them, and they responded in kind.[14]

These examples illustrate the power of the *self-fulfilling prophecy*, which is simply a belief that leads to its own fulfillment. When we expect other people to like us, we behave warmly, which in turn leads other people to like us. The same thing happens when we expect rejection: we behave coldly, which leads others to reject us.[15] In short, we tend to get from others what we expect. This research points to a simple yet powerful strategy for building connection: *expect the best in social situations.*

Correcting Our Errors

The fundamental attribution error, confirmation bias, and the self-fulfilling prophecy are all products of quick, automatic thinking. All are more likely to happen when we're distracted, tired, or unmotivated to put forth mental effort. We believe that simply knowing about these tendencies can be helpful. Also, recognizing times when we're likely to fall back on these easy modes of thinking is useful. Just like we know that we can't put forth our best physical effort at the gym when our body is exhausted, we should acknowledge that our minds can lead us to erroneous snap judgments when they're tired or distracted.

Short of becoming telepathic, is there any other way to correct for these biases? "Put yourself into the shoes of another" is common advice, and it sure *sounds* good. But the research reviewed in this chapter suggests that this sort of perspective-taking might be easier said than done, because it is so prone to error. Social psychologist Tal Eyal and her colleagues experimented with the idea that understanding another person's mind actually requires perspective *getting* rather than taking.[16] In a series of twenty-five different studies, they found that even the most dogged attempt to take another person's perspective led to errors, and this applied to a variety of scenarios (identifying fake smiles, lie detection, assessing nonverbal bodily cues, and more). Notably, some participants were asked to take on the perspective of a stranger, but others were given a seemingly easier task: to take on the perspective of their long-term romantic partner. Even this led to significant errors, despite participants' high degree of confidence in their ability to know their partners' minds. Well-intentioned as it may be, perspective-taking does not appear to increase interpersonal understanding.

What does work, the research found, was *simply asking the other person* what their actual opinions and feelings were. Don't try to read their minds; even if you are motivated to be accurate, and even if you know the person extremely well, you'll be better off going straight to the source. For example, if you're sitting across from a friend at a restaurant, trying to gauge how much he is enjoying his meal, you would do well to *simply ask him*, rather than attempting to guess. This seems obvious, but the researchers themselves noted that the most surprising thing they learned from these twenty-five studies is the fact that participants didn't appreciate the effectiveness of this simple strategy.

Distorted Social Cognition in Loneliness

So far in this chapter, we've seen that there are some predictable blind spots in how we make sense of the social world, even when we very much want to be accurate. This social thinking becomes even more distorted when we feel *lonely*—and the cause of this distortion is one of the most surprising and fascinating things about the science of connection. If you're struggling with loneliness right now, we hope you'll read this section carefully. It could be a game changer for you, as it was for Natalie (you can read her story in the Preface if you missed it earlier).

As we mentioned in Chapter 1, loneliness is the aversive feeling that arises when you perceive that your social relationships are inadequate in some way. It's when your expectations for your social life fall short of your perceived reality.[17] Many people equate loneliness with social isolation, but the two constructs are actually very different. Isolation involves being alone, whereas loneliness involves *feeling* alone, regardless of how many people are around. You can be surrounded by other people—on a college campus, at a bachelorette party, or in a vibrant coworking space—and still feel lonely. You can be in a romantic relationship and still feel lonely. On the other hand, you can be phys-ically alone—or go days without seeing your friends—and be perfectly con-tent. The triggers are different for everyone, but loneliness is a nearly universal condition. Virtually everyone has experienced the pain of loneliness at some point in their lives, and a growing number of people are dealing with loneli-ness on a regular basis. In recent surveys of US adults, 58% of respondents reported feeling lonely at least some of the time, and 17% reported that they felt lonely "a lot of the day yesterday."[18] If you're feeling lonely, you're in good company.

What's surprising about loneliness is that it's much more than an unpleasant feeling. Loneliness researcher John Cacioppo likened it to an iceberg: "we are conscious of the surface but there is a great deal more that is . . . so deep that we cannot see it."[19] In addition to making us miserable, loneliness triggers a number of changes in the brain and body that, left unchecked, can nega-tively impact our mental and physical health. Over time, loneliness is associ-ated with anxiety, depression, suicidal thoughts, fragmented sleep, increased blood pressure, increased inflammation, and impaired immune functioning. With its wear and tear on the body, loneliness also increases the risk of early mortality by 26%, which is equivalent to the risks associated with smoking.[20]

To understand what's happening beneath the surface, we need to consider where loneliness comes from. According to the evolutionary theory of lone-liness, developed by John Cacioppo and his colleagues, loneliness evolved to serve as a signal that we need to pay more attention to our relationships, much like pain sends a message that we need to tend to the body.[21] Consider our early ancestors who depended on other people for their survival. When they wandered too far from the tribe and found themselves alone in the wild, they were more likely to be eaten by a sabertooth tiger or giant hyena, be killed by a member of a rival tribe, or fall prey to some other misfortune. Being alone equaled being at risk. So, nature developed a biological alarm system—loneliness—to make them more cognizant of the dangers of being alone and motivate them to return to the safety of their tribe or to make new connections. The alarm system also triggered the fight-or-flight response to help them defend against any threats they might face on their way home.

This system was a brilliant way to ensure our ancestors' survival. And, today, the alarm system lives on, helping to ensure that we don't neglect our basic need for connection. In this way, loneliness is good for us (in the same way that an annoying seatbelt alarm is good for us). But the system often backfires in the modern world, where millions of people are living with persistent feelings of loneliness, unable to find their way back to their "tribe." For them, the alarm has been sounding for weeks, months, or even years. It's wreaking havoc on their bodies and distorting their social cognition in ways that only perpetuate their loneliness.

The Paradox of Loneliness

While loneliness increases our motivation to connect with others, it also triggers a conflicting motivation to avoid others who might harm us. Part of us leans in, and another part withdraws in self-defense. This happens because our brain interprets real or perceived isolation (loneliness) as a threat to survival and it snaps into a self-preservation mode. In this mode, we become hypervigilant to social threats, bracing ourselves for the possibility that someone might harm us.[22] This defensive reaction makes sense in the ancestral environment, where interacting with a stranger could prove fatal. But it's less helpful in the modern world, where social threats are rarely a matter of life and death. We're more likely to be ignored by a stranger or excluded from a friend's wedding than to face mortal combat. And, while modern-day social threats like criticism, rejection, and exclusion can be tremendously painful, they probably won't kill us.

The fact is that the hypervigilance borne out of loneliness is not particularly useful in modern social life, but we're stuck with it, nonetheless. It's part of our ancestral history. And it can lead to cognitive biases that distort our perception of the social world. We tend to see what we expect, and when we expect social threat, we see it *everywhere*. When a friend doesn't return a text, we assume that she doesn't really like us. When our boss doesn't mention one of our accomplishments, we feel like we're not valued at work. Remember the "bad is strong than good" effect mentioned earlier? It might just hit harder when we're lonely. Indeed, loneliness amplifies our normal concerns about being liked and accepted—and creates a fear of rejection, which can lead to anxiety, self-doubt, and even feelings of inferiority.[23]

When we're lonely and fear being evaluated negatively by others, it doesn't just change our beliefs. It also changes our behavior. We're more likely to adopt a cautious or avoidant interaction style. For example, we're less likely to share our opinions or disclose personal information. We're less likely to ask people questions. We're less likely to enjoy physical touch, and we prefer to stand farther away from those in our inner circle. The irony is that these cautious behaviors—designed to protect us from negative evaluation—can make us seem less friendly and likeable.[24]

The fear of negative evaluation created by loneliness can also undermine our social performance, causing us to "choke under pressure" in social settings. Although loneliness is not associated with a social skills deficit, the fears created by the lonely mind can make us less likely to *use* our social skills when we need them. And there's something about our behavior that allows both strangers and loved ones to sense that we're feeling lonely.[25]

Ultimately, this kind of distorted social cognition—and the defensive behaviors that flow from it—can create a self-fulfilling prophecy. Imagine a woman who's lonely at work. When she arrives at an office party, she automatically assumes that others won't be interested in talking to her, so she keeps her distance, standing in the corner of the room and staring down at her phone. Her behavior sends the message that she's not open for connection, so no one approaches her and she leaves feeling more alone than ever.

Worse still, when we're lonely, we're often unaware that we're sabotaging our efforts to connect. Research shows that the hypervigilance associated with loneliness often happens outside of our conscious awareness so we don't even realize that we're putting up walls between us and the very people we wish to connect with.[26] All of these factors can make it difficult to escape the confines of loneliness, but there *is* a way out.

Overcoming Loneliness

You might think the way to overcome loneliness is to "get out there" by joining a new club, downloading a dating app, meeting your neighbors, or reconnecting with an old friend. These strategies might work for you, but they could also backfire if your social cognition has been distorted by loneliness. For example, you might join a club, meet some cool people, and feel resentful that they seem to be already well-connected. So, in many cases, the antidote to loneliness is not as simple as reaching out to other people.

We must start by *changing our minds*. When researchers studied the effectiveness of different interventions to reduce loneliness, they found that interventions targeting people's maladaptive social cognitions were more effective than other common strategies—like enhancing social support or increasing opportunities for social interaction.[27] As John Cacioppo put it,

> the secret to gaining access to social connection and social contentment is being less distracted by one's own psychological business—especially the distortions based on feeling of threat. When any of us feels connected, the absence of social pain and the sense of threat allows us to be truly *there*: in sync with others. This lack of negative arousal leaves us free to be more genuinely available for and engaged by whatever real connection might develop.[28]

So, if you're feeling lonely, our advice isn't to join a club or make new connections (not yet, anyway). We recommend that you start by taking care of your "psychological business." How do you do that? Let's break it down.

Recognize and Acknowledge the Signal

First, it's important to recognize the signal of loneliness for what it is—not anger, not sadness, not grumpiness, but a longing for more meaningful social connection. If you're not sure whether you're lonely, consider whether you've been wanting more from your social life—maybe more friends, more time to socialize, or deeper conversations. These longings could be an expression of loneliness. Remember that loneliness is simply the perception that your social life is falling short of your expectations. It doesn't have to look like the opening scene of *Bridget Jones's Diary* where Bridget (Renée Zellweger) sits alone on her couch, drinking wine and singing along to the ballad "All by Myself."[29]

Once you recognize the signal for what it is, it's important to acknowledge it. Most of us admit when we're feeling hungry or sleepy, or when we're in physical pain. Why should it be any different when we're feeling lonely? There is a social stigma surrounding loneliness, which makes admitting loneliness feel like we're admitting that we have no friends, or that something's wrong with us.[30] But this can change. As more people open up about it—like Justin Bieber did in his hit song "Lonely"—people's perceptions will begin to change. And, if you open up about your own experiences, you might be surprised at the number of people who say, "Me too!" If you remember from the previous chapter, one of the best ways to combat harmful social norms is to stand up against them. Talking openly about loneliness is no exception!

Correct Your Cognitive Distortions

The next step is to recognize how loneliness distorts your perception of the social world, and then take steps to correct those cognitive distortions. When you're judging other people (*Does he* really *like me, or is just being nice because he wants something?*), give them the benefit of the doubt. All of the things we talked about in this chapter should help. Remember the confirmation bias: we tend to see in people what we expect to see, even if it's incorrect. And as research on the self-fulfilling prophecy suggests, we might act in a way that pulls those things out of them. We can set the stage for a positive interaction just by having a positive expectation. Yes, you might be wrong, but the consequences of being wrong are probably less serious than the consequences of persistent loneliness.

When you're judging *yourself*, have compassion. It's hard to navigate modern social life, even if your brain isn't playing tricks on you. So go easy on yourself. And be aware of the story you're telling yourself. Research shows that we tend to develop a self-defeating attributional style when we're lonely.[31] This means that we tend to chalk up negative social events to internal factors (like our personality), and positive social events to external factors. For example, if we're excluded from a party, we might assume that we're not very fun to hang out with (an internal factor). If we *are* invited, we might assume that the hosts are nice people who try to include everyone (an external factor). So, the next time you catch yourself making a self-defeating attribution, consider an alternative explanation. Maybe your neighbor didn't return your wave because he doesn't like you . . . but maybe that wasn't the reason at all. Practice considering alternative explanations and they will hopefully become more believable with time.

Also, pay attention to the story you tell yourself about your loneliness. Many people attribute their loneliness to some perceived personal flaw— like being too shy, too introverted, or not "good with people." We encourage you to make a different attribution. This strategy was examined in a series of studies conducted by social psychologist Megan Knowles. She asked lonely and nonlonely college students to complete a test of social skills: they looked at a series of facial expressions on the computer screen and had two seconds to label each one as anger, fear, happiness, or sadness. The students were led to believe that the task was related to social aptitude ("People who do well on this task tend to perform well in social situations") or not ("People who do well on this task tend to perform well in problem-solving situations"). Knowles found that lonely students performed just as well as nonlonely students when the task was framed as a nonsocial one, but they "choked under pressure" and underperformed when they believed it had social implications. Knowles discovered that this choking effect is a result of lonely people's heightened anxiety during social situations.

But the good news is that Knowles found that the choking effect disappears if lonely people can attribute their anxiety to something other than their personal attributes. In a second study, participants drank a caffeine-free beverage. However, some were led to believe they were drinking "a new sugar-free energy drink that is highly caffeinated . . . so, you may experience trembling, a fluttering of the heart, increased perspiration, and some feeling of anxiety during the tasks." Those in the control group were simply told that they were drinking a new sugar-free beverage. Knowles found that lonely participants in the control condition exhibited the choking effect, as expected. But lonely participants who were able to attribute their anxiety to the beverage did not.[32]

The results of this work have important implications for everyday life. If you're lonely, and also feel anxious, uncomfortable, or defensive in social settings, don't blame yourself. Don't second-guess yourself and think *I'm so bad at this*. Instead, attribute your feelings to the lonely brain. As neuroscientist Stephanie Cacioppo says, "Think of chronic loneliness as a malfunction of the social brain's alarm system."[33] The brain is trying to help you meet your needs, but it's being overly sensitive to perceived threats. Attributing your anxiety to a faulty alarm system—instead of a personal fault—might help you relax and be less anxious around others.

Disarm the Alarm

Once you realize that your alarm system is on the fritz, you can change the way you respond to the signal—or "disarm" the system entirely. Practicing *mindfulness* may be especially helpful with this. Mindfulness usually involves two components: monitoring and acceptance. Monitoring involves paying attention to the thoughts, feelings, and sensations you're experiencing in the present moment. Acceptance involves welcoming these experiences with an attitude of nonjudgment, openness, and receptivity. In other words, acceptance involves a willingness to remain present with your experiences without trying to change them. In the specific case of loneliness, it involves noticing that you feel lonely and allowing yourself to experience the loneliness without pushing it away. It's relaxing with it instead of resisting it.

One study led by Emily Lindsay found that a two-week program of mindfulness training (delivered through a smartphone app) reduced participants' loneliness and motivated them to increase their social contact. The authors stress that their mindfulness program was only effective when it focused on both monitoring *and* acceptance. In fact, a comparison group that practiced monitoring, but not acceptance, did not show these benefits (and neither did a group who did no mindfulness work at all).[34] In plain language, it's not enough for your internal conversation to be "I feel lonely right now." It should be, "I feel lonely right now . . . and that's okay."

How does mindful acceptance ease loneliness? Lindsay and her colleagues believe that acceptance reduces perceptions of social threat. As renowned meditation teacher Sharon Salzberg says: "mindfulness helps us get better at seeing the difference between what's happening and the stories we tell ourselves about what's happening."[35]

Want to give it a try? You can check one of the many smartphone-based mindfulness meditation apps (like Headspace, Calm, on Insight Timer), or follow the guidance we provide in Chapter 7.

Stop Thinking about Yourself

If you're in an emergency situation (you get lost on a hike through the desert, for example), you won't be able to stop thinking about yourself. Your brain will go into survival mode and you'll spend most—if not all—of your time focused on yourself and your needs. Something similar happens in loneliness. Research shows that lonely people are much more likely to agree with statements like "I can sometimes be a little self-centered" and "I think about myself a lot."[36] This makes sense when you realize that the brain considers loneliness a dire situation. If reading this makes you realize that you've been overly focused on yourself, don't feel badly about it (it's not you; it's your lonely brain). But do your best to counteract this tendency and spend more time thinking about other people. Volunteering or simply performing acts of kindness are great ways to turn the focus to others, and research shows that these strategies might also help reduce your feelings of loneliness.[37]

Choose Your Mindset

Some people argue that loneliness is a choice. After all, loneliness is the *perception* that something's not right with your relationships, and you can change your perception. It's true that you can lessen feelings of loneliness and strengthen your sense of connection even if your external circumstances don't change (through mindfulness and other strategies discussed in Chapter 7). But we don't think it's as easy as saying, "Yes, I'd rather feel happy than lonely, so I choose to be happy from this moment on." If it was that easy, wouldn't everyone choose to be happy and socially contented? Having said that, we do think you can choose to adopt a less lonely mindset in every social encounter. You can remind yourself that you're safe. You can choose to lean in instead of pulling away. And, if you find these choices too difficult at the moment, consider working with a therapist.

Once you're in the right state of mind, and you no longer feel threatened by the social world, you're ready to connect with other people. We offer lots of research-based strategies for doing so throughout the rest of the book, including successfully talking to new people, discovering similarities, expressing gratitude, showing vulnerability, and engaging in deeper, more meaningful conversations. Turn the page to get started.

Takeaways

- Remember that we don't see the world as it actually is; we see it through the lens of our expectations.
- Beware the spotlight effect: People are paying attention—and judging—less than you think. After all, they are living life in their own spotlight!
- If you get anxious in social settings, remember that people can't read your mind. You're probably hiding your anxiety better than you think you are.
- Catch yourself when you're engaging in the common practice of social comparison. How is it making you feel? And is the comparison even valid? In a quote widely credited to author Anne Lamott, "Never compare your insides to everyone else's outsides."
- Give people the benefit of the doubt and expect the best in social interactions.
- Acknowledge that not everyone is going to like you. Some people just don't mesh, and sometimes people aren't in a place where they are open to connection. This is truly okay! Remember, you don't always know what is fully going on with people.
- If you want to know what people are thinking and feeling, don't "put yourself in their shoes." Just ask.
- If you're lonely, remember that loneliness often changes the way you think about yourself and other people. You may become anxious in social settings, but this is the brain's (faulty) way of trying to protect you. You can overcome this by "disarming" the faulty alarm system.
- Lonely or not, remember that developing more accurate and positive ways of thinking about others can ultimately improve your social relationships.

4

Faulty Mind-Reading

Why We Underestimate Others' Desire to Connect

The single biggest problem in communication is the illusion that it has taken place.

—**George Bernard Shaw**

From *Pride and Prejudice* to *Friends* to *Abbott Elementary*, misunderstanding is a classic trope of romantic comedy. Two characters have palpable chemistry and—to us, the outside observers—share an obvious romantic interest. Sure, they might *think* they're clearly communicating this interest, maybe with a lingering glance, a kind gesture, or a heartfelt compliment. But, somehow, their signals get missed or are misinterpreted. And so the two characters bumble along, awkwardly trying to connect, as we root for them to bridge the gap that exists between them and to live happily ever after.

Consider a hilarious, real-life example of this kind of missed connection. In 2002, megastar Nicole Kidman, who had just been named "the world's most beautiful woman" by *People* magazine, was interested in meeting *Saturday Night Live* comedian Jimmy Fallon. (Both were single at the time.) After expressing her interest, a mutual friend spontaneously brought her by Fallon's New York City apartment to see if they'd hit it off.

Spoiler alert: romance failed to blossom, and they both went on to marry other people.

Fast-forward to 2015. Kidman was still a megastar, and Fallon had ascended to the coveted role of host of *The Tonight Show*. Kidman comes on as a guest, and in her interview, reminds Fallon that they had met once before, over ten years earlier. He claims to remember it well. They each proceed to share their version of the encounter. Fallon says, "I'm walking down the street in New York City, and my friend Rick calls me and says . . . 'I have Nicole Kidman with me and she wants to meet you . . . I can be in your apartment in like 10 minutes.' I go, 'You're going to bring Nicole Kidman over to my apartment? OK.'"

Kidman recalled, "I just remember I really liked you . . . Our mutual friend was like, 'Jimmy really wants to meet you. You can go over to his apartment.' I'm single and I'm like, 'OK!' " Fallon, at this point in the interview, looks completely shocked, upon learning that Nicole Kidman had romantic interest in him.

He clearly hadn't picked up on her cues at the time. Laughing, Kidman recalls, "You put a video game on or something and I was like, 'This is so bad.' . . . And you didn't talk at all. So, after about an hour and a half I thought, 'He has no interest, this is so embarrassing.' So, I left, and went, 'OK, no chemistry.' " Kidman took his wardrobe—sweatpants and a baseball cap—as further evidence of his complete lack of interest in her. Fallon, red-faced, stammers, "This is unbelievable! This is unbelievable!"[1] Despite their best intentions, the two interpreted the exact same situation in completely different ways. In this way, celebrities are just like us.

Looking Ahead

In this chapter, we'll explore the all-too-common experience of misreading another person. As socially astute as we might be, no one is a mind-reader. As such, social interaction will always involve a little bit of guesswork. This means that it is difficult or even impossible to bridge the gap between what happens in our own minds versus what is happening in the minds of others. This natural gap in perspectives prevents us from accurately assessing what other people think or feel, leading to mistaken (or "miscalibrated") expectations about our social interactions. Such *social miscalibration* inhibits us from doing some of the very things that create connection, including talking to new people, offering words of support, kindness, and gratitude, and broaching deep topics of conversation.[2] We'll examine how social miscalibration creates a barrier to connection, and what we might do to overcome it. We'll also explore the hopeful idea that people tend to like us more than we think they do!

Let's start off with what might be the biggest gap of all—the one that exists between us and people we don't yet know at all.

Talking to New People

We run into new people all of the time. Depending on our lifestyles and routines, it could happen while shopping, attending a class, visiting a coffee shop, commuting on public transit, or going for a walk around our neighborhood. There is no "one right way" to connect with them. You might consider a friendly smile and a genuine "how's your day going?" or a compliment, a request for directions, or a comment on the situation you're both sharing. The conversation could peter out from there, or it could lead to something deeper. (After all, let's remember that all of our friends were once strangers!) Regardless, research indicates that we tend to underestimate just how connected and happy it can make us to interact with strangers.[3] We tend to miss out on a surprisingly powerful source of social connection that is present all around us.

For example, one series of studies done by Nicholas Epley and Juliana Schroeder examined commuters on the buses and trains in the Chicago metro area.[4] Some were asked to interact with a fellow passenger, while others were asked to either sit in solitude or just do what they normally do on their morning commute. Epley and Schroeder found that those who made small talk with new people during their commute were in significantly better moods afterward than those who sat in solitude. The researchers also replicated their findings in people who rode in a taxicab after landing in Chicago's Midway airport (they were in better moods after making conversation with their driver compared to sitting in silence), and in a sample of Chicago adults sitting near a stranger in a waiting room (they, too, were in better moods after making conversation with a stranger versus sitting in silence). Across multiple studies, these benefits held up even for introverts. Finally, to make sure their findings generalized beyond Chicago, they replicated their findings in the stereotypically more reserved city of London, finding a similar pattern of results.[5] Commuters on public transit felt happier when initiating conversations with those around them, rather than sitting in solitude or doing what they normally do, and more so than they expected.

Did you read the last paragraph and think, *There's no way I'm talking to strangers on the subway!* If so, you're not the only one. For many of us, this seems like an intimidating way to begin the healthy habit of talking to new people. Many of us are taught from an early age about "stranger danger." Plus, approaching someone in a public space like a bus, train, or waiting room and striking up a conversation is fairly unusual in some places and the very thought of it might be a bit overwhelming. The people sitting near you might not give off a warm, welcoming energy. They may be engrossed in a book, scrolling through their phone, or wearing headphones. And there's no clear "script" for this: What do you say, exactly? Take heart: there are still countless opportunities to talk to new people in your everyday life; you just need to find the right time and place for you.

For a more approachable idea, consider this: in a 2014 study, Elizabeth Dunn and Gillian Sandstrom's research team approached people as they were entering a Starbucks in a busy shopping area and asked them to participate in a study.[6] Those who agreed were instructed to either have a genuine interaction with the cashier ("smile, make eye contact to establish a connection, and have a brief conversation"), or to get their coffee in an efficient manner and avoid any unnecessary conversation. As they were leaving the area, everyone was given a mood scale, and it was revealed that the people who had a brief social interaction with the cashier were in significantly better moods than those who hadn't. They also felt a stronger sense of belonging. You might notice that, compared to talking to people on public transit, casually chatting with a friendly cashier, someone you're interacting with anyway, might feel much more manageable and safe.

But regardless of who it's with and where it happens, perhaps it surprises you to hear how beneficial it can be to talk to people who are completely new to you. If so, you're in good company. In both the Chicago and London commuter studies, some people were asked to just *predict* what would make them happier: time spent talking to a new person, or time spent in solitude. And the majority of participants guessed that they'd be happier in solitude! This is another example of social miscalibration in action—people were often reluctant to reach out because they guessed that other people didn't want to be bothered. For the most part, this prediction was just plain wrong.

So why is it that even a brief encounter with a new person can give us a surprisingly big boost? It's because these interactions can be novel, stimulating, and can teach us something new.[7] They can encourage laughter, acknowledgment of a shared emotion or experience, a moment of commiseration, or a brief distraction from our worries. These interactions can pull us out of a funk—we tend to perk up and try to make a good impression when interacting with new people, while those we're close with may allow us to fruitlessly wallow in our bad mood.[8] These brief interactions might also brighten someone else's day. On a more existential level, they remind us that we're not alone in the world. Once again, this demonstrates how we undervalue conversations with new people. And you never know: a new person may offer a moment of casual chatter, or they could turn into something more. Again, it's helpful to remember that all of our friends—and our romantic partners—were once strangers.

It can take multiple pleasant encounters with new people to begin to learn these lessons, though. With this in mind, Gillian Sandstrom and her colleagues designed a week-long experiment where participants navigated their college campus as part of a scavenger hunt.[9] All participants were instructed to go out and find people who met certain, very specific criteria (examples might be someone wearing a purple hat, someone walking a small dog, or a member of a different racial or ethnic group). However, half of the participants were asked to actually strike up conversations with these people, while the others simply observed them from a distance.

At the start of the study, the researchers measured all participants' fear of social rejection, their beliefs in their ability to successfully engage in conversation and make a positive impression, and their expectations of awkwardness. They were curious to see if having multiple interactions with a variety of new people might improve participants' social confidence and reduce their fear of rejection over the course of this week. And that is what they found. Compared to how they felt at the beginning of the study, those who interacted with new people showed reductions in their fear of social rejection and awkwardness, increased confidence in their ability to make conversation and create a positive impression, and more enjoyment in talking to new people. These improvements tended to build up over the course of the week, and the results lingered for at least a week after the study ended. Participants who interacted with strangers also noticed opportunities for casual social interactions that they hadn't noticed before. Meanwhile, because they weren't getting the chance to socially engage first-hand, those who were told to merely *observe* new people did not experience these positive changes. From this research, we can learn that our reluctance to have interactions with unfamiliar others can be combatted through direct action. Putting ourselves out there, hopefully in a way that feels comfortable to us, can teach us vitally important lessons about the openness of others and about our own social aptitude.

Why Don't We Seize These Small Social Opportunities?

The main reason for this reluctance seems to be fear, and one study found that this fear can take many forms.[10] We might be afraid of social rejection, which stings even if it's coming from a total stranger. In short, we worry, *What if the person doesn't want to talk to me?* We fear awkward moments or sending the wrong message—*What if I say something off-putting? What if I offend them?* or *What if they think I'm hitting on them?* We believe we're too busy to stop and chat with someone and worry that it would be a poor use of time (although it's important to note that the participants in the London commuter study did not report feeling unproductive during their conversations). We also worry that *we* might not enjoy the conversation or we might not like the person we're talking to. Finally, we might not know the best way or the best time to end a conversation,[11] and that uncertainty might just prevent us from starting one at all.

While not all of these fears will apply to everyone, even one or two of them may lead to what is—on the surface—a reasonable conclusion: that it's easier to avoid talking to new people altogether. However, research has established that these common fears are often greatly exaggerated: most conversations with new people turn out to be quite pleasant.

Notice that we're not talking here about fears for your physical safety—in cases like that, absolutely listen to your gut instinct. What we are saying is that *social* fears—say, of awkwardness or of mild rejection—are worth questioning, because they can often be misplaced or exaggerated.

But the truth is that fears of talking to unfamiliar people *are* sometimes warranted. Some people and situations pose a realistic threat of physical or psychological harm. We must stress, put your safety first. Pushing past some general nervousness is to be expected when doing something new, but we'd never advise anyone to ignore gut feelings or actual signs of danger. A young woman riding a bus or subway alone at night might not feel physically safe striking up a conversation with someone new and potentially dangerous. A member of a marginalized group who's repeatedly experienced prejudice and discrimination might also feel unsafe or uncomfortable approaching new people in certain contexts. One general piece of advice is to choose a setting that feels approachable and nonthreatening to you. It could be as simple as talking to someone new in the safety of a group. Or it might mean talking to a new person in a familiar setting like church, when you're surrounded by others who share your values and cultural background. Or it could start with a passing smile as a nonthreatening way to potentially open the door to a conversation.

General Tips for Connecting with New People

The advice here may sound straightforward, but it's easier to understand than it is to execute. If this feels overwhelming, here are a few tips.

- First, start small. Begin by making eye contact with someone. Research suggests that simply acknowledging the people you cross paths with, using eye contact or a smile, can help you both feel a little more connected.[12]
- When you feel ready, strike up a conversation with a new person, in a time and place where you feel safe and comfortable. You might not even

need to create new opportunities for yourself; given how often we en-counter strangers, consider capitalizing on opportunities that naturally present themselves. For example, if you need to call customer service or go through the grocery store line anyway, why not seize that opportunity to briefly connect with the agent or the cashier?

- In the London commuter studies mentioned in this chapter, the way that people thought about their upcoming conversation mattered.[13] When asked to imagine *trying* to start a conversation with a new person, participants predicted that it would be more awkward than it was. However, when they imagined doing it successfully—rather than merely trying to—they didn't expect such a high degree of awkwardness. So, simply imagining an easy, free-flowing conversation may help reduce your anxiety and make it easier to approach that potential new friend.
- Focus on social situations that come with ready-made topics, where you might easily find some common ground on which to connect. The dog park is a prime example—it's very natural to ask someone what breed of dog they have or which groomer they use. Think about specific places in your life where you have things in common with those around you.
- Think about places where people have time to kill, like waiting in line at an amusement park or at the DMV. These people might be especially eager for conversation.
- Consider joining an organization or pursuing a hobby that you are in-terested in. This will connect you with like-minded people and give you natural topics of conversation.
- If this idea still makes you anxious, see if you can pinpoint why. If your fears take the form of *What will I say?* it might help to think of conversa-tional topics ahead of time. If you're worried that the other person won't want to talk to you, remind yourself that nearly everyone desires connec-tion and acceptance. That said, you might try approaching someone who looks open to conversation, as opposed to someone with headphones on or someone who is engrossed in their phone or newspaper.
- After you've tried it out, ask yourself the following: Were your fears exag-gerated? Did it go better, worse, or differently than you'd expected? Why? What would you change for next time?
- If the conversation didn't go well, remember the *fundamental attribution error* from the previous chapter. Consider the possibility that the person you reached out to was having a bad day, was rushing, or was dealing with a stressor you have no way of knowing about. You might never know for sure, but chances are, it had nothing to do with you. In these moments, it

might help to remind yourself of all of the people who really *do* like you, or of recent social interactions that went well.

- Finally, remember that practice makes all of this easier!

Connect through Positivity

Maybe you are eager to connect with new people, or to try to turn an acquaintance into a friend, but you're not quite sure how to do it. Maybe you're searching for a way in, or a good opener. Consider these three broad, tried-and-true techniques that will not only help you connect, but will also help infuse your new relationships with warmth and positivity. We are especially excited to share these strategies with you because, according to the research on social miscalibration, people systematically underestimate the power of these simple behaviors. As we mentioned earlier, one challenge of social connection is the natural gap between what we expect another person to think and feel, and how that person actually thinks and feels. Understanding this misperception will boost your confidence in social situations. If you feel some initial reluctance to try any of these techniques, consider the fact that your worries might just be exaggerated, largely due to the power of miscalibrated expectations. Also, remember that your attempts might have a huge impact, one that you might never fully see. In his book *Together*, Surgeon General Vivek Murthy says,

> Most of us are interacting with lonely people all the time, even if we don't realize it. And due to the state of hypervigilance that loneliness creates, many of these people will be anxious and on edge. For someone in such a state, kindness can be a disarming force. One never knows when a moment of appreciation or generosity can open the door to connection for someone who is struggling alone.[14]

Give Genuine Compliments

If you're trying to connect with a stranger or a casual acquaintance, consider offering them a genuine compliment. After all, this sort of expression of admiration speaks to a person's deep need for acceptance and belonging. When given thoughtfully, compliments convey that we're not only paying attention to someone, but also appreciating and acknowledging positive aspects of their character. Unfortunately, we tend to underestimate the power of compliments and, as a result, we can shy away from giving them. Researchers Erica

Boothby and Vanessa Bohns found that, across a series of studies, participants underestimated how good the recipients (all of whom were strangers) of their compliments would feel. They also thought that recipients would be more annoyed and uncomfortable than they actually were. In a different set of studies, Xuan Zhao and Nicholas Epley also found a reluctance to give compliments, largely because people underestimated how positive—and overestimated how awkward—the interactions would be. This effect held up across different types of relationships: romantic partners, friends, and casual acquaintances.[15] This specific type of social miscalibration—underestimating recipients' positive feelings while overestimating the negative ones—feeds into a reluctance to give compliments, inadvertently taking away a tool for genuine connection.

Why *don't* we fully appreciate the power of a compliment? It's often because we worry so much about saying that perfect thing: well-articulated, graceful, and charming. But those on the receiving end of our compliments don't care so much about that. Studies show that, in these situations, *people respond much more to warmth than to competence.*[16] In other words, maybe it's actually okay to stumble over our words a little bit, if the message is expressed in a heartfelt way. Remember the quote often attributed to Maya Angelou: "people will forget what you said, people will forget what you did, but people will never forget how you made them *feel.*" As you'll see, this misplaced focus on competence over warmth is a recurring theme in the literature on social miscalibration.

And, if you feel like you're being genuine in offering them, don't worry *too* much about the frequency of compliments, at least from one day to the next: one series of studies found that people often refrain from giving out multiple compliments, because they imagined the impact of the compliments would diminish over time.[17] In other words, they mistakenly guessed that, maybe the first or second compliment might be a lovely surprise to recipients, but eventually, that feeling would wear off. Additionally, people worry that multiple compliments will start to be seen as insincere by the recipient. However, at least over the course of one "compliment week" (a week-long event designed to encourage people to give one another compliments), this was not at all the case: recipients of a series of compliments from one person maintained their positive reactions over the course of the week, and did not start rating the compliments as insincere, so long as the compliments were at least slightly varied (for example, you aren't telling someone "I like your shoes" day after day). Do note that recipients got just one compliment a day for five days in a row. The research didn't examine how many compliments might be *too many* over the course of one interaction, so we hesitate to advise you to "max out" on giving many compliments in a very short period of time (say, in one interaction). Still, the general finding of these studies bears repeating: we tend to underestimate the positive impact of giving compliments.

Finally, it's worth noting that, in most of this research compliments were written out and delivered to recipients, giving the authors of these compliments ample time to think them out and phrase them just-so. In the rapid, spontaneous flow of an in-person conversation, we are seldom afforded this luxury. As a result, on occasion, compliments do run the risk of being inappropriate or off-putting. So, consider the following general guidelines:

- Don't compliment someone right before asking them for a favor, or you might come off as disingenuous or manipulative.
- Think twice about complimenting aspects of someone's physical appearance ("You look like you've lost weight—good for you!").
- Be mindful of your compliments being perceived as unwanted romantic advances.
- Avoid playing into stereotypes or making assumptions about someone's identity. These things can come off as microaggressions. ("For a young person, you're so good at your job," or "Your boyfriend's a lucky guy.").

As well-meaning as these compliments might be, they can easily come off badly. A safe bet is to offer a genuine compliment about how someone makes you feel. ("I feel really energized after talking to you," "your performance in that play was really touching," or "the comment you made in the meeting really inspired me.") Those kinds of compliments really convey that you're paying attention and valuing the person's efforts, character, and unique strengths.

Express Gratitude

A frequently mentioned way to inject more positivity into interpersonal relationships is through an authentic expression of gratitude.[18] Think about someone that you're grateful for but never adequately thanked. It could be someone very close to you or even a casual acquaintance: a patient teacher or coach, a caring medical professional, a helpful work colleague, or even someone who helped one of your loved ones. Imagine writing them a letter of gratitude, where you remind them of what they did for you, how it has impacted you, and how grateful you are for them.[19] Then imagine sending them this letter (or, if you dare, reading it aloud to them directly!). How does this make you feel?

Many people like this exercise in theory, but balk at it in practice. Researchers examined this reluctance in a series of studies.[20] In one study, participants wrote gratitude letters to someone who had affected them in a meaningful way. Recipients of the letters were later sent a survey to report their thoughts and feelings upon receiving the letter. They found that the letter writers significantly underestimated the positive impact that their expressions of gratitude would have (in terms of recipient's mood and in how surprised they were at receiving it), and also overestimated how awkward recipients would feel upon receiving their messages. In reality, the recipients seemed to love getting a heartfelt message of gratitude that they weren't expecting. (Wouldn't you? We certainly find that, as professors, a message of thanks from a student can absolutely make our day!) Yet, as the authors of those letters, people found this difficult to grasp. As was the case with the research on giving compliments mentioned previously, letter writers seemed to overemphasize the importance of expressing their gratitude with competence and undervalued the importance of conveying warmth. Pressure to get the words "just right" could deter people from expressing them at all. As a result, kind words that could have a real positive impact might just remain unsaid.

Ready to put your reluctance aside? Great! Think of someone to whom you'd like to express gratitude and simply start writing (or typing). If it's been a while, you might need to remind them of exactly what they did (they might not even realize that they'd done anything special!) Tell them how they have impacted you and continue to impact you. Write in a voice that is authentic to you and the nature of your relationship (meaning, for example, if you normally have a lighthearted sort of connection, don't feel the need to be excessively serious here).

How should you share your message of gratitude? Experts have long suggested that you deliver the message in person. However, recent research offers promising alternatives for people who find this approach just a bit too vulnerable, or simply too inconvenient (say, if the person lives far away). A sample of undergraduates was recruited and asked to express gratitude to a specific person, using one of three formats: some expressed gratitude privately, composing a letter but—importantly—not sharing the letter with anyone. Others composed and sent a text message of gratitude, while others made a public expression of gratitude for a specific person on social media.[21] They did their assigned activity four times over the course of a week, expressing gratitude to a new person each time (to help keep the activity novel). Compared to a control group, who did not express gratitude at all, those in all three gratitude-expression conditions—the private letter, the text message, and the social media post—felt more connected, less lonely, and were in better moods after completing this exercise. Results also indicated that texting a message of gratitude was surprisingly powerful, offering the biggest boosts in social connection and feelings of support. The take-home message of this research is both straightforward and encouraging: when you want to express gratitude, simply choose the means of communication that feels the most natural and least risky to you!

Help Out

Of all the strategies mentioned here, prosocial behavior—essentially, doing something to benefit others—may just be the most impactful for a variety of reasons. First, and most obviously, your thoughtful actions are having a direct benefit on someone else. Whether you're doing something casual, one-time, and informal, like holding the door for someone or showing a coworker how to use a new computer program, or something structured and formalized, like volunteering through an organization, you are taking action to make someone else's day a little brighter. But it goes further than that. Prosocial behavior doesn't just benefit the recipients of our kind acts; research shows that it might benefit the benefactor even more than the recipient. And it can be one of the best tools for social connection, for multiple reasons.[22] Let's explore why this sort of activity is so beneficial for our social lives.

First, when you engage in prosocial behavior, you can't help but put yourself into the mind of someone else. Your needs, concerns, and anxieties are pushed aside as you prioritize the needs of the person or group you're trying to help. This shift in focus can reduce the pressures associated with reaching out. Specifically, typical concerns, such as *What will I say?* and *Will they like me?* (which often plague us when we reach out to new people), are replaced by *How can I help?* and *What does this person need right now?* Notice how this might pave the way for a smoother social interaction as we worry less about our social aptitude and focus more on the task of helping.

Next, helping others fuels a positive self-image. It's a socially valued act, and it feels good to help someone else out. It also encourages a positive *public* image and makes you more likeable. In short, prosocial behavior does seem to set the stage for social connection.[23]

How can you capitalize on this? First off, think of the small opportunities that you are offered every day.

- What are you passionate about? What natural skills do you possess? Using your unique strengths to serve others will allow you to approach your prosocial efforts with confidence.[24] Identifying these passions and strengths is a necessary first step. (Need some help with this? Try taking the VIA Character Strengths Survey at www.viastrengths.org.)

- If your schedule and lifestyle permit, is there a volunteer organization that you might want to explore and consider joining? Maybe an opportunity through your church community, your children's school, or simply though a personal interest of yours? Joining an organization—ideally, one that meets regularly—has the added benefit of connecting you with like-minded people who share your interests, thereby giving you a natural entry point for conversation and connection.

- Consider channeling your energy into a cause that has in-person meetings or events (rather than a fully online group) so you can meet people and have the chance to connect.

This advice might seem straightforward, and yet, you can probably think of a time when you considered offering help but didn't follow through. Maybe you knew of a sick neighbor, or an overwhelmed coworker, or an acquaintance who had recently suffered a loss. Perhaps reaching out felt inconvenient or awkward. Maybe you told yourself that your support wouldn't make that much of a difference or might even be an imposition. Indeed, research suggests that we tend to undervalue just how impactful social support can be.[25] When imagining offering a message of support to someone in need, participants tended to underestimate how positively these messages would be received, and overestimated how awkward it would be to offer support (and this error was larger for people they knew less well). Once again, a key reason for this is that we tend to judge our actions based on competence (*Did I sound smart just now? Did I say the exact right thing?*), while those on the receiving end tend to focus on warmth (*What a nice thing to say! What a thoughtful person!*). This is yet another important example of social miscalibration: the disconnect between what we focus on and what the other person focuses on. And it can help explain why we don't always grasp the impact of reaching out to others.

Types of Support

Let's say you can push past this sort of misplaced reluctance. How can you help? Consider two broad types of social support: first, there's what we call *instrumental support*. Maybe this is the type of helping you naturally think about when you imagine volunteer work: the efforts that actively reduce someone else's burden in tangible ways—childcare, rides to appointments, helping to move a large piece of furniture, and so on. But there's also *emotional support*—this may be more subtle and less visible, and it includes sitting with someone and truly listening to them, offering advice if asked, and being the proverbial shoulder to cry on. Both types of support are helping in reducing stress, signaling care and concern, and promoting deeper connection.[26]

Emotional support may sound like something reserved for long-term, close relationships, but this is not necessarily the case.[27] Daily life provides many opportunities to offer small moments of emotional support. Imagine seeing a stranger crying in a public restroom, or visibly upset waiting at the endless airport ticket counter line. What about a young mom, obviously exhausted as she waits near you in the school pick-up line, or a colleague who is clearly annoyed by the malfunctioning copy machine? While you might not know these people well, or know them at all, this might be a chance for a small, subtle offering of support that helps alleviate the person's suffering. And while it might feel a little opportunistic to envision these moments as a chance to make a new friend, that can sometimes be the outcome.

The take-home here is that, if you see a person in need of some support, and you feel safe in offering it, try not to agonize over saying the perfect thing in the perfect way. A warm, genuine moment of connection and compassion will likely go much further than you may expect. And it doesn't need to be reserved for your closest friends and loved ones.

Of course, we have to mention one caveat. People don't always benefit from receiving social support. For example, if the support being offered is not responsive to their needs, it can lead to negative outcomes. In some cases, asking "What can I do to support you?" may be the best way to show support.[28]

The Ultimate Miscalibration?

We've all been there. We have a conversation with someone—maybe a potential new friend, a work colleague, or a new romantic partner—and, even if nothing particularly dreadful happened, we find ourselves excessively worrying about the kind of impression we've made.[29] These worries can take many forms: *Did I share too much? Did that comment sound pretentious? Did I ask enough questions? Did I ask too many questions?* or even *Did I have garlic breath?* Because of our deep desire to connect and be accepted, these worries make some sense. We want to perform well, look like we have it together, and be liked!

There is actually good news here. In general, our conversation partners aren't nearly as critical as we might expect. Even better news: they tend to like us and enjoy our company more than we think they do. Researchers call this discrepancy in perspectives—what you *think* someone thought of you versus what they *actually* thought of you—the *liking gap*. It's one key reason why social interactions can be a source of stress and worry, even after they're over. We underestimate just how much people enjoyed our company! This might be the ultimate form of social miscalibration, where our perceptions of others' thoughts and feelings don't match up with the reality. But unlike talking to strangers, giving compliments, expressing gratitude, or offering support, which are specific acts, the liking gap touches on a broader misunderstanding—how much people enjoy being in our company.

In a series of studies, researcher Erica Boothby and colleagues investigated the liking gap by examining several types of social interactions.[30] In one study, pairs of strangers met in a laboratory and performed a brief get-to-know-you task. In another, adults got acquainted as part of a personal development workshop. And to test how the liking gap plays out over longer periods of time, a third study looked at first-year college suitemates over the course of an academic year.

Across these different settings, types of people, and lengths of time, Boothby found evidence for the liking gap, where people guessed that their conversation partners liked them less and enjoyed the conversation less than they actually did. And the liking gap is persistent: for the first-year college suitemates, the liking gap persisted for the majority of the school year. (It did seem to be erased by May, just as students were packing up to go home for the summer.) Interestingly, while the liking gap was evident across a variety of situations and regardless of personality traits such as self-esteem and sensitivity to rejection, it seemed to be even more exaggerated for people who are shy. If this sounds like you, pay special attention to this message: People probably like you and your company more than you think they do.

A second series of studies examined the liking gap in people who were assigned to collaborate on a project in small groups.[31] Even while people were focused on their work, the liking gap existed here, too: many people thought that their group members liked them less than they actually did. And this had consequences for work-related outcomes. Those who guessed (wrongly) that others disliked them were less likely to ask their group members for help, were less likely to offer feedback to group members, and were less likely to want to work with the group again in the future.

Why Does the Liking Gap Exist?

To some extent, this error is driven by the negative, self-critical thoughts we often have during and after conversations, when we are feeling judgmental of things that our conversation partners couldn't possibly detect (our own well-hidden anxieties, for example) or just weren't paying attention to. This inner monologue is inaccessible to others, but extremely powerful for us. (Remember the illusion of transparency from the previous chapter? We think our internal states are more visible than they are!)

Note that, on the surface, this self-criticism can seem well-intended. We want to be liked, and we are exquisitely sensitive to any social blunders that we might make, so that we can repair them and hopefully perform better in the future. But—as this research points out—we can take these concerns a bit too far and spend a lot of time and energy worrying about conversational missteps that no one even picked up on! We can also carry these worries forward into future social interactions, making subsequent social encounters even more difficult. Plus, we often forget that our conversation partners may be grappling with their own self-criticisms as well. Instead of judging our blunders, they are probably focused on their own.

Closing the Gap

Next time you catch yourself being self-critical after a social interaction, pay attention to your thoughts. For example, you might catch yourself thinking, *I talked too much about politics during that conversation* or *I didn't maintain eye contact.* How likely is it that your conversation partner *actually* noticed these things? How likely is it that they were bothered by them? You probably won't know for sure, but make your best guess.

Next, can you come up with anything that *they* might have said or done that they could be worrying about? And simply reminding yourself of the findings of this research might even be comforting next time you catch yourself in a spiral of self-criticism. You are not alone in your need to be liked and to perform well in social situations. So, while you are worrying about your own performance, the person you interacted with is likely to be doing the same. The existence of self-criticism and social stress is not exactly good news, but it is hopefully comforting to know that it is something shared by most everyone.

Takeaways

- Remember that people often have miscalibrated expectations about the outcomes of reaching out to others, and these miscalibrations can create a barrier to connection.

- Start noticing the small moments for connection in your daily life—things like saying "good morning" to a neighbor, asking a coworker to lunch, or safely striking up a conversation with a stranger.
- If you're unsure how to connect, consider a genuine compliment, an act of social support, or a message of gratitude. We tend to undervalue the positive impact of these practices.
- In moments of self-doubt, remember that other people may also be plagued by their own self-doubt, and they are probably enjoying the interaction more than you think they are!

5
Liking, Demystified
Why Making Connections Can Be Surprisingly Simple

There are no strangers here; only friends you haven't yet met.
—William Butler Yeats

In 2021, actor Dwayne "The Rock" Johnson was profiled as "The Most Likeable Person in the World." What makes him so likeable? It helps that he has incredibly good looks (he was crowned 2016's "Sexiest Man Alive" by *People* magazine). He also seems to have natural-born charisma. And research shows that we tend to like people who are physically attractive and charismatic.[1]

But there are many factors that influence liking, and many have little to do with a person's unique attributes. In fact, research in social psychology suggests that liking is often triggered by simple, mundane factors, and Dwayne Johnson has a number of these factors at work for him. First, we like people we see often, and we see Johnson seemingly *everywhere*. He's starred in dozens of movies, has hosted *Saturday Night Live* multiple times, has a clothing line with Under Armour, and has over 388 million followers on Instagram. He also seems relatable, often pointing out similarities we might share with him (like a rough childhood or financial troubles). Additionally, Johnson conveys positivity—through his huge smile and warm sense of humor—and, as he told Oprah Winfrey, he strives to be a good listener. And this all feels *genuine*. On a somewhat personal note, Johnson owns a farm not far from us in Central Virginia and has been known to work out at a very unglamorous Gold's Gym in the area. In 2017, he posted a video on his Instagram account with some adoring fans outside of the gym. They discussed everyday topics (Taylor Swift and Virginia moonshine), and then he said, "I drive away feeling like the luckiest S-O-B on the planet to meet such amazing fans. This kinda stuff will always be the best part of fame."[2]

We may never achieve Dwayne Johnson's level of celebrity, get to host *Saturday Night Live*, or sit across from Oprah, but we can leverage some of these common factors—familiarity, similarity, positivity, and genuine interest in others—to draw people in and cultivate more connection in our own lives.

Looking Ahead

In this chapter, we'll unpack some of the simple factors that encourage likeability. For example, we like people who we see frequently—it seems to trigger a sense of predictability and comfort. We also tend to like people who are similar to us, partially because it signals compatibility and provides common ground on which to grow a relationship. And we like people who show interest in us and are pleasant to be around, because it just feels good! Since these factors *are* so simple, we suspect you don't fully realize the outsized role they play in shaping your social life.

This barrier—not realizing that the building blocks of liking are straightforward and within our control—can hold us back from using them to their full potential. As you read this chapter, we encourage you to reflect on the unique ways in which these factors have impacted you and ask yourself how you might make better use of them moving forward.

One caveat, before we get into the research: the goal of this chapter is not to help you "win friends and influence people."[3] It's also not designed to help you master the art of people-pleasing. Our goal is to share strategies for becoming more likeable and attuned to others, which will set the stage for more authentic, fulfilling relationships.

See and Be Seen

When we ask our psychology students how they came to know their closest friends in college, a common response is something along the lines of "they were my freshman roommate" or "they lived down the hall." In other words, they were *physically close*. Research supports the idea that many friendships start with proximity. In social psychologist Elliot Aronson's words, "the people who are geographically nearest to you are most likely to become dearest to you as well."[4]

There's nothing magical or mysterious about the power of proximity. The more you see someone, the more opportunities you have to smile at one another, say hello, strike up a conversation, and discover common interests. A 2019 survey from the Pew Research Center found that 35% of married or partnered people initially met through work or school.[5] Yes, Hollywood abounds with tales of serendipitous encounters that lead to love. But as much as we might like to romanticize the tales of how we formed our friendships or found love, most of our favorite people had the chance to fall into these roles simply because they were *around*. As social psychologist Sam Sommers quipped, " 'I love how familiar you are' doesn't sell many Valentine's Day cards,"[6] but the sentiment is true nonetheless.

In the 1950s, pioneering social psychologist Leon Festinger and his colleagues conducted a field study to examine the link between physical proximity and liking at a residential community for married students at the Massachusetts Institute of Technology (MIT).[7] Residents were interviewed and asked to report on which neighbors they had formed the closest relationships with within the community. One of the strongest predictors was simple physical distance: people liked those who lived close by—say, just one or two doors down. (The findings of this field study have been supported by more recent experimental data as well.[8])

Another strong predictor of liking in the MIT study was something the research team termed *functional distance*—or how often people's paths cross. They found that people who lived in high-traffic locations—near the stairwells, communal mailboxes, or bus stops—also tended to be more well-liked within the community at-large, because they had more natural opportunities to see and be seen. (Note that residents were randomly assigned to their units, eliminating the possibility that high-traffic areas were actively sought out by the friendlier tenants.)

This makes logical sense—after all, if you don't ever see someone, you have no chance to connect and become friends. Proximity provides natural opportunities for socializing. But the effects of proximity on liking may also be driven by something far more basic: a well-known phenomenon known as the *mere exposure effect*.[9] In short, the more we're exposed to something, the more we tend to like it (assuming it's not aversive to begin with). The mere exposure effect applies to foods, scents, songs on the radio, and—yes—people. Seeing a familiar person triggers a sense of comfort and security. This is so fundamental that we can fail to notice and appreciate it. In fact, every day you probably encounter people that you don't consciously consider. They are physically there, but you're not focused on them. They are essentially the background characters of your life. But if you were asked how you felt about one of these people, you might notice a vague sense of liking for them, even if you don't actually know anything about them!

Sound hard to believe? Consider a large college classroom, where students can't reasonably interact with every other student. To capitalize on this particular setting, one study examined mere exposure in a large university class of 130 students.[10] The researchers arranged for four women (who all looked somewhat similar to one another) to attend class sessions, pretending to be students in the class but not interacting with anyone. One woman attended 5 class meetings over the term, another attended 10, and another attended 15, while the fourth woman never attended the class at all. At the end of the term, students in the class were simply shown each woman's image and asked to rate each on familiarity, attractiveness, and perceived similarity. The findings were clear: the more often a woman had attended the class, the higher she rated on these three desirable outcomes, *even though she had never spoken up in class or interacted with any of her classmates.* Shy or quiet readers: take particular note of this. There are multiple ways to put mere exposure to work for you. Consider becoming a regular at the gym, coffeeshop, church, neighborhood park, or other public space. Just being around gives you a social advantage!

Mere exposure is easy to understand: we like who we repeatedly see, so let people see you! But it's not always easy to put into practice. For one, many people have found it difficult to get back out there, postpandemic. In a 2023 piece in *The Atlantic*, provocatively titled "How We Learned to Be Lonely,"[11] Arthur Brooks mentions that many Americans still work from home for various reasons, and according to a 2022 Forbes Health survey, many are reluctant to socialize like they once did. Why? A small percentage (9%) reported being worried about catching the virus, but many more—a full 59% of respondents—thought that forming relationships has gotten harder. Twenty-nine percent of respondents said they were nervous about not knowing what to say or how to interact, 26% were worried about embarrassing themselves, and 16% worried about saying the wrong thing.

Brooks argues that isolation and loneliness have become habits. He advises pushing through this reluctance to socialize so we can be reminded first-hand of the natural rewards of social interaction and, we might add, so that we might make good use of the mere exposure effect.

As a side note, you might wonder whether these findings extend to our virtual lives. In a 2011 study, researchers asked pairs of unacquainted college students to chat over email for a varying number of times.[12] The findings revealed that the more they chatted, the more they liked each other. So, yes, even virtual exposure seems to breed liking. We suspect that the mere exposure effect holds up on social media, too (though frequent *negative* posts can reduce liking).[13] Just keep in mind that there's a limit to the mere exposure effect— both in person and online. Too much exposure is not a good thing. How many social media posts are *too many*? Researchers haven't answered this question yet, so you'll have to rely on your intuition here.

Also, a corollary to the proximity principle is that it requires that you be available to see and interact with people. If you'd like to get to know your neighbors, but you're rarely home or seldom leave your house, you may not reap the benefits of proximity. The same logic applies if you belong to a variety of organizations but seldom attend meetings. You need to give yourself the opportunity to be seen. (That includes allowing the time to stop and chat.) It might be better to commit fully to one organization—be it a church, fitness group, or volunteer association—and to show up as often and as consistently as you can, than to be only nominally affiliated with many.

Finally, remember the importance of functional distance. In the MIT housing study, people who lived in high-traffic locations were generally more well-liked, presumably because they were more visible and had more opportunity to cross paths with people. Think about how visible you are in your pre-existing networks (to the extent that you can control these things). Do you see and say hello to neighbors and coworkers? At work, is your office door open? Is your cubicle in the center of the office layout, or tucked back into a corner? At the gym, do you choose the treadmill in the center of the room, or do you choose one away from others? Even at home: do you sit outside on the front porch, where you might encounter a passing neighbor? Or do you choose a more private space, like the backyard or back deck? In general: are you willing to physically move yourself into the sightlines of others? These small decisions might just have a surprisingly large impact on your social life!

Find Common Ground

Proximity will help set the stage for social success. But, then what? We suggest that you try and find some sort of common ground. Despite the cultural maxim that "opposites attract," research finds that we're actually more likely to hit it off with people with whom we share similar attitudes, demographics, values, and hobbies.[14] Like proximity, similarity is a powerful determinant of liking.

We encourage you to look for the similarities you share with others and point out the ones you discover (in a way that feels natural and authentic, of course). In talking to a new acquaintance, you might learn that you have children around the same age. Maybe you do similar work. You might enjoy the same local restaurants, bands, or vacation spots. Maybe you're even wearing similar shoes! It could be that you're visiting the same volunteer organization, taking the same Zumba class, wearing the same team jersey, or waiting in the same grocery store line. In an initial conversation, you don't need the extra stress of trying to be the most fascinating or hilarious person in the room. Let similarity set you up for connection.

The similarity principle might help explain why so many people—at least anecdotally—make friends at the dog park, at church, or in fitness communities. There, you can expect to connect with a fellow animal lover, spiritual person, or cardio-enthusiast, respectively. There are shared interests built in. Not only does this provide natural topics of conversation, but it also suggests a broader system of shared values. You can naturally capitalize on the joint power of proximity and similarity by joining a club or group that taps into one of your interests or passions. Ideally, it will meet regularly, giving you ample opportunity to show your face and connect with like-minded people.

Unearthing Hidden Similarities

Some similarities are easy to spot, but others can only be uncovered by interacting with and learning more about people. Unfortunately, we often don't give ourselves that opportunity. Research shows that we're quick at deciding who we won't mesh with. We might automatically dismiss someone based on a presumed characteristic: age, gender, race, and sexual or gender identity, or physical attractiveness, to name a few. A young professional might view her retired neighbor as an unsuitable friendship candidate simply because she's older. A straight, White man might assume he has nothing in common with a Black lesbian. Certainly, our unconscious biases come into play here, as we naturally gravitate toward people who we perceive as similar to us.[15] Unfortunately, this can keep us stuck in a social rut. (And it also reinforces stereotypes. For example, if you think that people who live in a certain area of your town are snobby, you might behave toward them in a way that pulls those very qualities out of them. If this sounds familiar, this is a perfect example of the self-fulfilling prophecy, which we presented in Chapter 3.)

By dismissing someone who seems different, we might sabotage or completely miss out on really rewarding conversations and potential friendships. To test how this might play out in cross-race interactions, social psychologist Robyn Mallett and colleagues recruited a sample of college students and told them that they were going to be having a conversation with a student of another racial group. Before meeting and interacting with this new person, participants made a prediction of how they thought the conversation would go. Most expected the conversation to go poorly, because they were focused on what was most salient to them—the obvious racial differences. But when they actually went on to have the conversation, their natural similarities were made apparent (after all, they were about the same age, all students at the same university, taking psychology classes). The conversations were far more enjoyable than they had expected. Mallett also found that when they asked the students to consciously focus on their similarities (rather than on their differences), they were more likely to (correctly) predict that the conversation would go well.[16] The advice here is clear: before entering a social interaction, particularly with someone who you judge as "different," think of all of the things the two of you might have in common, especially if those similarities aren't visible on the surface.

In fact, we want to challenge you to push past your initial impressions and open yourself up to people who, on the surface, seem quite different from you in terms of age, race, culture, sexual orientation, and so on. If you do, you'll find that there may be similarities and a "spark" that you can't initially see. Plus, you might experience a broadening of your perspectives as you open yourself to new and different people.

For example, one of us (Jaime) often takes part in a Sunday morning run with a group of local people of all ages and backgrounds. Although this group is united by a common love of running, we don't seem to have all that much else in common, at least not on the surface. For one, the group ranges from graduate students in their early 20s to middle-aged parents to retirees in their 70s. It's easy to see how, in other contexts, we might inadvertently self-segregate by stage of life, using age to draw ingroup/outgroup distinctions. But on Sunday mornings, this hardly matters. We are all runners, period. And as we sit and chat over post-run coffee, other commonalities are revealed—a mutual love of travel, dogs, our local college basketball team, *Ted Lasso*—which transcend generational boundaries. A few of us have even put together a jazz quartet after realizing we had several musicians in the group. Enduring cross-generational friendships have emerged from this running group, and we have to wonder if this would have happened in a different setting.

We'd like you to consider the idea that ingroup ("people like me") and outgroup ("people not like me") distinctions are largely artificial and socially constructed. As such, they are malleable and can be broadened to be more inclusive. First, though, we'd like you to take a moment and do something that might feel a little strange: make a mental list of the many groups that you belong to (your ingroups). Think about demographics—say, middle-aged, college-educated, Democrat, Californian, Asian-American, and middle class. Those ingroups imply the existence of a corresponding outgroup: young and old, non-college-educated, Republican, non-Californian—you get the idea. Given that we are drawn to the safety and predictability that similarity affords, you might naturally gravitate to your ingroup members. Some of this is due to physical proximity (as in, it's much easier to meet fellow Californians than people who live out-of-state). But it's also because of the powerful pull of similarity.

This is likely borne out in your own social network: it's full of people who are similar to you—at least on the surface. Are we right?

But maybe the boundaries we draw can be broadened. Instead of middle-aged, why not think of yourself as "adult"? Instead of Californian and Asian-American, why not think of yourself as "North American"? Your ingroups have just grown! This redrawing of boundaries is what social psychologists John Dovidio and Samuel Gaertner refer to as crafting a *common ingroup identity*.[17] Their research shows that this mental shift predicts lower levels of stereotyping and prejudice toward those who would have otherwise been labeled as an outgroup member. We also think it will set the stage for unearthing similarities that you may have otherwise missed.

We stress all of this because we tend to be fairly quick to dismiss someone as "not for me," and we often do this based on perceived differences. Once these unfortunate first impressions are made, they are pretty difficult to change (thanks in large part to the confirmation bias and self-fulfilling prophecy that we discussed in Chapter 3). And yet, having a diverse set of social ties is actually related to greater well-being, possibly due to the greater sense of connection, social support, and broadened perspective they can provide.[18]

Start with a Smile

We are generally drawn to people who are positive—those who convey a sense of lightness, zest, optimism, and happiness. And one of the easiest ways to express positivity is simply to smile. As a signal of positivity, a genuine, bright smile can immediately make us more likeable, attractive, and memorable. It signals warmth, approachability, and even intelligence. It's no surprise that naturally happy people tend to be more well-liked.[19] They have a natural social advantage.

So, the advice is clear. Smile. You don't have to do it forever. But it's simply one of the easiest and most important ways to make a positive first impression. Laughter tends to operate similarly. While we don't suggest doing this spontaneously, in the absence of anything humorous, laughing at a funny statement or moment is another way to convey a positive, lighthearted nature. Genuine laughter is playful. It eases tension, conveys understanding, can act as a compliment ("I think you're funny and clever!"), and can serve to draw people together. Shared laughter also increases perceived similarity which, in turn, enhances relationships.[20]

What If You're Not Feeling It?

As you consider this advice—smile! laugh!—and think about exactly how you might use it, you may have a nagging sense that some of it might feel disingenuous. For example, we just advised you to smile more, because smiles draw people in and signal warmth and approachability. This is true. But what if that's not your natural tendency? What if you just don't feel happy? To be honest, we have struggled with this issue ourselves. We want to be "real," but we also want to be likeable. Fortunately, research shows that there are situations when forcing a little positivity can set us up for success, both internally and in our interactions with others.

During graduate school, social psychologist Elizabeth Dunn observed this phenomenon first-hand. When her then-boyfriend (Benjamin) was in a bad mood, she would do her best to offer him support and understanding, yet she wasn't always able to cheer him up. On the other hand, if they were out socializing with acquaintances, he would pull himself up, and his bad mood would disappear, as if by magic. In other words, people who were practically strangers seemed able to repair his mood, while his own girlfriend could not!

As a budding happiness researcher, Dunn decided to more systematically investigate "the Benjamin effect." In one study, she asked heterosexual dating couples to come to the lab, two couples at a time. They were randomly assigned to interact with their romantic partner or with the opposite sex stranger from the other couple, and their conversations were recorded so research assistants could later analyze them. The results showed that the participants were more likely to "put their best face forward" for the stranger, and this positive self-presentation led participants to feel pleasant, happy, and cheerful after the conversation—and much more than expected. In fact, they felt just as good after interacting with the stranger as after interacting with their loved one, although they expected to feel much better with their partner. In other words, they underestimated the impact of conveying positivity.[21]

In an interview for NPR's *Hidden Brain*,[22] Dunn further explained the results:

> What we see in our study is that when people engage in this positive self-presentation, acting pleasant and cheerful around someone they don't know, it actually has benefits for their own mood in a way that they themselves don't seem to foresee. It provides this unexpected boost to our moods when we just act pleasant and cheerful for the benefit of somebody else.

Meanwhile, our loved ones don't inspire us to manage impressions, given that they keep coming back even though they often see us at our worst. They already love us! Therefore, we're less likely to do the work needed to repair our moods and—in short—we stay moody. However, another of Dunn's studies shows that when we *do* engage in positive self-presentation with a loved one, this can yield surprising mood boosts, too.[23]

The results of this work suggest that we might want to put our best face forward in our relationships. Of course, we don't mean to suggest that we should *always* feel compelled to "fake happy," and certainly not when going through tough times. In fact, sometimes sitting with an accepting loved one, feeling our feelings, and knowing we're supported through it all is exactly what we need to process and cope with difficulty. We're talking here about those more minor feelings of sadness, lethargy, and annoyance, when there's nothing to really "work through." It's just a passing mood. Also consider those neutral moments when we're not feeling particularly bad but could still use a little boost. In those cases, we can underestimate the emotional benefits provided by strangers and shallow connections. The happy display that may feel exaggerated or phony at first can quickly become real.

And from there, initial expressions of positivity can engender an "upward spiral," giving rise to more and more positive emotions. Expressing positivity in a social interaction often pulls a smile, a laugh, or some other kind of positive response from the other person. This leads to even more positivity, and so on and so on. In this way, you're giving other people a "social gift" by expressing positivity.

So, we hope that you will smile at someone, even if you're not feeling truly happy. Maybe it doesn't feel truly genuine at first. But imagine that you get a smile back. Maybe it's accompanied by a conversation or small moment of connection—which then actually *does* make you feel genuinely happier, and it boosts your confidence for next time. So, what initially may have felt disingenuous quickly becomes real and takes on a life of its own.

The Art (and Science) of Conversation

How many times a day do have this exchange?

> "Hey! How are you?"
> "I'm good! How are you?"
> "I'm great."
> "Good to hear."

This sort of conversation happens mindlessly and is governed by a few implicit rules: we don't *really* say how we are, we don't disclose anything significant, and—if we're already in motion—sometimes we don't even stop walking! While we might feel like we're making more of an effort than we would by just nodding or smiling, the tacit understanding is that neither person really cares to know what's *actually* going on with the other.

In an effort to acknowledge the emptiness of this sort of exchange, Claire Bidwell Smith, therapist, grief expert, and host of the podcast *New Day*, always starts off by asking her guests, with genuine warmth and curiosity, "How are you doing . . . but how are you *really* doing?" The responses she gets are often fascinating and revealing. That's one great tip—stop, take a beat, and infuse the normal, mindless "How are you?" exchange with authentic interest. And if you don't have the time or attention to do that, consider not asking.

What if you're on the receiving end of the "how are you?" routine? How would it feel to give a genuine answer? One of our social psychology undergraduates (we'll call her Ally) made a point of doing just that as part of a social norm–breaking project. When the cashier at her coffee shop mindlessly asked her how her day was going, Ally said, "Honestly, I'm really stressed and overwhelmed." The cashier was thrown off for a second—*that's not how this exchange is supposed to go!*—but she quickly recovered, looked Ally in the eye, smiled in solidarity, and said, "You know what? Me too. Let's both get through it and hope tomorrow is a little better." Ally was initially nervous at the thought of breaking this conversational norm and was shocked at how much this brief encounter lifted her spirits and made her feel less alone. We advise you to give it a try, and you might just be equally surprised.

Show Your Interest

In informal polls, we asked our social psychology students which leads to greater liking: playing hard to get, or letting someone know that you like them (in a natural, noncreepy way). Every semester, the majority of students think that playing hard to get is the way to go. And it does make sense: an element of uncertainty is exciting! And isn't it more rewarding to learn that someone likes you after a drawn-out period of wondering, rather than having it revealed immediately?

When it comes to a nail-biter of a sporting event or a tense mystery novel, yes: uncertainty is thrilling. But when it comes to *people*, our students'—and many people's— intuitions are a bit off. While there is always an exception, we like people who like us, plain and simple. Being liked is inherently rewarding and taps into our basic need for acceptance and belonging. Meanwhile, those who string us along and make us guess where we stand can be among the most stressful types of relationships, exerting a measurable toll on health and well-being.[24]

This principle—sometimes called *reciprocal liking*—could hardly be more simple, but the implications are profound. *Let people know you like them.* In one experiment, when participants were led to believe that their interaction partner (a stranger) liked them, they tended to open up more and expressed greater liking for them in return. In another study, those who were told their interaction partner (also a stranger) liked them were more likely to interpret their somewhat ambiguous behavior as having good intentions, when compared to those who were *not* told that they were liked.[25] Being liked, even by a stranger, doesn't only feel good, but seems to set the stage for future positive interactions.

A simple way to convey liking is through straightforward warmth and friendliness. In one of the studies on reciprocal liking mentioned above, participants were given this written feedback from their interaction partner: "I enjoyed reading my partner's responses. She seems like a really fun and interesting person. I would really like to get to know her better."[26] Is there a natural way to send this sort of message in everyday life? Children tend to be pretty direct about it: "I like you; let's be friends." Maybe you're the kind of socially gifted person who can make that one work. (And you don't know unless you try!) Or perhaps a more subtle version, like, "I had fun tonight, let's do it again." Or a simple compliment: "You're hilarious!" or "I love your sense of style." There are countless ways to express liking.

Here's another tip: try to remember people's names—and other important details about them—because it signals that they are important to you.[27] Of course, cognitive psychologist Daniel Willingham confirms that remembering people's names is inherently difficult for many. You often learn a person's name while also navigating a complex social situation. For example, imagine a cocktail party or a business function. You're meeting many people at once, it's noisy and overstimulating, and maybe you're also a bit nervous.[28] All of that makes a hard thing even harder. So, if you really, truly can't remember someone's name, it offers an opportunity to be vulnerable: "I'm so sorry . . . the night we met was so crazy. Can you remind me of your name again?" This conveys that it's not that the person doesn't matter to you. The forgetting is due to external circumstances. If you can recall any other details about the person, you might try to bring them up as a way of compensating ("We met a few months back at Bobby's bar mitzvah! Can you remind me of your name again?"). And hopefully you'll remember their name the next time you interact.

Another, related tip is to show that you remember your previous interactions with people. In a subsequent conversation, you might say something like, "I remember you saying you were remodeling your kitchen. How did that go?" or "How was the beach? Your photos look incredible!" Also, try to remember their birthday and significant events in their lives—and let them know that you remember. (You might need to put these things on your calendar or find other handy ways of remembering. Does that make it any less meaningful? Would it matter to you? Personally, it's touching to think about a friend putting "Jaime's birthday" or "Natalie's trip to Ireland" on their calendar of important events!)

The Gift of Attention

In a scene from the 2017 film *Lady Bird*, the title character (a high school student played by Saoirse Ronan) meets with her guidance counselor, who compliments her college admissions essay about her hometown. She remarks, "You write about Sacramento so affectionately and with such care . . . it comes across as love." Lady Bird shrugs, saying, "Sure, I guess I pay attention" to which her guidance counselor muses, "Don't you think maybe they are the same thing? Love and attention?" Lady Bird is stunned, as she claims disdain for all things Sacramento and voices a fierce desire to escape to a far-off college. And yet, the comment hits home.[29] What is love, if not focused attention? And how better to convey it than through open, intentional listening?

In her 2020 book *You're Not Listening*, journalist Kate Murphy thoughtfully remarked, "In our modern life, we are encouraged to listen to our hearts, listen to our inner voices, and listen to our guts, but rarely are we encouraged to listen carefully and with intent to other people."[30] However, this kind of *active listening* may be the best outward display of focused attention, a sign that you are really "with" someone, fully present with their emotions, thoughts, and needs. To best appreciate the importance of focused attention and active listening, it might help to imagine its absence. As we have probably all learned first-hand, a person can certainly *hear* without really *listening*. Signs include seeming distracted or restless (checking one's phone or smartwatch is an obvious clue), looking around the room, not asking us any questions, interrupting, regularly turning the conversation back to themselves, or not remembering what we've said. Almost all of us been on the receiving end of this, and it doesn't feel good.

The good news is, most everyone can learn to be a better listener. How? To set the stage, if you're able, put distractions—that means your phone and smartwatch—out of sight. To convey that you're actively listening, try to provide nonverbal cues like eye contact, nodding and smiling, and maintaining an open posture. But merely nodding and smiling in response is not enough. While nonverbal cues like these can easily be faked (as in, you can look like you're paying attention when you're really not), it's much harder to fake the verbal cues.[31] You need to really take in what a person is saying in order to say something appropriate in response. To convey active listening through words, you might give affirmations, refer back to other things the person has said, and show verbal signs of compassion if appropriate.

Dale Carnegie once said, "You can make more friends in two months by becoming interested in other people than you can in two years by trying to get other people interested in you."[32] While this seems a bit hyperbolic, the sentiment is clear: one of the best ways to indicate attention and interest is by *asking questions*, and then by fully listening and being present for the person's response. Journalist Kate Murphy, who has interviewed countless subjects during her long career in reporting, argues that "good listeners are good questioners." (Once again, the self-fulfilling prophecy is relevant here: if you go into a conversation thinking that the person is interesting, you're more likely to pull interesting things out of them!) Make an active choice to be curious. As Murphy said, "everybody is interesting if you ask the right questions."

Of course, Kate Murphy is a reporter . . . and we don't want our conversations to sound like interviews. If you wonder if you're asking *too* many questions in your conversations, social cues (such as the person looking bored or annoyed, or giving extremely short answers) might give you your answer. But know that most people enjoy being the focus of someone's interest! (Also worth noting: people who are lonely tend to ask fewer questions of others, and spend more time talking about themselves![33])

Just to drive home the role of engaged, active listening in a quality conversation, consider a sampling of survey items from the Connections During Conversations Scale.[34] In answering these, you might think back to the last conversation that you had, focusing specifically on the person you were talking to. To what extent do you agree with these statements?

They really understood who I am.

They were able to relate to my experiences.

I was interested in their thoughts and feelings.

I felt that my energy was drained during the interaction.

If you agreed with the first three and disagreed with the last, we bet you'd call it a pretty pleasant conversation, one with a mutual sense of understanding. Notice the role of focused attention and listening here. A good conversation requires them.

To further gauge the quality of a conversation, Kate Murphy offers this advice: "When you leave a conversation, ask yourself, 'What did I just learn about that person? What was most concerning to that person today? How did that person feel about what we were talking about?'"[35] You might check in with yourself and see if you're able to answer these. And—and always—we hope your efforts lead to some natural give-and-take, because you'd surely like to be the object of someone else's interest, too!

It Takes Time

Undervaluing the simple principles presented in this chapter can be a barrier to connection. Also, as much you might understand these principles in theory, you may still struggle to cultivate connection if you don't invest enough *time* when putting them into practice. As we mentioned in the introduction to the book, researcher Jeffrey Hall found that it takes about 40 to 60 hours to turn acquaintances into casual friends, around 80 to 100 hours to transition from casual friend to friend, and more than 200 hours to become good or best friends. Given that many of us spend less than an hour a day socializing, we can expect the process to be somewhat slow.[36] And once you establish those friendships, you have to invest time and energy to maintain them.

What about the times when you meet someone and feel like you instantly "click?" This concept—what researchers call *interpersonal chemistry*—has captivated poets, authors, and filmmakers, as well as singles looking for love, for centuries. Chemistry doesn't need to be romantic or sexual in nature, though. It can and does exist between friends, teammates, creative partners, and so on. Also, as much as we equate it with an instant spark, researchers think about chemistry as something that *gradually* emerges in a relationship context (and, as such, maybe we shouldn't be quick to immediately decide whether or not we have it with a new person). The more time people spend together, the more opportunity there is to see if chemistry exists.[37]

So, give it time.

Next Level

For a variety of reasons, some relationships won't proceed past the early stage. Maybe you had a pleasant but one-time interaction with a stranger. Maybe you are work colleagues and want to keep things friendly but professional. Maybe you realize you don't have much in common. Maybe you don't have the time or energy to develop a more in-depth relationship. This is not necessarily a bad thing. You can still feel moments of joy, laughter, comfort, and connection with relationships that exist at the level of acquaintanceship.

But when you do feel a spark—or simply a desire to get to know someone better—we hope that your conversations and feelings of connection will evolve. As you get to know someone more, you'll hopefully feel more secure in your relationship and able to reveal the more nuanced aspects of yourself—these include the funny stories and moments of triumph, but also your past experiences of struggle and setback. Insecurities. Troubled relationships. And all of the rich, complex emotions that go along with them.

In this chapter, we focused on the simple but underappreciated factors that predict liking in the early stages of a relationship. Proximity promotes social opportunities by allowing you to see and be seen. Discovering similarities and conveying positivity leads to enjoyable first conversations. Making the person you're talking to feel appreciated and heard really drives home the fact that you value them. Because these factors are fairly basic, some of the research in this chapter may seem obvious or straightforward. The real challenge lies in the *execution*. In the next chapter, we'll discuss strategies for creating greater depth in relationships . . . and we'll challenge the barriers to closeness that can keep us stuck.

Takeaways

- Consider your social network—perhaps your romantic partner, friends, and loose acquaintanceships. Note the roles that proximity, similarity, positivity, and genuine interest have played in crafting this network. This will help you see just how impactful these simple factors truly are.
- Become a regular in a public space that feels like "you"—comfortable and full of people you might want to connect with. Think of the big ideological sorts of things (political views, religious beliefs, deep passions) but also consider unique tastes and interests (salsa dancing, gardening, or gourmet cooking).
- Remember that we are quick to rule people out as potential friends, often based on surface features. Try to find things in common with people who may seem very different from you.

- When possible, bring more positivity into your interactions. What does this look like for you? When does this feel easy or natural? Try and capitalize on these moments.
- Practice giving the gift of genuine, focused attention. Put away distractions, ask questions, and really listen to the person. How does it feel?

6

Beyond Casual Connection

The Rules and Rewards of Building Intimacy

To know that you are seen and loved for who you are, and to perceive someone else in all of their vulnerability and love them as they are, may just be one of life's most fulfilling experiences.

—Emma Seppälä

If there's ever an activity that forces a person to reflect on their social network, it's drawing up their wedding guest list. Who'll receive an invitation? Who won't? And, of these people, who gets elevated to the role of bridesmaid or groomsman?

As she found herself planning her own wedding, one Nashville, Tennessee-area blogger realized,

> I could make a 500-person guest list, easy . . . I have tons of people to invite and that I love, but none that I am super close with. I have so many acquaintances, but no one that I call on a regular basis just to talk. No one that I talk to about heavy things. No one I cry to if I have a horrible day.

She laments the fact that she's been to over forty weddings but was a bridesmaid in just one of them. And she, in turn, has no idea who to ask to be *her* bridesmaid . . . despite having a vibrant, active social life.[1]

You might have been struck by a similar realization at one time or another. You may have a large social network, maybe even a lot of people you'd call friends. But, deep down, you might also feel that these people don't really, truly *know you*. Perhaps it's because you just don't spend enough quality time together, or when you do, you're too distracted to really give them your full attention (or vice versa!). Perhaps your conversations are made up of small talk and they seldom hit upon anything revealing or meaningful. Or perhaps you're afraid to let your guard down and put your true self—the good, the bad, and even the ugly—on display.

If you find yourself lacking in deep connections, know that you're not alone. Since 1990, Americans have reported having fewer and fewer close friends. In 2021, interviews conducted by Gallup and the Survey Center for American Life revealed that an alarming 12% of Americans reported having no close friends at all, which was a fourfold increase from 30 years prior (and it's not just a function of the COVID-19 pandemic, as the number had been increasing for years). Of the friends they *do* have, Americans report seeing them less frequently and relying on them less and less for support. Only about half of respondents said they were satisfied with the quality of their friendships. Additionally, around the world, there's evidence that people are marrying later in life or not at all.[2]

Looking Ahead

The reasons for the decline in close relationships are surely complex and multifaceted. But in this chapter, we'll focus on two key *psychological* barriers to closeness. First, there's a reluctance to letting yourself truly be known and second, a difficulty in being responsive to the deep needs of others. But with a bit of knowledge, courage, and practice, we believe that these challenges can be overcome. To that end, we hope to motivate you to better understand and push past these barriers as we discuss several specific research-based strategies. As a result, you might come to realize that, while modern life does pose real challenges to closeness, achieving it may be easier than you initially believed.

Defining Closeness

Exactly what makes a relationship close and intimate? How do you know you've gone from the level of casual acquaintanceship to something more emotionally rich? Researchers define a close relationship as one in which both partners are *responsive* to each other—they understand, validate, and care for one another.[3] But you don't need a definition to know whether you have a close relationship. You probably just *know*.

Think about those close people in your life. Take a minute and see if you can identify what distinguishes them from people you know and like but don't feel particularly close with.

It may just be a feeling you have, along the lines of *this is a person I trust, who makes me feel safe and secure.* Or there might be a more specific signal you've picked up on. Our students pinpointed idiosyncratic indicators of closeness in their own relationships, such as sharing clothes, opening someone's refrigerator without permission, disclosing secrets or gossip, having private lingo, inviting someone over without obsessively tidying up, and being able to sit comfortably with someone in silence. Other signals may convey a sense of validation and understanding (they "get" what makes you feel loved, and also what makes you feel angry or hurt, without judgment). Others still might convey care (you feel comfortable asking the person for a favor or coming to them with a problem). You might have some signifiers of your own as well, maybe things you've never really noticed before, which are unique to the personality of your relationships.

Personality psychologist Dan McAdams has a different perspective: he argues that knowing a person deeply means that you know *their life story*, the unique narrative they weave together from all of the different chapters of their life.[4] This is much more than just a list of personality traits, along the lines of "Angie is hard-working, punctual, and serious." By knowing these things, you know Angie a little, but certainly not in-depth. For example, you don't know why she sees lateness as the ultimate sign of disrespect, why she doesn't touch alcohol, or why she is prickly when you bring up Mother's Day. But when you know elements of her life story, you might understand that some of her earliest memories are of waiting after school, alone and uncertain, for her mother, who struggled with substance abuse, to come pick her up. You might also have more of a grasp of inconsistencies in her behavior: for instance, why she is often open and receptive to new people but shuts down immediately when she sees a sign of flakiness. By knowing even some of her life story, you can understand why she thinks, feels, and acts the way she does in different situations. More concisely, you feel like you know her. It follows, then, that sharing elements of *your* life story is one way to foster emotional intimacy.

The amount of time you've spent with someone is one predictor of closeness, but it's certainly not a perfect indicator. We're sure you can think of someone with whom you've bonded very quickly, opening up about the details of your lives and letting your guards down. On the other hand, you might be acquainted with someone for years and still not really *know* them. Or as Jane Austen put it, "Seven years would be insufficient to make some people acquainted with each other, and seven days are more than enough for others." As we mentioned in the previous chapter, Jeffrey Hall's work has found that truly close friendships require over 200 hours of shared time, but what you do, say, and reveal in your time together matters tremendously. That is what we will explore in this chapter.[5]

We want you to note that this advice transcends any particular type of relationship. It's not exclusive to romantic pairings, or to friendships, or to families. You might use these tips to connect more deeply with a neighbor or a coworker that you like but don't know well. You might use them to liven up a stale romantic connection or reconnect with a friend you haven't talked to in years. You may be surprised by who is open and receptive to your attempts to connect on a deeper level.

Show Your Whole Self

Self-disclosure—intentionally revealing information about yourself—may be the most direct way to build deeper social bonds.[6] Researchers describe the self-disclosure process as akin to peeling back the layers of an onion, where you gradually move past the superficial layers to the more substantive ones. Eventually, if it feels right, you'll reveal the core: the real you, the part that only a privileged few may get to see. Ideally, this is a reciprocal process, where both people share increasingly revealing information with each other as their trust and connection grow.

While some might prefer to immediately dive right in to the big, deep topics, self-disclosure typically happens gradually. People often start by sharing surface-level things about themselves—tastes, preferences, basic background information, maybe a lighthearted anecdote. They often note the similarities that they share, as we emphasized in the previous chapter. Imagine the sort of conversation you might expect on a pleasant first date, as you feel each other out and try to decide if you want to reveal more.

If you desire an even closer connection, and if the initial disclosures have gone well (meaning they were well-received and reciprocated), you may begin to open up more about your feelings and values and share more privileged information. (Imagine the process of a new couple getting to know one another more deeply, over multiple dates, as they establish trust.) If you feel safe in your relationship, you may start to let your guard down even more and share aspects of yourself that you're not proud of, like failures, setbacks, and unpleasant past experiences. Eventually, if the relationship continues to develop, you might disclose with one another much more freely and spontaneously, as self-disclosure has become a natural part of the relationship.[7]

What have researchers learned about self-disclosure? First, self-disclosure is important in all stages of relationships, from first encounters to long-term relationships. Also, self-disclosure leads to increased liking and closeness—both for the person making a disclosure and the person receiving it (although receivers tend to report *more* liking). Self-disclosure also tends to be reciprocal. When the self-disclosure is one-sided (when one person opens up and the other doesn't), it's less likely to cultivate connection. This has important implications for people who are shy, lonely, or socially anxious: you might be tempted to simply ask questions and listen to your partner's responses, but this might not make a good impression. Make sure there's some give and take.[8]

So, this all sounds great in theory. Share a little, feel good about it. Share a little more. Feel good about that. Get closer, share more, and suddenly, you're deeply connected! But what if it's not so easy?

A Little Mess Is OK—Really.

Are you nervous at the thought of opening up? Do you tend to keep people at arm's length, and keep conversations at a surface level? We fully acknowledge that there may be a valid reason for this reluctance, and we encourage you to reflect on why this might be the case for you. Take note of when the desire to clam up hits you the hardest. It's very possible that you've attempted self-disclosure in the past and experienced judgment, betrayal, or rejection. Or maybe you prefer to maintain a polished persona, with your messier, more complex layers neatly hidden away. Or maybe—as Brené Brown's research has found—you view vulnerability (broadly defined by Brown as "uncertainty, risk, and emotional exposure") as a sign of weakness, something to be avoided at all costs.

The fact is, it's hard to experience deep connection when you can't or won't let your guard down. As Brown argues, "there is no intimacy without vulnerability." Breaking down this particular barrier to connection is challenging for many people, yet the rewards are plentiful.[9]

If avoidance of vulnerability resonates with you, maybe this will provide some comfort: those on the receiving end of your vulnerability probably really, truly appreciate it. However, we tend to view showing vulnerability as a strength in others, but see it as a weakness in ourselves, a common discrepancy that researchers call the *beautiful-mess effect*.[10] Across multiple studies, Anna Bruk and colleagues found that imagining *other people* expressing vulnerability was viewed favorably. But imagining doing it *ourselves* was seen as a weakness. In other words, the exact same behavior is viewed as beautiful when others do it, but messy when we do.

For example, we might find it really hard to confess that we've been doing a poor job at work in recent weeks, overwhelmed and unable to meet deadlines. Revealing that sort of thing *is* hard! Even with our close friends, we like to look like we have it all together. Doesn't admitting otherwise suggest some level of weakness or incompetence? However, what if a friend came to us with that same problem? We would most likely be flattered by their obvious trust. We would embrace their momentary slip-up, remind them that everyone goes through tough times, and maintain our respect for them. We might even feel closer to them as a result of this disclosure.

In Bruk's research, the beautiful-mess effect was evident in a variety of common situations, including expressing feelings of love, asking for help, admitting a mistake, and sharing insecurities about one's physical appearance. This startling disconnect happens partially because, when it comes to our own moments of vulnerability, we are subject to all of our internal, private discomforts and self-doubts. But we don't see any of that when receiving the vulnerability of others. From that outside perspective, it just looks *brave*. To sum it up, Brené Brown states, "We love seeing raw truth and openness in other people, but we are afraid to let them see it in us . . . vulnerability is courage in you and inadequacy in me."

To push past this, we challenge you to put yourself in the mindset of a loving friend when trying to be more vulnerable. Remember that you will likely look brave to them—not at all like a mess—and might even inspire them to be more vulnerable themselves. Also try to have compassion for yourself, as research shows that people who accept their slip-ups see their displays of vulnerability in a more positive light.[11] (We'll talk about strategies for developing more self-compassion in the next chapter.)

When you're willing to risk it and show your vulnerabilities, avoid making two important mistakes. First, don't tone down your vulnerable moments. People often express their fears or weaknesses by couching them in humor or by minimizing them. They want or even *need* to share something vulnerable, but they serve it up in a way that's palatable—a strategy that psychologist Marisa Franco calls *packaged vulnerability*. It's when "the words seem vulnerable but the delivery doesn't." For example, imagine wanting to tell a friend that you're worried about your relationship with alcohol. You say, "I drink wine every night and I'm starting to worry that I can't stop," but you say it in a playful tone and laugh it off. Your friend picks up on the lightness of your tone, laughs along with you, and moves on to a new topic. You're left feeling frustrated, unseen, and unsupported. But they weren't able to pick up on your distress, because you didn't make it known! You packaged your vulnerability to avoid really putting your true, messy self out there and, as a result, your emotional needs weren't able to be met and your sense of closeness with this friend may have even taken a hit.[12]

Another mistake is to make *too many* negative self-disclosures. If you're really struggling with something—maybe you're depressed or you feel stuck in a bad relationship—and you decide to share the struggle with a friend, that's a beautiful act of vulnerability. But sharing the struggle *repeatedly* may backfire. Research shows that people who frequently disclose negative information are perceived less favorably by friends and receive less support from their romantic partners. It might be better to express excessive negativity in a safe, therapeutic context.[13]

Despite the potential pitfalls, we encourage you to embrace vulnerability. As an act of emotional and interpersonal courage, vulnerability is the very thing that allows us to form close, meaningful, and authentic connections with others. As you go about your everyday life, you might take notice of all of the opportunities you have to practice true, unpackaged vulnerability. For example, when someone asks, with genuine interest, "How's your new job going?" do you answer with a knee-jerk "Oh, it's fine" and abruptly change the subject? Or do you make a joke about counting the days until the weekend, perhaps to mask your unhappiness? What if you gave a more honest (yet socially appropriate) response like "I'm feeling a little overwhelmed by all there is to learn" or "My new boss is pretty demanding"? And just see what happens next.

Beyond "How's the Weather?"

Particularly in Western cultures, small talk is a fact of everyday life. In fact, only about a third of people's daily conversations involve an exchange of meaningful information.[14] Knowing how to smoothly chitchat about the weather, a favorite sports team, or your recent vacation is a valued skill in the workplace or at a cocktail party. There *is* a time and place for this kind of light, easy conversation. Let's not forget that, as we discussed in previous chapters, even brief moments of small talk with strangers provide a surprising burst of happiness.[15] But *never* going beyond this, out of fear or lack of skill or both, can ultimately lead to unsatisfying social connections, where you don't feel known, don't feel like you know others, and also don't feel well-practiced in the art of conversation.

Quality, deep conversations often require self-disclosure. But when you think about going deeper, maybe it would help to frame it not as a heavy-handed "opening up" or "being vulnerable" but as something lighter and lower-stakes. Think, "skipping the small talk" or "being more interesting." It's true, after all. While they might feel emotionally safe, surface-level conversations can be dull and emotionally unfulfilling when compared to deeper ones. After all, people are fascinating! Why do we think that a conversation about the weather or a sports team would be more compelling than personal anecdotes, opinions, or revelations about oneself? Indeed, people report wanting to engage in deeper conversations, but they are reluctant to initiate them.[16] Is it purely the fear of vulnerability that's driving this? While that is part of it, it's not the whole story.

Consider this: researchers Michael Kardas, Amit Kumar, and Nicholas Epley conducted a series of studies examining what keeps people from having more deep conversations. In the first set of studies, they asked participants to engage in either a deep or a shallow conversation with another person. In some studies, the researchers provided the questions (a shallow question was "Do you like to get up early or stay up late?" while a deep question was "Can you describe a time you cried in front of another person?"). In other studies, they asked participants to come up with their own questions to more closely capture what happens in real-life, unscripted conversations. In all of these studies, participants tended to overestimate how awkward deep conversations would be compared with shallow conversations. They also underestimated how connected they would feel to their conversation partner when they discussed deeper topics. It's important to note that this mismatch happened with both strangers and close friends, but the effect was more pronounced when connecting with new people. Also important to note is that these findings held up for both introverts and extraverts.

In yet another study, Kardas and his colleagues asked participants to engage in both shallow and deep conversations. Although participants expected to prefer the shallow conversation, they actually preferred the deeper one. So, why is there a such a discrepancy between people's expectations and their actual experiences? In short, it's because *we underestimate how much people care about what we have to say*. Fortunately, the researchers did uncover one simple way around this problem. They asked some of their participants to imagine their conversation partner as being "very sociable, caring, and considerate of others" while others were asked to imagine the person as "rather indifferent toward others, who isn't very caring or considerate." Imagining the person as sociable, caring, and considerate seemed to encourage the participants to choose deeper topics of conversation, ultimately leading to a more rewarding interaction.[17] So, unless you have clear evidence to the contrary, *assume that people care.*

In a separate but similar line of research, Todd Kashdan and colleagues explored the role of curiosity in encouraging deep conversation, finding that naturally curious people tend to experience more interpersonal benefits from deep conversations with strangers than do less curious people.[18] While curiosity is often thought of as a stable quality of a person, approaching a conversation with an open and inquisitive mind (*"What can I learn here?"* or *"What might be interesting about this person?"*) might just help transform conversations from superficial and dull to revealing and intimate, while also mitigating the anxiety that these deeper conversations can bring.

In sum, researchers have identified several broad reasons why we shy away from self-disclosure. We tend to equate vulnerability with weakness, even as we value it in others. We also overestimate the awkwardness of deep conversation and underestimate how much others care about what we have to say. But even if we can overcome these misplaced beliefs, a very real challenge still exists: exactly *how* do we self-disclose? How do we have deeper, higher-quality conversations? How do we shift from conversations about the weather or something equally mundane to something revealing? And how do we do it in a socially appropriate way?

We might draw inspiration from a well-established technique casually known as "fast friends."[19] It was developed by social psychologist and relationships researcher Art Aron and is essentially a list of open-ended questions designed to get people to open up and share increasingly deep information about themselves, their pasts, their values, their hopes and fears, and more. Questions are presented in three sets, and they get more revealing as you proceed. A few examples of the first set of questions include:

> *What would constitute a perfect day for you?*
> *For what in your life do you feel most grateful?*
> *When did you last sing to yourself? To someone else?*

The second set of questions goes a bit deeper and includes:

> *What roles do love and affection play in your life?*
> *What is your most terrible memory?*
> *Is there something that you've dreamed of doing for a long time? Why haven't you done it?*

Finally, the third set goes the deepest, including:

> *What, if anything, is too serious to be joked about?*

Complete this sentence: "I wish I had someone with whom I could share_____."
Tell your partner what you like about them; be very honest this time, saying things that you might not say to someone you've just met.

In the original study of this technique, college students, who were strangers before the experiment began, were put into pairs and given a list of questions to talk through. Half of the pairs were given the "fast friends" questions, while the others were given questions or prompts to encourage more shallow small talk (things like "Describe the last time you went to the zoo"). Those who went through the fast-friends questions showed significantly more feelings of closeness when spending 45 minutes talking through them, compared to students assigned to spend an equal amount of time making small talk. Anecdotally, some in the fast-friends condition were even seen exchanging contact information, presumably because they wanted to maintain contact with this person who no longer felt like a stranger. One pair even ended up getting married!

This concept or even these specific questions might sound vaguely familiar to you. If so, it's probably because they enjoyed a moment of fame in 2015, when they were featured in *The New York Times* weekly Modern Love section.[20] The author of the piece used the questions to connect with—and ultimately fall in love with—her husband-to-be. Pair that outcome with the headline "To Fall in Love with Anyone, Do This" and it's no wonder that this column was the most-read Modern Love piece of all time.

During a normal conversation, maybe it initially sounds strange to pull out preplanned questions to liven things up. (Although there are card games you can play that are inspired by these questions, such as *We're Not Really Strangers!*) Still, there is much to learn from the fast-friends research. Notice how the questions increase in intensity and sensitivity. Rather than jumping right into a very deep and personal conversation, consider a more gradual escalation. Ideally, feelings of trust and safety can grow slowly and naturally as the conversation expands. Or, you have an "out" if these feelings aren't developing over the course of the conversation. And you can feel free to ask follow-up questions. If someone responds to "what would constitute a perfect day for you?" with "I'd love to have a few quiet hours to read this book I'm really into," ask them what they're reading! Consider committing a few of these questions to memory so you can ask them when it feels natural to do so. It doesn't need to be as scripted as the fast-friends research seems to be.

Walk and Talk

Still struggling to open up? Consider taking a walk with someone! In a piece for NPR's program *On Being*, journalist Jeffrey Bissoy lamented the difficulty men have in expressing deep emotion (which you might recall us discussing in Chapter 2), while also noting the conversational ease that can happen while walking. He writes,

> To all the men and boys reading this: If you find yourself frustrated or crying out for help, invite your closest friend on a walk. I'm not talking about a walk around the block or a brisk walk around the lake. I'm talking about an hour-long (or more) walk with your closest male friend around the city. Pick a destination, maybe somewhere in your town you've never been, venture downtown, or just walk aimlessly walk, talk, and connect.[21]

As he reflected on an hour-long, late-night walk with an old friend, he adds, "In the past, he'd always smoothly evade [my] questions, but on this walk he was transparent about his dreams and vulnerabilities."

Corroborating this with research, members of a British walking group were interviewed and asked about the specific benefits the group had brought into their lives. A common theme that emerged was that walking with others makes them feel more relaxed about talking to a variety of people, shifting from one conversation to another, and experiencing moments of silence without feeling awkward.[22] As one woman in her early 60s remarked: "It might be easier to talk about difficult things, you know, because you're looking ahead, you're not giving eye contact, you've got time to have gaps in the conversation or go slowly." For many people, this lack of eye contact might just make it easier to open up, at least at first. The shared environment also provides natural topics of conversation: nearby buildings, the landscape, an upcoming hill, and so on. If you're not into walking, consider a similar activity: a casual bike ride, a long drive, or even gathering around a campfire might also help ease conversational awkwardness.

Break Out of Your Routines

Even people we know extremely well have hidden layers. Sometimes we fail to see them. We might get into ruts over time, doing the same things over and over: we wear ratty sweats, cook the same kind of dinner, watch the same TV programs, scroll our phones, and run after the kids. Routines surely provide us with comfort and stability, but they can also be dull, and from this we can conclude that our relationships lack spark. However, Art Aron's work on novel and exciting activities reveals that not only can we inject new excitement into long-term relationships, but we might also unearth hidden strengths, commonalities, or complexities in the people we know best.

To test these ideas, Aron and his team brought adults in long-term relationships into his laboratory. Some of these couples were randomly assigned to do a mundane, ordinary activity (slowly rolling a ball around), some didn't do any activity at all, and others were asked to perform what was—on the surface—rather strange: their leg was attached to their partner's with a strap of Velcro, and they were asked to crawl together around the laboratory as quickly as possible.[23] (Actually, there is nothing special about this activity; the key was that it was new and different, a way to shake things up that could be performed in a laboratory setting. In other words, you don't need to do this specific task to reap the benefits . . . unless you really want to.)

Compared to the couples who did the mundane activity or no activity at all, those who did the novel activity reported higher relationship quality. Additionally, observers who were unaware of which experimental condition the couples were in noted greater nonverbal signs of closeness in the couples who had done the novel activity. Survey research also conducted by Aron's team corroborated these findings: long-term, committed couples who report having a high degree of novelty and excitement in their relationship reported greater relationship satisfaction and less boredom.

So, perhaps more time together doing pleasant but unexciting things, like watching a movie or eating at your favorite neighborhood restaurant, isn't always sufficient, especially if you are feeling a bit bored or disconnected in your relationship. Consider doing something new and exciting that will work for *you*. Cook a new cuisine together. Play a new sport together. Take a dance lesson or an improv class. Doing something to safely push your boundaries can help encourage positivity and feelings of closeness.[24] And we see no reason why this wouldn't apply to nonromantic long-term relationships as well.

Be Responsive

In the classic romantic comedy *When Harry Met Sally*, the movie ends with the character of Harry revealing his love for Sally. He says:

I love that you get cold when it's seventy-one degrees out. I love that it takes you an hour and a half to order a sandwich. I love that you get a little crinkle above your nose when you're looking at me like I'm nuts. I love that after I spend a day with you, I can still smell your perfume on my clothes and I love that you are the last person I want to talk to before I go to sleep at night.[25]

In this now-famous declaration, he doesn't merely *acknowledge* Sally's imperfections (such as her highly sensitive and fastidious nature, which he has come to know deeply over many years of friendship). This is because he doesn't love her *in spite of* her flaws; these things are actually part of what he loves about her. Here Harry is embodying a key characteristic of satisfying, supportive relationships, which social psychologist Harry Reis has termed *perceived partner responsiveness*. It is a sense of being understood by another person and also being validated by them, and it's a key component of a close, fulfilling relationship.

Here are a few sample items from a commonly used measure of perceived responsiveness.[26] While this measure is most often used in romantic partnerships, the authors encourage users to adapt it for other relationship types: close friendships, familial bonds, and so on.

Think of someone in your life. Is each statement not at all true of them? Moderately true? Or is it completely true?

This person really listens to me.

This person sees the "real" me.

This person values my abilities and opinions.

This person seems interested in what I am thinking and feeling.

This person is responsive to my needs.

Notice the core components of perceived responsiveness here: feeling understood, validated, and cared for.

Exactly how do we respond to others in order to convey this sense of value and understanding? We want to refer back to the previous chapter's discussion of asking good, curious questions and really listening to the responses we receive. Given the effort involved in simply paying attention, we want to reiterate: what conveys the message "I love and value you" more than attentive, active listening?[27] In short, perceived responsiveness starts with simply *paying attention*, and the elements of quality listening that we explored in the previous chapter absolutely apply here. In addition, we'll next focus on more specific, relationship-enhancing styles of responding.

Make the Most of the Good Times

For decades, relationship researchers focused almost solely on strategies for getting through tough times, like offering social support and managing conflict. But what about all of the *good* things that happen in a relationship? Current researchers are quick to point out that feeling understood and loved in a relationship isn't just about how you weather the tough times, but also how you respond to one another when things go *well*.

Celebrate Life's Wins, Together

Research by Shelly Gable, Harry Reis, and others has established that people often have a distinct pattern of responses to someone else's good news. Let's say that Andrea comes home from work and excitedly tells her husband, Mark, that she received a much-desired promotion. She is unequivocally proud and exuberant. The question is, how does *he* respond to her good news?

It's possible that he responds dispassionately, mumbling some vague approval and turning the conversation back to himself. It's also possible that he actively points out the downsides of the promotion: longer hours, more stress, and so on. Needless to say, either reaction may leave Andrea feeling unloved, misunderstood, or unappreciated. With these kinds of negative responses, relationship quality can suffer as the person with good news feels deflated and devalued. That's not shocking. What may be more surprising is that even positive but low-energy support can be damaging. Here, that might be something like, "Great news, honey" paired with a tepid smile. It's *technically* positive but lacks the enthusiasm the event warrants. In short, how we respond to someone's good news matters, and there are multiple ways to do it wrong. So, how *should* Mark respond if he wants Andrea to feel good? He should adopt what researchers called an "active-constructive" response, expressing involvement or excitement toward the event.[28]

For example, he might say something like, "Wow, this is incredible news! I know how hard you've worked for this and how much you wanted it. Let's go out and celebrate! I want to hear all the details." With this positive and engaged response, he is conveying several key things. First, he expresses that he understands Andrea and how important this promotion was to her. Second, he has witnessed and admired her commitment and hard work toward achieving this goal. And third, he is amplifying and prolonging her positive feelings by having her relive the experience and by celebrating it. (This is very different from offering social support, where the desire is to alleviate negative feelings.) And if this sounds related to the idea of perceived responsiveness, that's because it is! One of the key things happening here is that the sense of

"I understand you and validate you" is being conveyed through this genuine expression of enthusiasm.

This process of sharing good news with someone is called *capitalization*. When people share good news and receive an active-constructive response from their partner, both parties experience emotional benefits. Capitalizing with a responsive partner also has positive relationship outcomes like a deeper sense of intimacy, closeness, and commitment, and greater relationship satisfaction. Research suggests that these relationship benefits exist because capitalization, paired with an enthusiastic response, increases the couples' sense of "we-ness" or togetherness, at least for romantic couples.[29]

Though most of the research done on capitalization is correlational (it examines what naturally unfolds in real-life relationships), there is some experimental evidence that capitalization is what causes all of these desirable outcomes. In one study, participants were asked to think of a personal highlight from the past few years and share it with another person (who was actually a research assistant trained to respond in different ways). When the research assistant provided an active-constructive response (versus responding in a neutral way), participants expressed more liking, trust, perceived responsiveness, and willingness to discuss personal topics with them in the future. This study adds to the growing evidence that capitalizing with a responsive partner is good for relationships—and not just romantic ones.[30]

So we encourage you to give it a try. Capitalize on your successes, both big and small, and celebrate your loved one's good news, too. Do it in a way that feels honest and natural to you and true to your relationship dynamic. And we are willing to bet that, over time, this process will help you cultivate deeper connection.

Gratitude's Deeper Power

We've mentioned the power of gratitude before, but it does hold a special place within the context of close relationships. In fact, emotion researcher Sara Algoe convincingly argues that gratitude is a *relational* emotion, one that exists to promote and sustain connection.[31] Research by Algoe, Emily Impett, and others finds that, much like capitalization, gratitude for a partner's kind acts injects feelings of positivity and perceived responsiveness into a relationship. It can encourage an upward spiral, where an initial experience of gratitude can foster ever-greater feelings of connection and appreciation. In a romantic relationship, gratitude is even related to a desire to meet a partner's sexual needs.[32] And as we explore below, *expressing* your gratitude, not just keeping it inside, and openly receiving other people's expressions of gratitude, are both key.

In one laboratory task, college students who had been dating for at least six months were asked to recall something that they were grateful for, that their partner had done, no matter how big or small, and to express that gratitude. All participants reported how responsive they perceived their partner to be during these conversations. (A genuine smile might indicate responsiveness, while shrugging and saying, "no big deal" would indicate nonresponsiveness.) Participants completed a few follow-up questionnaires six months later, which assessed their relationship satisfaction. What was fascinating was this: how one's partner responded to an expression of gratitude was predictive of relationship satisfaction six months later.[33] In other words, if your attempts to show your appreciation go unnoticed or are not taken well, your relationship is unlikely to benefit. This makes logical sense, but we think it's important to stress this when applying research findings to one's own life. We encourage you to not only express gratitude, but also be open and receptive when people express gratitude to you. If someone close to you offers you a heartfelt "thank you," don't dismiss it with a nonchalant "oh, it was nothing." Hear them and acknowledge their feelings of gratitude.

Make It Work for You

Both of these positive practices—capitalization and gratitude—may seem straightforward, but research does suggest a few caveats. First off, when you're feeling lonely, you perceive others to be less responsive than you might otherwise, so capitalization attempts don't tend to be as effective.[34] They may be more impactful when you're already feeling somewhat upbeat and connected.

Remember that your capitalization attempts need to feel genuine and in keeping with the broader dynamic of your relationship. If you're not an exuberant person, suddenly expressing extreme enthusiasm may be jarring to your partner. Practice expressing it naturally. Also, in a committed relationship, a person might actually have genuine reservations about their partner's good news and how it impacts them. What if an exciting job promotion, like Andrea received in our previous example, requires working weekends or even moving to a new city? Her husband Mark might not be on board with that, and a display of unbridled enthusiasm may feel dishonest. In these moments, it might be wise to say something like, "We know this is going to be complicated, but we can talk about that later. Tonight, we celebrate." Capitalization doesn't trump honesty.

With regard to gratitude, we should remember that much of the research—compelling as it is—is correlational.[35] In one experimental study, there was a sense that instructing couples to express gratitude could at times feel artificial. This is because gratitude generally emerges organically within a relationship dynamic. Let it happen naturally when the time feels right. And let it be driven by your authentic emotions—when you *truly* feel grateful and want to say so.

Also note how you frame your gratitude expressions. Let's say that a loved one generously offers to drive you to the airport, something that you very much needed and also something that was inconvenient for them. You have two things you could focus on when you thank them: how they were responsive to your needs in that moment *and* just how much of a hassle it was for them to take time out of their day. Which should you focus on? One study, which followed participants over the course of two weeks, found that expressing gratitude for having someone respond to their needs was related to enhanced positive feelings, while expressing gratitude for someone's costly, high-hassle efforts had no such benefit.[36] It may well be that acknowledging how well someone noticed and responded to your needs feels more relational ("you see me!") than acknowledging the costs they're incurring by helping you. It also speaks to the importance of perceived responsiveness.

Note that while we have presented these two positive practices—capitalization and gratitude—separately, they can and often do operate in tandem. A recent study found that capitalization encouraged later expressions of gratitude and vice versa, suggesting that these practices inject positivity into a relationship in a broad sense, opening us up to deeper, more positive connections going forward.[37] Also note that you might have a positivity-boosting practice that works for you that we don't mention here, but operates similarly: exercising together, laughing together, creating together, or looking back fondly on your shared memories. If it draws you closer and makes you both feel valued and loved, have at it!

Finally, and once again, remember that while much of the research in this section focuses on romantic partnerships, these tips can be applied to any kind of close relationships—friendships, family relationships, and so on. Responding to another's needs, actively listening and valuing them, providing support, and expressing positivity are valuable tools in any close relationship.

Let's Not Forget the Tough Times

Knowing what to say to a struggling loved one is extremely difficult. There's simply no perfect nugget of wisdom to impart in a time of difficulty. Or to quote a recent book title on navigating tough times with others, "There is no good card for this." In practice, because we lack that perfect nugget of wisdom, we fear saying the wrong thing. As a result, we might opt to say nothing at all. However, this only serves to makes the person feel unsupported while also widening the gap between the two of you. We encourage you to remember the findings that we presented in Chapter 4: people appreciate your genuine care and concern much more than you realize, and your attempts to offer support probably aren't perceived to be as awkward as you think they are.[38]

Researchers acknowledge that each relationship and each struggle is unique, but when offering social support, certain basic principles do apply. Using active listening, of course, is particularly affirming and compassionate in tough times. Try to validate the person's emotions ("I understand why you feel this way" or "that sounds really difficult") as opposed to telling someone how they "should" feel. Relatedly, telling people to "calm down" or "stop being so angry" tends to consistently backfire.[39]

Refraining from giving advice unless it's truly asked for can also be wise (and challenging for all of the "fixers" among us). People tend to be more open to advice if they feel like they are truly being listened to and affirmed, so be sure that message is being conveyed.[40] In a 2023 *New York Times* piece, author David Brooks reflects on his lifelong friendship with Pete, who struggled with crippling depression and had recently succumbed to suicide. While Brooks knew of Pete's depression, in conversations with him, he found himself almost reflexively reminding Pete about all of the wonderful things about his life in an effort to positively reframe his circumstances and change his perspective. This only served to alienate Pete and make him feel even more inadequate. Brooks concluded, "I learned, very gradually, that a friend's job in these circumstances is not to cheer the person up. It's to acknowledge the reality of the situation; it's to hear, respect and love the person; it's to show that you haven't given up on him or her, that you haven't walked away."[41] While this example is extreme and tragic, the basic idea of perceived responsiveness is evident.

Final Thoughts

If we had to summarize all of our research-based advice for connecting more deeply with other people, we'd say: *Reveal yourself and show up for others.*

Self-disclosure is essential for creating more depth in our relationships, yet many people shy away from this behavior. You might think that people won't be interested in learning more about you, or that they'll reject you when you're most vulnerable. But research suggests that these concerns are often overblown. To overcome this barrier to connection, we encourage you to take a risk and share more of yourself with others.

Also remember that perceived responsiveness is a cornerstone of close relationships. One of the best ways to cultivate deeper connection is to be fully present, engaged, and responsive to the person you're with. This might be difficult to do, especially in the modern world, but consider it a practice. The more you work at it—by removing distractions, actively listening, celebrating good times, and sitting with your people through tough times—the better you'll be. Another strategy that might help is to ensure that you're fully centered and connected to *yourself* before you interact with others. This is a topic we'll explore in the final chapter.

Takeaways

- Don't be afraid to open up and be vulnerable. Remember that people appreciate vulnerability and enjoy deep conversation more than we think they do. Can you identify any new opportunities for deeper connection? You might start small, broaching topics that go beyond small talk while still feeling safe and okay to share. If this goes well, you can open up more as your trust and confidence grow.
- Consider how much attention you bring to your social interactions. Are there specific ways that you can minimize distractions to be more present?
- Can you find more ways—big and small—to make your loved ones feel seen and valued?

7
Connection on Demand

How to Feel Connected Even When We're Alone

I have a great deal of company in my house; especially in the morning, when nobody calls.

—Henry David Thoreau

If we were to ask you to think of a recent time when you felt truly connected, where would your mind naturally go? Probably to other people. You might imagine laughing with friends over beers, having a heart-to-heart with a trusted confidante, or snuggling with your grandchildren. It's true that some of our best moments of connection happen in the presence of other people. But in this final chapter, we are going to challenge you to broaden your definition. Connection isn't just a byproduct of great relationships; it's also a feeling that you can cultivate on your own. It's something you can experience *on demand*.

Want to try it now? Reflect on the last time you felt a strong bond with someone. What were you doing in that moment? What made you feel connected to them? What emotions did you experience at the time? Stop reading for moment and savor those feelings of togetherness.

This thought experiment demonstrates that social connection is a feeling you can generate on your own, with just your thoughts. And, as we'll see, there are many other ways to create connection on demand.

Looking Ahead

As we've argued thus far, decades of research suggest that we absolutely need other people in our lives. But we're not *dependent on them* to feel a sense of connection. In this final chapter, we'll explore how we can strengthen our inner sense of connection with a variety of practices that can be done even when we're alone. Some of these will strengthen our sense of connection to *ourselves.* These include the practices of mindfulness and self-compassion, which we explore in the first part of the chapter. We will also introduce you to activities that will help you feel more connected to others, even in their absence, such as gratitude expression, loving-kindness meditation, and nostalgic reflection. Finally, we will explore ways you might connect to the broader world beyond yourself through the experience of awe and other spiritual practices.

We Need Self-Connection, Too

Researcher and best-selling author Brené Brown argues that connecting with *ourselves* is just as important as connecting with others. In fact, after analyzing the data from thousands of interviews with research participants, she concludes that "our connection with others can only be as deep as our connection to ourselves."[1]

What does it mean to connect to ourselves? It might sound like a modern idea (something akin to "me-time" or "self-care"), but it's actually an ancient one—one that shows up in various religious and spiritual traditions. For example, over two thousand years ago, the Buddha taught the practice of *attadipa saranam* (taking refuge in the island of self). As the modern-day Buddhist teacher Thich Nhat Hanh explained, there is an island within each one of us—a home where we truly belong. If we feel disconnected, it's because we have wandered too far from this home. To reconnect, we must return to the island of the self.[2]

While the concept of self-connection has ancient roots, it has just recently come to the attention of scientific psychology. There are only a handful of quantitative research studies on the topic, and there's not yet even a consensus on the precise definition of the term. However, we do think it's important to consider the concept of self-connection and how it might facilitate greater connection with others.

Researcher Kristine Klussman and her colleagues define self-connection as *awareness* of oneself, *acceptance* of oneself based on this awareness, and *alignment* of one's behavior with this awareness. This will likely be refined as the science progresses, but we can use it as a working definition. First, self-connection involves knowing our own internal states—our beliefs, values, emotions, and so on. According to Brené Brown, knowing ourselves is an important prerequisite for connecting with others. She says, "If I don't know and understand who I am and what I need, want, and believe, I can't share myself with you." What's more, research shows that people who have a strong sense of who they are tend to be more satisfied with their romantic relationships and feel happier in the company of friends than those who lack this clarity.[3]

The second component of self-connection is self-acceptance. Of course, mainstream culture conditions us to believe that we *shouldn't* accept ourselves the way we are, that we should continually strive to be *more*: more physically fit, more attractive, more intelligent, or more successful. This conditioning can make us feel as if something's wrong with us. In her book *Radical Acceptance*, psychologist and Buddhist teacher Tara Brach says that we're caught in a trance of unworthiness and "feeling unworthy goes hand in hand with feeling separate from others, separate from life." According to Brach, radical self-acceptance is the key to breaking free from our cultural conditioning and discovering wholeness and true belonging.[4]

The final component of self-connection is self-alignment. This involves acting in line with your "true self"—that is, the person you really are, deep down, regardless of your outward behavior. According to Klussman, you live in alignment when you make choices that reflect your internal states, values, preferences, goals, and intuitions. When you tune in to your body and give it what it needs. When you spend your time wisely, in ways that reflect your values. And when you're honest with yourself and with other people.

So, our working definition of self-connection involves knowing and accepting yourself, and living in alignment with that self. You might still be wondering: *how* exactly do I do these things? First, let's consider an intuitive approach. You can connect to yourself in the same way you connect with others—by paying attention, being curious, expressing care, and providing support. And if it helps, consider the opposite. When you're *not* connecting with yourself, you might be mindlessly scrolling your phone. You might numb your feelings with drugs or alcohol. You might not be aware of the physical tension or discomfort your body is holding. You could be talking to yourself in a way that is harsh and self-critical, rather than open and accepting. You might be unwilling or unable to listen to your inner voice, thereby denying or suppressing your true feelings and desires. And when people genuinely ask you how you're doing, you might not have the insight to honestly answer their question.

In this chapter, we offer some specific suggestions for connecting with yourself. Some of them have been tested in rigorous scientific studies, while others haven't yet caught researchers' attention. We encourage you to test them all in the laboratory of your own life.

Spend Some Quality Time with *Yourself*

Throughout the book, we've talked about the importance of being in the company of other people. But occasionally retreating from the demands of social life (that is, spending time in *solitude*) is important, too. Intentional solitude has been embraced by both secular and religious people across the ages—from the Buddha to Jesus to Henry David Thoreau—and modern science is beginning to examine the nature and benefits of solitude.[5] The evidence suggests that solitude can provide time and space for relaxation, self-reflection, and growth. This was certainly true for Jaime, who took daily solitary hikes during the COVID-19 lockdown. With no one to answer to, she allowed herself to bask in the beauty of springtime in Virginia. She moved at the speed she felt like, sometimes listening to music or a podcast, but more often just being present in nature. The silence, solitude, and immersion . . . all were natural stress relievers. Natalie had a similar experience when she went on a solo camping trip to the Mojave Desert. It was one of the most rejuvenating experiences of her life!

Research shows that solitude can also increase one's sense of self-connection. A group of researchers in the United Kingdom conducted in-depth interviews with a diverse group of people, asking them to reflect on their experiences with solitude. Most of the participants described solitude as a space where they could attend to their "inner world" and connect exclusively with themselves. For some participants, true solitude required physical separation from others and freedom from external distractions (so working on their laptop in Starbucks wouldn't bring the same benefits as sitting alone with their thoughts). Many of the participants talked about the importance of striking a balance between solitude and social time. This was true even for extraverts, who, just like introverts, experience fatigue after too much social interaction.[6] The researchers concluded that, when people achieve the right balance, "solitude transforms into a space that opens introspection and connection to internal experiences in a positive way."[7]

It's clear that there are individual differences in the desire for solitude. Some people love spending time alone, and they might even feel like they're not getting enough of it at times (a feeling that researchers call *aloneliness*).[8] Other people will choose to do anything *other* than spend time with themselves. In one well-known study, people found sitting alone with their thoughts so aversive that many opted to give themselves an electric shock instead![9]

If you don't like the idea of spending time alone, we encourage you to reframe it as an opportunity to connect with yourself.[10] Find a time to sneak away from the distractions of everyday life, and focus on your inner world. Tune in to your thoughts, feelings, and sensations. Find your way back to the island of the self. If you try out this reframing strategy, and it doesn't help, you might try one of the other strategies in this chapter or work with a therapist. At the end of the day, you should feel comfortable with the person you spend the most time with: you!

Finally, we want to stress that it's important not to spend *too* much time alone. Even if you enjoy long stretches of solitude, remember that you have a hard-wired need for connection. People who spend lots of time by themselves are at higher risk for health problems and premature death, even if they don't necessarily feel lonely. Also, people who express a strong preference for solitude are at higher risk of being ostracized by others. So, again, the key is to find the right balance between "me time" and social time.[11]

What Would You Say to a Friend?

Many people have an internal monologue or "inner voice" inside their head. What tone does your inner voice tend to take? *How* do you talk to yourself? (This might require a little reflection. We'll wait.) Do you speak to yourself as you would speak to a friend—warmly and generously? Or are you harsh and critical? Especially note how you talk to yourself in a moment of failure or setback, even if it's a small moment, like spilling your coffee or running late for an appointment.

Researcher Kristin Neff, who has pioneered this area of study, has found that many of us fall into the easy, culturally reinforced habit of self-criticism, believing that it provides motivation and prevents complacency. If we're not hard on ourselves, the reasoning goes, how will we ever achieve anything? This logic is wrong. What encourages us to keep going is actually a mindset of *self-compassion*, where we talk to ourselves like we would talk to a cherished friend, *particularly* in times of struggle.[12] While the basic concept is fairly straightforward, self-compassion is actually thought to contain three distinct factors: mindfulness, self-kindness, and common humanity (or connectedness). Mindfulness here involves having an objective awareness of how we talk to ourselves. Self-kindness is the tendency to offer ourselves compassion, and common humanity is possessing the understanding that no one is perfect, everyone experiences ups and downs, and struggle is a shared human experience.

Neff's research reveals that self-compassionate people are happier and more optimistic, and less susceptible to anxiety and depression, less likely to ruminate, and less prone to that "I'll never be good enough" type of perfectionism that ultimately leaves you frustrated. More to our point, though, self-compassion is associated with greater feelings of social connectedness and less loneliness.[13] Why might self-compassion, an internalized mindset about the self, have these social outcomes? One explanation is that self-compassion actually makes a person less sensitive to social rejection. This, in turn, makes social interaction less intimidating. In plain language, if you're able to forgive yourself your social blunders or accept that not every person you meet will like you, you'll feel freer to put yourself out there, with comfort and ease. Socializing is less risky and scary to the self-compassionate person, and it's more likely to lead to success. Another interesting connection exists between self-compassion and tolerance of others.[14] The common-humanity element is especially linked to this attitude: understanding that slip-ups and weaknesses are a part of the human condition encourages people to have patience and compassion for others as well as for themselves.

Unfortunately, self-compassion doesn't come easily to many of us. If you struggle to be kind to yourself, there's good news: you can train yourself to become more self-compassionate. Noticing how you talk to yourself, particularly in difficult moments, is an important first step. If you do notice a need for more self-compassion, there are some tried-and-true practices, developed by Kristin Neff and her colleagues, that you can consider.

- In a moment of self-criticism, imagine you're talking to a good friend.[15] Could you imagine saying those harsh words to them? If not, what would you say instead? Probably something warm and supportive. Can you turn that kind, compassionate voice toward yourself? (And if you can't, it's worth examining why this is so tough.) If you're so inclined, you could even write yourself a letter of support and encouragement, like you might to a loved one. A similar idea involves imagining someone who loves you a lot. What would that person say to you in this moment of difficulty? Try to get their voice in your head. Over time and with practice, this voice might just start to merge with your own.
- Recall that one element of self-compassion is connectedness, or common humanity. It's the idea that everyone makes mistakes and has their weaknesses; it's part of being human. To see how this plays out in your own life, Neff suggests making a list of your best and worst traits. Look at your list and notice how it comprises a whole, complex person who has gone through many ups and downs. You might also think about your favorite people and notice that they too struggle and have their own personal weaknesses . . . and you love them anyway.

- You could also try out a guided self-compassion meditation, which encourages you to sit quietly with your feelings of guilt, inadequacy, fear, and so on.[16] Rather than harshly judging these feelings, you practice accepting them. You wish yourself well, perhaps repeating a phrase like "May I forgive myself" or "May I learn to accept myself as I am" and are invited to reflect on the struggles you share with all of humanity.

Connect with Others—Even When Alone

The worst of the COVID-19 pandemic in 2020 and 2021 forced many people into a state of social isolation that was unlike anything they had ever experienced. Some experts predicted that there would be a steep rise in the prevalence of loneliness, but that's not what happened. A meta-analysis of 34 studies and more than 215,000 participants showed that loneliness increased during the pandemic, but only slightly.[17]

We suspect that an important buffer against loneliness was the ability to create connection on demand, even in the absence of others. One study found that practicing gratitude over a two-week period (specifically, thinking of three good things that happened each day) increased participants' feelings of social connectedness during pandemic lockdowns (compared to a control group). Thinking optimistically about the future also enhanced feelings of connection. For another example, community members had more positive emotions and a stronger sense of connection after participating in an online dance class, even though they danced alone.[18] These findings suggest that there are multiple ways a person can reap the benefits of connection even in times of isolation.

Thankfully, the worst of the pandemic is behind us. But there may be other times when you're socially isolated and missing other people. You might work two jobs and have little time or energy left for your friends. Or you might have a severe chronic illness that prevents you from leaving the house or even your bed. In these situations, you can still cultivate a sense of social connection by using some of the practices below.

The Power of Meditation

One strategy to enhance feelings of social connection, even when you're alone, is meditation. According to psychologist and meditation teacher Sharon Salzberg, this technique is "essentially training our attention so that we can be more aware."[19] There are many different techniques you can use, but the goal is to direct your attention so that you can see clearly what's happening in the present moment and choose how to respond to it.

A classic meditation practice involves focusing on the in and out breath. We're not meditation teachers, so we'll share some of Sharon Salzberg's guidance:

- Sit comfortably on a cushion or a chair, with your spine erect.
- Close your eyes or, if you prefer, gaze gently a few feet in front of you.
- Start paying attention to your breathing. Don't try to control it; just *feel* it.
- Notice where you feel your breath most vividly—at the nostrils, chest, or abdomen—and rest your attention there.
- As you focus on the breath, you'll notice that countless distractions will arise—thoughts, emotions, sensations, etc. As Salzberg says, "Just be with your breath and let them go. You don't need to chase after them, you don't need to hang on to them, you don't need to analyze them. You're just breathing."
- The moment you realize that you've been lost in thought, bring your attention back to your breath. Don't get mad at yourself. Simply bring your attention back to your breath, as many times as necessary.[20]

One of the most important things to realize is that you're not going to stop your mind from wandering. It will wander. It's its *job* to wander, to notice things and let you know what's happening in the world around you. So, be kind to yourself in these moments, maybe note where your mind went, and then return your attention to the breath. Salzberg tells us, "If you have to let go of distractions and begin again thousands of times, fine. That's not a roadblock to the practice—that *is* the practice."[21]

There are many different categories of meditation—mindfulness meditation, body-scan meditation, gratitude meditation, walking meditation, or one we'll talk about shortly called loving-kindness meditation. These and many other variations are free and readily available to you as audio recordings and videos. Start by typing any of these keywords into a Web browser and see what you find. Or try one of the popular apps, like Headspace or Calm. The biggest challenge might just be sorting through the countless offerings to find the one that suits you.

The effects of meditation on outcomes like physical well-being, stress management, and attentional processing have been well-documented.[22] But for what is often a solitary practice, you might be surprised to know that it has *social* consequences as well. One study, which employed a real-life test of helping behavior in a laboratory waiting room, examined how participants responded to a person walking into the room while on crutches. Those who had just taken part in a three-week, online mindfulness meditation program were significantly more likely to offer up their seat, compared to a control group.[23] Other research (mentioned in Chapter 3) found that a two-week program of mindfulness practices reduced participants' loneliness and increased the number of social interactions they had each day.[24]

Cultivate Loving-Kindness

Loving-kindness meditation (or *metta* in the Buddhist tradition) is an ancient practice that has been shown to encourage a warm, caring attitude toward yourself and others.[25] (Very closely related is compassion meditation, which focuses on alleviating the suffering of the self and others. We'll discuss research on both.) In its simplest form, it might involve spending a little time getting calm and grounded, often by focusing on the breath. In a guided version (which we definitely recommend for beginners), when instructed, you are asked to think about a specific person in your life. You might really try to put yourself in their shoes, imagining what their life might be like and what they might be thinking and feeling. As you envision this person, you will be asked to repeat key phrases, such as "may you be happy," "may you be healthy," "may you live with ease" and "may you be free from suffering." Next, you might think of someone you love or feel very close to and repeat the key phrases with them in mind. Then, you might be prompted to think of a more shallow acquaintance, a stranger, or even someone you find difficult. Some versions might also ask you to repeat the key phrases, thinking of all living beings everywhere. And some will have you send these warm wishes to yourself as well (and if this sounds like a self-compassion meditation, you're right. Self-compassion is like sending loving-kindness to yourself!).

As you repeat the phrases, out loud or in your head, you should allow yourself to feel the full range of emotions they evoke, openly and without judgment. You may feel a strong sense of love and warmth, or (particularly in the case of the difficult person) a sense of sadness or guilt. These feelings are all worth noting (although do take a break if any negative emotions start to overwhelm you). What you will most likely feel is a heightened sense of understanding and compassion. Taking a moment to consider the unique situation and complex humanity of another person, while you're feeling calm and open, is a documented way to create compassion.

Indeed, there is a surprisingly large body of research on loving-kindness meditation. And for all of its simplicity—it really just takes a little time, focus, and commitment—the interpersonal effects are impressive. For instance, in one three-week study by Brian Don and colleagues, a sample of midlife adults was split into three groups: some received general mindfulness training, others received loving-kindness meditation training, and others were in a control group and received no training. Findings revealed that the loving-kindness participants—but not the others—showed an increase in social-approach goals (essentially, wanting to connect and be in social situations) and less of a tendency to avoid social situations.[26] (Earlier research shows that mindfulness training can increase people's desire to connect, so it's not clear why it didn't increase social-approach goals in this study. Don and colleagues argue that the explicitly *social* focus of loving-kindness meditation confers a special benefit.)

Other research has shown that just a two-week program of compassion meditation (delivered online for 30 minutes a day) led to greater prosocial behavior toward a victim of injustice in a lab-based resource-allocation task (this was compared to a control group who spent two weeks performing a more self-oriented task for similar amounts of time). Participants in this study also viewed images of people in distress while in an fMRI brain scanner. Notably, compared to how they responded at the very start of the study, compassion-meditation participants showed increased neural activity in brain regions associated with emotion regulation, perspective-taking, and empathy. A similar study found increased activity in brain regions known to be involved with positive emotion and social affiliation after just one intensive, in-person day-long training session.[27] Finally, one 2012 review article concluded that loving-kindness and compassion meditations are among the most effective tools for increasing feelings of compassion. While long-term, dedicated practitioners certainly show a heightened degree of compassion for others' distress, other results suggest that even a short-term practice is beneficial. One study found that even a single ten-minute session had a significant impact on people's feelings of social connectedness and positive feelings toward strangers.[28] As researcher Helen Weng said, "It's kind of like weight training . . . we found that people can actually build up their compassion 'muscle' and respond to others' suffering with care and a desire to help."[29] If you want to develop more compassion or strengthen your sense of connection to others, we encourage you to go online to find a guided loving-kindness meditation that suits you, and then do it regularly!

Practice Gratitude

In previous chapters, we discussed the power of *expressing* gratitude—of offering a heartfelt "thank you." But there are also many benefits of simply *feeling* gratitude for the good things in your life. Research shows that gratitude can improve your emotional and even your physical well-being.[30] It's also good for your social life. Feeling grateful for all of the people who show up for you—the stranger who returned your grocery cart to the corral, the friend who helped you move furniture on the hottest day of the year, or the colleague who volunteered to cover your responsibilities while you were out sick—can shine a spotlight on these people, highlighting just how valuable they are to you. Gratitude can also help strengthen your relationships and make you feel more connected. Research shows that, after feeling grateful to someone, people are more motivated to spend time with them.[31] In one experiment, participants who felt grateful to a stranger who had helped them out (who was actually a part of the experiment) elected to work with them on a subsequent task, while those who were not helped preferred to work on the task alone. Further, the feeling of gratitude drove this effect (as opposed to, say, a sense of obligation or politeness). Indeed, other research has established that, at its core, gratitude serves the all-important function of bonding us with others.[32]

So, even if—or especially if—you're physically alone, spend some time thinking—or writing—about the people you're thankful for. Consider beginning a practice of gratitude journaling. A simple way to start is to list three things that you're grateful for. They can be big things, like your health or your home, or they can be small things, like a delicious croissant or a soft pillow. While this practice will likely feel good, we encourage you to focus specifically on *people*. *Who* are you grateful for? Why are they such a blessing in your life? What have they done for you? What do they bring into your life? Let the feelings of gratitude wash over you.

If you feel stuck, you might also ask yourself questions like, "What good things or people often go by unnoticed?" or "Is there anyone who hasn't helped me directly, but who has helped one of my loved ones?" or even "What would I miss if it wasn't here, in this particular time or place?" Noticing and appreciating the ordinary good things that constantly surround us isn't always easy or natural, so it's not unusual to need prompts like this. Of course, if you aren't in the headspace for gratitude at a particular moment, that's perfectly normal. Simply consider picking the practice up when you're feeling a bit more receptive.[33]

Ask "What If . . . ?"

Take a moment and call to mind the single most important person in your life. Now, imagine what your life would be like without them. Further imagine that, for whatever reason, you had just never met. What would your life look like? Really try and dwell in this mindset.

This exercise, called *mental subtraction*, has surprising interpersonal benefits. In one study, all participants had been in a satisfying, committed romantic relationship for at least five years (arguably an adequate amount of time to start taking your partner for granted a bit).[34] All were told that they would be writing about an assigned topic for 15 to 20 minutes. A third of them were randomly assigned to "mentally subtract" their partner from their lives, describing in writing "how they might never have met their partner, how they might never have started dating, and how they might not have ended up together." A second group wrote about how they *actually* met their partner and came to be in a relationship with them (generally a pleasant thing to think about), and a third set of participants wrote about a more neutral topic (a typical day, or how they met a good friend). Afterward, the mental subtraction group reported the greatest satisfaction with their partner. As Joni Mitchell famously sang in "Big Yellow Taxi," "You don't know what you've got 'til it's gone," or as this research shows, 'til you imagine it to be gone.

Connect with Your Past

In the early days of the COVID-19 pandemic, when many people were in lockdown, Spotify reported a large increase in the streaming of music from the '50s, '60s, '70s, and '80s, and in the creation of nostalgic playlists. Also during this time, viewings of classic television shows such as *Friends* surged. These trends may have occurred because the pandemic triggered a wave of *nostalgia*.[35]

Nostalgia is a sentimental longing for the past, and it often involves memories of specific time periods (like childhood) or important events that you shared with close others (like your college graduation, your engagement, or your favorite family vacation). Research shows that people use nostalgia as a refuge when they experience psychological discomfort (like loneliness, social anxiety, or even boredom) and that nostalgia, in turn, soothes the discomfort. In this way, nostalgia serves to maintain psychological equilibrium.[36]

Nostalgia can also reconnect you with the people that have contributed to your life story. In fact, participants who were asked to reflect on a nostalgic (versus ordinary) event from their past reported heightened social connectedness and perceived social support. Other studies show that nostalgia can also increase interpersonal competence and comfort with social interactions.[37]

So, one strategy to increase your sense of social connection is to get nostalgic. How exactly do you do it? Music is one of nostalgia's strongest triggers, but nostalgia can also be elicited by looking at cherished photographs and mementos, reflecting on favorite memories, eating foods that are linked to such memories, or even smelling evocative smells from one's past.[38]

To add one final layer of complexity, nostalgic reflection *does* run the risk of making a person feel badly, if it elicits harmful comparisons with one's present life.[39] So, if looking back on the "good old days" makes you feel worse about where you are now, this might not be the best strategy for you. In short, as a bittersweet emotion, nostalgia is emotionally complex, with elements of both happiness and sadness built into it. It won't work for everyone. But if looking back on your past *does* appeal to you, nostalgia is a wonderful tool to help you feel more connected even when you are physically alone.

Transcend the Self

The 13th-century mystic Rumi said, "Doing as others told me, I was blind. Coming when others called me, I was lost. Then I left everyone, myself as well. Then I found everyone, myself as well." Rumi seems to suggest that leaving—or transcending—ourselves can help us find our way *back* to ourselves and to each other. Research confirms this centuries-old wisdom: certain practices that encourage us to transcend our needs and desires and to focus on the world beyond ourselves can improve our well-being and make us feel more connected to others.

Connect with the Natural World

Mounting evidence shows that exposure to nature—walking through the woods, observing a beautiful sunset, or simply tending to a plant—improves our psychological and physical health. What's more surprising is that nature is also good for our social well-being.

Why? First, nature encourages prosocial behavior. People who are exposed to nature—particularly *beautiful* elements of nature—exhibit greater prosocial tendencies than others. One reason for this is the simple fact that nature encourages the sorts of positive moods that tend to lead to prosocial behavior. When we feel good, we tend to also do good.[40]

Nature also strengthens our sense of social connection, even when we're experiencing it alone. One group of researchers asked college students to be mindful of either the natural elements or the human-built objects they encountered in their everyday lives for two weeks. At the end of the two weeks, students who paid attention to natural elements—like the beautiful rosebushes they passed on their way to class—had a stronger sense of connectedness (to other people, to nature, and to life as a whole) and a greater prosocial orientation than students who paid attention to lifeless objects.[41]

It's possible that nature orients us toward others by decreasing self-focused thought. In a study done at Stanford University, researchers asked people to go on a 90-minute walk in a green space overlooking the beautiful San Francisco Bay, or on a busy city street. When they climbed into an fMRI scanner after the walk, the people who walked in nature showed reduced activity in a part of the brain that's involved in self-focused thought. Those who walked in nature also reported lower levels of rumination during the walk. It's possible that "getting out of our heads" increases our capacity for other-focused thought and makes our interconnectedness more salient, though more research is needed to examine this possibility.[42]

Does reading this section make you want to get outdoors? Great! Just keep in mind that you don't have to go to the Pacific Coast or somewhere similarly striking to enjoy nature's benefits. You can go to a local park, botanical garden, or hiking trail. If you live far away from natural settings, and don't have the means to get there, you can connect with the nature in your own backyard or neighborhood. Walk barefoot in the grass. Listen mindfully to the sound of leaves rustling in the wind. Look up at the clouds. Watch in awe as the sky turns gorgeous shades of red, orange, and pink during sunset. If you live in an urban environment, see if you can find a community garden (where you might also meet new people!).

If you're homebound with a chronic illness or stuck inside during a harsh winter, you can always bring nature to you. You might put a bird feeder outside of your window. Or buy some beautiful indoor plants. Research suggests that you can even benefit from looking at images or videos of nature. Many of the ultra-high definition nature documentaries available today make you feel like you're fully immersed in nature. You never know: watching the BBC's documentary *Planet Earth* might just help you feel more connected to the other humans who inhabit the planet.[43]

Open Yourself to Awe

Can you think of a time when you were emotionally moved by something vast or magnificent? It might have happened on a dark winter's night, when you looked up at the sky and were stunned to see a canopy of stars, shining down from millions of light years away. Maybe you hiked to an overlook and were treated to a sweeping landscape lying below. Or it could have happened in a human-made structure, such as a massive Gothic cathedral or a packed stadium of cheering fans. In these moments, you were quite possibly feeling the emotion of *awe*.[44] Awe is a self-transcendent emotion, elicited by things or experiences that challenge your basic assumptions about the world. It can come with a sense of bafflement and even fear as you struggle to make sense of what lies before you. You might feel small as you stand in wonder, utterly un-self-conscious as your eyes widen, your mouth hangs open, and you mumble "wow."

As described here, awe is an internal experience, yet mounting research is establishing its clear social consequences. For example, researcher Paul Piff and colleagues took participants to a grove of towering eucalyptus trees on the campus of the University of California-Berkeley. Some participants were asked to spend one minute looking up at the awe-inspiring trees while others were asked to face a different direction and look up at an adjacent tall building. Compared to the control group, those who gazed at the trees reported greater feelings of awe and lower levels of entitlement. They also offered more help to an experimenter in need. This is believed to happen because awe takes the spotlight off of the self and self-related concerns, and makes people feel like they're a small part of something greater than themselves.[45]

To further test the social effects of awe, researchers took advantage of a 2017 solar eclipse. They examined over 8 million Twitter posts that used certain keywords and hashtags (such as eclipse, eclipse2017, and solareclipse2017). They also tracked the location of respondents: some were in the path of a truly awe-inspiring total eclipse, where the sun was fully covered by the moon (thereby making the sky go briefly dark), while others saw only a partial eclipse—still interesting, but arguably less awesome. Textual analysis of Twitter posts revealed that those who saw the total eclipse used more awe-inspired language ("amazing!" "mind-blowing!"), but also more humble, helpful, and affiliative language. Examples include more use of "we" and "us" rather than "I" or "me" and use of words like "care," "together" and "grateful." Moreover, use of awe-words predicted the use of the humble, helpful, and affiliative language, suggesting—once again—that the feeling of awe is what triggered this prosocial mindset.[46]

Finally, to use an even more dramatic example, astronauts peering down on earth often report a deep sense of awe, and also a seismic shift in their perspective. From their rarefied vantage point, they are struck by the oneness of human nature (researchers term this "the overview effect"), which contributes to a profound sense of connection with humanity.[47]

A question that naturally follows is *"Well, what about me?"* Is awe reserved for far-flung vacations, arduous hikes, rare celestial events, or even space flight? No! Opportunities for awe are all around us, argues Dacher Keltner, awe researcher and author of *Awe: The New Science of Everyday Wonder and How It Can Transform Your Life.* In his book, Keltner describes "eight wonders of life" that can elicit awe in everyday life.[48] These are:

- *Nature.* One of the most reliable sources of awe is nature, as we've discussed. Many of us experience awe while viewing natural wonders, but we can also experience it during cataclysmic events like thunderstorms, lightening, and floods. Have you ever watched a thunderstorm rolling in over the ocean? Truly awesome. Everyday nature experiences can fill us with wonder, too—like watching thousands of fireflies light up a summer evening, or noticing the moonlight glisten on ice-coated tree branches after a winter storm.

- *Moral beauty.* Another wonder of everyday life is *other people*—specifically, their kindness, courage, or persistence in the face of adversity (what Kelter calls "moral beauty"). We get goosebumps when we see a young girl shave her head in solidarity with her brother battling cancer, or when we see a man jump into a frozen lake to save a dog. We're brought to tears watching a student walk across the stage to receive his diploma, eight years after a shooting left him paralyzed from the neck down.[49] Witnessing these acts of moral beauty can be contagious, inspiring us to do beautiful things as well.

- *Collective effervescence.* The third wonder of life is collective effervescence—which, in Keltner's view, is the unique feeling that arises when you move in unison with a large group of other people. You might feel it at a Taylor Swift concert, when you're swaying in unison with thousands of other fans. Or at a South American soccer game, when you're jumping up and down with half of the arena. Or at a night club, where you're dancing in synchronized rhythm with the crowd. Collective effervescence often involves a feeling of connection to the other people present—and a feeling of sacredness. And research suggests that you don't have to go a stadium or a nightclub to have this type of experience.

Collective effervescence can arise from smaller, everyday moments like playing pickleball with a neighbor or walking with friends.[50]

- *Music.* For many of us, listening to music can inspire awe and even transport us "from the present to the past, or from what is actual to what is possible." (It happens for Jaime whenever she listens to Broadway star Audra McDonald linger on a glorious high note.) Listening to music with others can also bring us closer together. As Keltner explains: "when we listen to music with others, the great rhythms of our bodies—heartbeat, breathing, hormonal fluctuations, sexual cycles, bodily motion—once separate, merge into a synchronized pattern. We sense that we are part of something larger, a community, a pattern of energy, an idea of the times—or what we might call the sacred." If music moves you, Keltner recommends that you spend five minutes a day listening to music for awe. Don't just play it in the background of your life. Spend some time *really* listening—until you feel the chills run down your spine.

- *Visual art.* Keltner argues that visual art—like painting, sculptures, or a cathedral's stained-glass windows—has inspired awe for tens of thousands of years. And, like other forms of awe, it can contribute to a sense of interconnectedness. Does visual art inspire awe in you? If so, when's the last time you went to a museum or browsed through a photography collection? Perhaps you could make more time for these activities. Or, perhaps you could add inspiring artists to your social media feeds to get a daily dose of awe.

- *Spiritual experiences.* Spiritual or religious experiences can trigger mystical awe—the feeling of encountering what many people call the Divine. With mystical awe, you might feel like you've merged with something larger than yourself. Natalie felt that way while hiking through the deserted canyons of Death Valley National Park, and also while sitting quietly in a 1,000-year-old European church. Studies suggest that mystical experiences deactivate the default mode network, a part of the brain involved in self-focused thought. So, with mystical awe, the personal self dissolves. And, as spiritual teacher Adyashanti says, "when you let go of the . . . self, what you are getting in exchange is the whole universe."

- *Life and death.* Many of us are awestruck by the beginning of life. Parents might experience awe when they hear their baby's heartbeat for the first time. Friends and grandparents might experience awe as they watch the mother's belly grow—and move with signs of life inside. Those who witness the baby's birth might feel the emotion quite intensely. But, the feeling of awe can happen on the other side of the life cycle, too. As Kelter notes, we can be "moved in transcendent ways by watching the end of life." Kelter experience this first-hand as he watched his younger brother, who was dying of colon cancer, take his last breath. It was an incredibly sad moment for him, but also one filled with wonder.

- *Epiphanies.* The eighth wonder of life involves epiphanies or "big ideas" that transform the way we see the world. You might be awestruck by a personal realization, scientific discovery, or philosophical insight. One thing that left *us* awestruck is learning that our sun is just one of 100 billion stars in our galaxy, and there are billions of galaxies in the universe.[51] Wow! That certainly makes us feel like a small part of a larger whole.

Keltner's work demonstrates that there are many ways to experience awe in everyday life. In many cases, it's about finding the extraordinary in the ordinary.

Awaken Your Spiritual Side

Many spiritual and wisdom traditions are rooted in the belief that everything in the universe is interconnected—that everything is *one*. People who have a belief in oneness feel more connected to humanity, and are more concerned about others' welfare, than those who don't have this mindset.[52] Perhaps you can increase your sense of social connection by tapping into your spiritual side. Regardless of your religious beliefs, you can start to ponder the interconnectedness of all of life. Think about how you're connected—or at least related—to everyone else on the planet: we're all living a human existence, we're all dependent on our planet's natural resources, and we can all get a sunburn from a star that's 93 million miles away. Try to see yourself as part of a human family or a global community. The next time you're struggling with something—maybe sitting in a chemotherapy chair or comforting your child who's been bullied by the other kids—try thinking of all of the people around the world who are currently struggling with the same thing.

Even if you don't have spiritual beliefs, certain spiritual practices may help you feel more connected. Breathwork (also called yogic breathing or *pranayama*) is an ancient practice that's believed to promote mental, physical, and spiritual well-being. Breathwork refers to any practice in which you consciously manipulate the breath in order to achieve some desired state. For example, in "box breathing," you might inhale for 4 seconds, hold for 4 seconds, breathe out for 4 seconds, and then hold for 4 seconds.

Researchers have started to examine the benefits of breathwork in controlled studies. A study done by researchers at Yale University found that a breathing-based program called *Sudarshan Kriya Yoga* decreased students' anxiety and increased their feelings of social connection. Another study found that a breathwork technique called *cyclic sighing*—characterized by deep inhales followed by relatively longer exhales—practiced daily for 4 weeks led to an increase in positive affect, a decrease in anxiety, and a reduction in respiratory rate. Researchers have yet to study the impact of cyclic sighing on feelings of social connectedness, but the calming effect might affect your experiences in social interactions, especially if you tend to feel a little nervous about socializing.[53]

Want to give breathwork a try? Sudarshan Kriya Yoga is available from a nonprofit organization called The Art of Living. Neuroscientist Andrew Huberman has a guided video of cyclic sighing available on his YouTube channel. You might also find a breathwork class at your local yoga studio. Regardless of where you do it, we encourage you to try it. It's a simple but powerful way to cultivate greater connection and increase your overall well-being.[54]

Takeaways

- The next time you're feeling disconnected, remember that you have the power to generate connection *on demand*.
- Remember that connecting with yourself may be just as important as connecting with others.
- Find a good balance between social interaction and "me time." Solitude is an important ingredient in connection.
- Practice being kind to yourself, especially in the face of a struggle or a failure.
- Give meditation a try. It might be hard at first, and you might not immediately feel the benefits. Keep going. They call it a practice for a reason!
- When you're alone, take time out to think about the people who have brought goodness into your life. Because gratitude journaling is especially powerful here, write about what these people have done for you and why it's been so beneficial. And consider visualizing what your life might look like if these people hadn't entered into it.
- Spend time in the natural world. Remember that you yourself are nature.
- Bask in everyday awe. Let yourself be swept away by natural beauty, visual art, music, or the energy of a crowd. Look up at the stars on a clear night

and contemplate the fact that you're actually seeing what they looked like light years in the past.

- Embrace the ancient wisdom that we're all part of the same whole. Even if you can't fully embrace this idea, you can engage in some spiritual practices that have proven benefits.

Conclusion

In the modern world, it can be really hard to find meaningful social connection. It's hard for people across the globe and across the lifespan. The problem has become so common that the US Surgeon General released an advisory about the need to make loneliness a public health priority in America, and the World Health Organization launched a commission to foster social connection in countries around the world. It's clear that this is a societal problem, not an individual one. In other words, it's not really our fault if we feel disconnected!

The problem is that there are all sorts of barriers that block our efforts to make and strengthen relationships in today's world. Some of these barriers are byproducts of our psychological makeup, while others are the result of social forces that seem to be driving us apart. But, as daunting as they may initially seem, we firmly believe that these barriers can be overcome. Often, it starts with a seemingly small gesture, the sort of thing that you can do every day—smiling at a stranger, sending a text to an old friend, turning off your phone during social gatherings, and expressing gratitude, to name a few.

With technology advancing and the population growing, social life is likely to get even more complicated in the future. Adapting to it is something we'll have to continually practice. As your authors, who are also just regular people, we want you to know that we've been practicing right along with you. Jaime notes,

Write a book on social connection and you'll naturally catch yourself reflecting on your relationships in new ways. In social situations, I've always strived to be amusing, upbeat, and full of entertaining anecdotes to share. But lately I've come to be much more appreciative of the simple gift of another person's attention. Those people in my life who will sit with me and hear me, without defensiveness, without turning the conversation back to themselves as quickly as possible, and without checking their devices—these have become the people I have come to cherish and seek out the most. And I, in turn, have been trying to intentionally give that gift to others, hopefully offering them the space to feel authentically heard (although I still relish sharing an amusing anecdote every now and then!). As we quoted in Chapter 5, "Don't you think maybe they are the same thing? Love and attention?" Personally, I do think that, and I've been trying to live more in line with that statement.

Natalie says,

While writing about the barriers to connection, I started to notice barriers *everywhere*. Sitting in a noisy coffee shop with a friend, I had trouble hearing what she was saying. Feeling stressed about a deadline at work, I wasn't fully present at the dinner table. Trying to schedule a weekend getaway with friends, I couldn't find a date that worked for everyone. For a while, noticing all of these barriers was a bit discouraging. Then I realized that noticing the problem is the most important step in overcoming it. *Noticing* has helped motivate me to make simple but important changes in my life—things like meeting up with friends for a walk instead of coffee, saying "no" to social and professional opportunities that ultimately leave me feeling depleted, putting fewer things on the calendar, and making time for daily meditation and other practices that help me stay connected to myself.

So, like us, we hope that you feel encouraged and empowered to make change. Exactly what that change looks like is up to you. Maybe it's prioritizing relationships by investing more time in them. Maybe it's identifying and challenging the social forces that keep you isolated and divided. Maybe it's acknowledging the biases that we all have and entering into your social interactions with more positive expectations. It could involve overcoming your fear of reaching out to people in order to create more intimacy in your relationships. Or it could be strengthening your inner sense of connection.

As you make changes, consider how your actions might have a ripple effect. A smile, a compliment, or a kind word might just touch the life of someone in the depths of despair. Subtly challenging social norms by, say, putting your phone away or hosting a casual potluck in the midst of a fairly busy week can be a small but meaningful step on the road to change. Expressing vulnerability can help to signal emotional safety, encouraging others to share more of themselves too. Many of the practices we shared here won't just benefit you . . . they'll benefit others around you, too and—if enough of us commit to them—might just help to shift social norms toward our very human need to authentically connect.

Our final piece of advice is to open up a dialogue about social connection with the people in your life. We all but guarantee that you're not alone in your desire to connect, and talking openly about it might be one of the best ways of all to foster deeper bonds.

We wish you the best on your journey.

Remember, we're all in this together.

Acknowledgments

Over the past two years, we've read countless research studies on gratitude, but the most powerful lessons we learned came not from the academic literature, but from *life*. As it turns out, writing a book requires a lot of support and encouragement. And, as we reflect back on this journey, we have a renewed sense of appreciation for so many people who have helped and bolstered us along the way.

We're both grateful for our colleagues and students who helped shape our ideas about the book, including Ben Blankenship, Emily Bowles, Scout Bowman, Alyssa Bryars, Sarah Caufield, Kevin Cottrell, Elizabeth Dunn, Jack Gilmore, Sophie Kay, Lydia Killos, Catherine LeHanka, Devon Lussier, Kala Melchiori, Ryan Murphy, Shige Oishi, Jenny Olcott, Claire Peterson, Holly Schiffrin, Brianna Thomas, Emily Triplett, Suzanna Turanyi, and Ashleigh Williams. We also appreciate insights from Louise Hawkley, Livia Tomova, two anonymous peer reviewers, and the editorial team at Oxford University Press, especially Nadina Persaud and Emily Benitez, for their expertise and enthusiasm for this project.

Natalie would like to thank her friends for sharing their personal stories of connection and disconnection, giving feedback on the book, and validating the claim that connection is the key to a happy life: Eleanor Baker, Stephanie Baller, Kim Duvall, Amanda Garber, Wendy Lushbaugh, Katie McConnell, Andrea März, Cara Meixner, Misty Newman, Liz Shoop, Abby Herr, and Melinda Walton. She'd also like to thank Jaime, who said "yes" to the crazy idea of writing a book, and her earliest connections—Brenda, Ed, Susan, and James Kerr—for their steadfast love and support. Finally, she'd like to thank her husband, Ed, for providing lots of encouragement and doing more than his fair share of after-school pickups; her daughter, Katie, for bringing chocolate to the office and sharing the Generation Z perspective; and her daughter, Kara, for joining in ecstatic dance breaks and giving great back rubs. She couldn't have written this book without them.

Jaime would like to thank Natalie for inviting her to take part in this challenging, eye-opening, and rewarding project. She also thanks her friends for their enduring support over the past two years, whether in the form of a long Saturday morning run, an evening of jazz, a shared bottle of cabernet, a weekend getaway, or even just a silly or encouraging text message: Kate

Lambert Cadaret, Amelia Camacho, Jessica Irons, Michelle Majorin, Hung Cam Thai, Jeanine Wolanski, Tracy Zinn, Brooke Zoller, and the Harry Landers Quartet. And special thanks to her family: Tiffany Smith, Vevi Smith, Peanut Smurtz, Mary Kurtz, and Ryan, Kelly, and Griffin Kurtz for the encouragement, laughs, and love.

Notes

Preface

1. Cacioppo, J. T., & Patrick, W. (2008). *Loneliness: Human nature and the need for social connection*. Norton.

Introduction

1. Gallup. (2023). *The global state of social connections*. https://www.gallup.com/analytics/509675/state-of-social-connections.aspx
2. Office of the Surgeon General. (2023). *Our epidemic of loneliness and isolation: The U.S. Surgeon General's advisory on the healing effects of social connection and community*. U.S. Department of Health and Human Services. https://www.hhs.gov/sites/default/files/surgeon-general-social-connection-advisory.pdf
3. Pollan, M. (2009). *In defense of food: An eater's manifesto*. Penguin.
4. Holt-Lunstad, J., Smith, T. B., & Layton, J. B. (2010). Social relationships and mortality risk: A meta-analytic review. *PLoS Medicine, 7*(7), Article e1000316. https://doi.org/10.1371/journal.pmed.1000316
5. Perrin, A., & Atske, S. (2021, March 26). *About three-in-ten U.S. adults say they are "almost constantly" online*. Pew Research Center. https://www.pewresearch.org/fact-tank/2021/03/26/about-three-in-ten-u-s-adults-say-they-are-almost-constantly-online/; Cox, D. A. (2021, June 8). *The state of American friendship: Change, challenges, and loss*. Survey Center of American Life. https://www.americansurveycenter.org/research/the-state-of-american-friendship-change-challenges-and-loss/; Bellezza, S., Paharia, N., & Keinan, A. (2017). Conspicuous consumption of time: When busyness and lack of leisure time become a status symbol. *Journal of Consumer Research, 44*(1), 118–138. https://doi.org/10.1093/jcr/ucw076; Coleman, J. (2021, April 18). Parents are sacrificing their social lives on the altar of intensive parenting. *The Atlantic*. https://www.theatlantic.com/family/archive/2021/04/intensive-parenting-bad-parents-social-lives/618629/
6. Hall, J. A. (2019). How many hours does it take to make a friend? *Journal of Social and Personal Relationships, 36*(4), 1278–1296. https://doi.org/10.1177/0265407518761225

Chapter 1

1. Behr, Z., Bree, D., George, D., Green, Z., Malhotra, K., McCarroll, R., Monserrate, R., Montgomery, B., Palek, G., Pender, R., & Witt, S. (Executive Producers). (2015–Present). *Alone* [TV series]. Leftfield Productions.
2. Baumeister, R. F., & Leary, M. R. (1995). The need to belong: Desire for interpersonal attachments as a fundamental human motivation. *Psychological Bulletin, 117*(3), 497–529.

3. Lieberman, M. D. (2013). *Social: Why our brains are wired to connect.* Crown.

4. Tomova, L., Wang, K. L., Thompson, T., Matthews, G. A., Takahashi, A., Tye, K. M., & Saxe, R. (2020). Acute social isolation evokes midbrain craving responses similar to hunger. *Nature Neuroscience, 23,* 1597–1605. https://doi.org/10.1038/s41593-020-00742-z

5. Holt-Lunstad, J. (2021). The major health implications of social connection. *Current Directions in Psychological Science, 30*(3), 251–259. https://doi.org/10.1177/096372142 1999630

6. Cacioppo, S., Grippo, A. J., London, S., Goossens, L., & Cacioppo, J. T. (2015). Loneliness: Clinical import and interventions. *Perspectives on Psychological Science, 10*(2), 238–249. https://doi.org/10.1177/1745691615570616; Hawkley, L. C., Gu, Y., Luo, Y. J., & Cacioppo, J. T. (2012). The mental representation of social connections: Generalizability extended to Beijing adults. *PLoS One, 7*(9), Article e44065. https://doi.org/10.1371/jour nal.pone.0044065; McWhirter, B. T. (1990). Factor analysis of the revised UCLA Loneliness Scale. *Current Psychology, 9,* 56–68. https://doi.org/10.1007/BF02686768. Cacioppo et al. (2015) argue that the three types of connection roughly correspond to what evolutionary psychologist Robin Dunbar (2014) calls the inner core, sympathy group, and active network.

7. Chelsom, P. (Director). (2004). *Shall we dance?* [Film]. Miramax.

8. Bonos, L. (2018, December 4). "You're my person": How "Grey's Anatomy" created a stand-in for "soul mate." *Washington Post.* https://www.washingtonpost.com/lifestyle/2018/12/ 04/youre-my-person-how-greys-anatomy-created-stand-in-soul-mate/

9. Hawkley, L. C., Hughes, M. E., Waite, L. J., Masi, C. M., Thisted, R. A., & Cacioppo, J. T. (2008). From social structural factors to perceptions of relationship quality and loneliness: The Chicago Health, Aging, and Social Relations Study. *Journal of Gerontology: Social Sciences, 63*(6), S375–S384. https://doi.org/10.1093/geronb/63.6.s375

10. Cacioppo, J. T., & Patrick, W. (2008). *Loneliness: Human nature and the need for social connection.* Norton.

11. Cohen, S., & Janicki-Deverts, D. (2009). Can we improve our physical health by altering our social networks? *Perspectives on Psychological Science, 4*(4), 375–378. https://doi. org/10.1111/j.1745-6924.2009.01141.x; Sandstrom, G. M., & Dunn, E. W. (2014). Is efficiency overrated? Minimal social interactions lead to belonging and positive affect. *Social Psychological and Personality Science, 5*(4), 437–442. https://doi.org/10.1177/194855061 3502990

12. Lieberman, M. D. (2013). *Social.*

13. Eisenberger, N. I., Lieberman, M. D., & Williams, K. D. (2003). Does rejection hurt? An FMRI study of social exclusion. *Science, 302*(5643), 290–292. https://doi.org/10.1126/scie nce.1089134

14. Lieberman, M. D. (2013). *Social.*

15. Matthews, G. A., Nieh, E. H., Vander Weele, C. M., Halbart, S. A., Pradhan, R. V., Yosafat, A. S., Glober, G. F., Izadmehr, E. M., Thomas, R. E., Lacy, G. D., Wildes, C. P., Ungless, M. A., & Tye, K. M. (2016). Dorsal raphe dopamine neurons represent the experience of social isolation. *Cell, 164,* 617–631. https://doi.org/10.1016/j.cell.2015.12.040; Matthews, G. A., & Tye, K. M. (2019). Neural mechanisms of social homeostasis. *Annals of the New York Academy of Sciences, 1457*(1), 5–25. https://doi.org/10.1111/nyas.14016

16. Tomova, L., et al. (2020). Acute social isolation evokes midbrain craving, 1597–1605.

17. Waldinger, R., & Schulz, M. (2023). *The good life: Lessons from the world's longest scientific study of happiness.* Simon & Schuster. https://www.ted.com/talks/robert_waldinger_what_makes_a_good_life_lessons_from_the_longest_study_on_happiness/c

18. Pinker, S. (2014). *The village effect: How face-to-face contact can make us healthier and happier.* Random House Canada.

19. Holt-Lunstad, J. (2021). The major health implications, 251–259; Holt-Lunstad, J., Smith, T. B., & Layton, J. B. (2010). Social relationships and mortality risk: A meta-analytic review. *PLoS Medicine, 7*(7), Article e1000316. https://doi.org/10.1371/journal.pmed.1000316

20. Diener, E., & Seligman, M. E. P. (2002). Very happy people. *Psychological Science, 13*(1), 81–84. https://doi.org/10.1111/1467-9280.00415; Sandstrom, G. M., & Dunn, E. W. (2014). Social interactions and well-being: The surprising power of weak ties. *Personality & Social Psychology Bulletin, 40*(7), 910–922. https://doi.org/10.1177/0146167214529799

21. Boothby, E. J., Clark, M. S., & Bargh, J. A. (2014). Shared experiences are amplified. *Psychological Science, 25*(12), 2209–2216. https://doi.org/10.1177/0956797614551162

22. Miller, M., & Fry, W. (2009). The effect of mirthful laughter on the human cardiovascular system. *Medical Hypotheses, 73*(5), 636–639. https://doi.org/10.1016/j.mehy.2009.02.04

23. Coan, J. A., Schaefer, H. S., & Davidson, R. J. (2006). Lending a hand: Social regulation of the neural response to threat. *Psychological Science, 17*(12), 1032–1039. https://doi.org/10.1111/j.1467-9280.2006.01832.x

24. Lambert, N. M., Stillman, T. F., Hicks, J. A., Kamble, S., Baumeister, R. F., & Fincham, F. D. (2013). To belong is to matter: Sense of belonging enhances meaning in life. *Personality and Social Psychology Bulletin, 39*(11), 1418–1427. https://doi.org/10.1177/0146167213499186; Stillman, T. F., Baumeister, R. F., Lambert, N. M., Crescioni, A. W., Dewall, C. N., & Fincham, F. D. (2009). Alone and without purpose: Life loses meaning following social exclusion. *Journal of Experimental Social Psychology, 45*(4), 686–694. https://doi.org/10.1016/j.jesp.2009.03.007

25. Buss, D. M. (2000). The evolution of happiness. *American Psychologist, 55*(1), 15–23. https://doi.org/10.1037/0003-066X.55.1.15

26. Santos, H. C., Varnum, M. E. W., & Grossmann, I. (2017). Global increases in individualism. *Psychological Science, 28*(9), 1228–1239. https://doi.org/10.1177/0956797617700622

27. Bureau of Labor Statistics (2023). American time use survey summary. https://www.bls.gov/news.release/atus.nr0.htm.

28. Murthy, V. (2023, April 30). Surgeon General: We have become a lonely nation. It's time to fix that. *The New York Times.* https://www.nytimes.com/2023/04/30/opinion/loneliness-epidemic-america.html

29. Smillie, L. D., Kern, M. L. & Uljarevic, M. (2019). Extraversion: Description, development, and mechanisms. In D. P. McAdams, R. L. Shiner, & J. L. Tackett (Eds.), *Handbook of personality development* (pp. 118–136). Guilford Press.

30. Smillie, L. D., et al. (2019). Extraversion; Zelenski, J. M., Sobocko, K., & Whelan, D. C. (2014). Introversion, solitude, and subjective well-being. In R. J. Coplan & J. C. Bowker (Eds.), *The handbook of solitude: Psychological perspectives on social isolation, social withdrawal, and being alone* (pp. 184–201). Wiley Blackwell.

31. Donnellan, M. B., & Lucas, R. E. (2008). Age differences in the Big Five across the life span: Evidence from two national samples. *Psychology and Aging, 23*(3), 558–566. https://doi.org/10.1037/a0012897

32. Wilt, J., Noftle, E. E., Fleeson, W., & Spain, J. S. (2012). The dynamic role of personality states in mediating the relationship between extraversion and positive affect. *Journal of*

Personality, 80(5), 1205–1236. https://doi.org/10.1111/j.1467-6494.2011.00756.x; Wilt, J. A., Sun, J., Jacques-Hamilton, R., & Smillie, L. D. (2023). Why is authenticity associated with being and acting extraverted? Exploring the mediating role of positive affect. *Self and Identity, 22*(6), 896–931. https://doi.org/10.1080/15298868.2023.2246672

33. Margolis, S., & Lyubomirsky, S. (2020). Experimental manipulation of extraverted and introverted behavior and its effects on well-being. *Journal of Experimental Psychology: General, 149*(4), 719–731. https://doi.org/ 10.1037/xge0000668

34. Jacques-Hamilton, R., Sun, J., & Smillie, L. D. (2019). Costs and benefits of acting extraverted: A randomized controlled trial. *Journal of Experimental Psychology. General, 148*(9), 1538–1556. https://doi.org/10.1037/xge0000516; Zelenski, J. M., Santoro, M. S., & Whelan, D. C. (2012). Would introverts be better off if they acted more like extraverts? Exploring emotional and cognitive consequences of counterdispositional behavior. *Emotion, 12*(2), 290–303. https://doi.org/10.1037/a0025169

35. Zelenski, J. M., Whelan, D. C., Nealis, L. J., Besner, C. M., Santoro, M. S., & Wynn, J. E. (2013). Personality and affective forecasting: Trait introverts underpredict the hedonic benefits of acting extraverted. *Journal of Personality and Social Psychology, 104*(6), 1092–1108. https://doi.org/10.1037/a0032281.

36. Cain, S. (2012). *Quiet: The power of introverts in a world that can't stop talking.* Random House.

37. Lawn, R. B., Slemp, G. R., & Vella-Brodrick, D. A. (2019). Quiet flourishing: The authenticity and well-being of trait introverts living in the West depends on extraversion-deficit beliefs. *Journal of Happiness Studies, 20*, 2055–2075. https://doi.org/10.1007/s10 902-018-0037-5

38. Gillath, O., Karantzas, G. C., & Selcuk, E. (2017). A net of friends: Investigating friendship by integrating attachment theory and social network analysis. *Personality and Social Psychology Bulletin, 43*(11), 1546–1565. https://doi.org/10.1177/0146167217719731; Lee, J., & Gillath, O. (2016). Perceived closeness to multiple social connections and attachment style: A longitudinal examination. *Social Psychological and Personality Science, 7*(7), 680–689. https://doi.org/10.1177/1948550616644963

39. Franco, M. G. (2022). *Platonic: How the science of attachment can help you make—and keep—friends.* Putnam.

40. Fraley, R. C., Gillath, O., & Deboeck, P. R. (2021). Do life events lead to enduring changes in adult attachment styles? A naturalistic longitudinal investigation. *Journal of Personality and Social Psychology, 120*(6), 1567–1606. https://doi.org/10.1037/pspi0000326; Stanton, S. C. E., Campbell, L., & Pink, J. C. (2017). Benefits of positive relationship experiences for avoidantly attached individuals. *Journal of Personality and Social Psychology, 113*(4), 568–588. https://doi.org/10.1037/pspi0000098

41. Office of the Surgeon General. (2023). *Our epidemic of loneliness and isolation: The U.S. Surgeon General's advisory on the healing effects of social connection and community.* U.S. Department of Health and Human Services. https://www.hhs.gov/sites/default/files/surg eon-general-social-connection-advisory.pdf

42. Cigna Corporation. (2021). *The loneliness epidemic persists: A post-pandemic look at the state of loneliness among U.S. adults.* https://newsroom.thecignagroup.com/loneliness-epidemic-persists-post-pandemic-look; Gorczynski, P., & Fasoli, F. (2022). Loneliness in sexual minority and heterosexual individuals: A comparative meta-analysis. *Journal of Gay and Lesbian Mental Health, 26*(2), 112–129. https://doi.org/10.1080/19359705.2021.1957 742; von Soest, T., Luhmann, M., Hansen, T., & Gerstorf, D. (2020). Development of

loneliness in midlife and old age: Its nature and correlates. *Journal of Personality and Social Psychology, 118*(2), 388–406. https://doi.org/10.1037/pspp0000219 Shukla, A., Harper, M., Pedersen, E., Goman, A., Suen, J. J., Price, C., . . . Reed, N. S. (2020). Hearing loss, loneliness, and social isolation: A systematic review. *Otolaryngology Head and Neck Surgery, 162*(5), 622–633. https://doi.org/10.1177/0194599820910377; Hymas, R., Badcock, J. C. & Milne, E. (2022). Loneliness in autism and its association with anxiety and depression: A systematic review with meta-analyses. *Review Journal of Autism and Development Disorders.* https://doi.org/10.1007/s40489-022-00330-w

43. https://www.facebook.com/honytheseries/videos/304877943347249/

Chapter 2

1. Cialdini, R. B., Kallgren, C. A., & Reno, R. R. (1991). A focus theory of normative conduct: A theoretical refinement and reevaluation of the role of norms in human behavior. *Advances in Experimental Social Psychology, 24*, 201–234. https://doi.org/10.1016/S0065-2601(08)60330-5; Göckeritz, S., Schultz, P. W., Rendón, T., Cialdini, R. B., Goldstein, N. J., & Griskevicius, V. (2010). Descriptive normative beliefs and conservation behavior: The moderating roles of personal involvement and injunctive normative beliefs. *European Journal of Social Psychology, 40*(3), 514–523. https://doi.org/10.1002/ejsp.643

2. Santos, H. C., Varnum, M. E. W., & Grossmann, I. (2017). Global increases in individualism. *Psychological Science, 28*(9), 1228–1239. https://doi.org/10.1177/0956797617700 622; Kannan, V. D., & Veazie, P. J. (2023). US trends in social isolation, social engagement, and companionship—nationally and by age, sex, race/ethnicity, family income, and work hours, 2003–2020. *SSM—Population Health, 21*, 101331. https://doi.org/10.1016/j.ssmph.2022.101331; Rainie, L., & Zickuhr, K. (2015, August 26). *Americans' views on mobile etiquette.* Pew Research Center. http://www.pewinternet.org/2015/08/26/americans-views-on-mobile-etiquette/; Dotti Sani, G. M., & Treas, J. (2016). Educational gradients in parents' child-care time across countries, 1965–2012. *Journal of Marriage and Family, 78*, 1083–1096. https://doi.org/10.1111/jomf.12305

3. Anderson, L., Washington, C., Kreider, R. M., & Gryn, T. (2023, June 8). *Share of one-person households more than tripled from 1940 to 2020.* U.S. Census Bureau. https://www.census.gov/library/stories/2023/06/more-than-a-quarter-all-households-have-one-person.html#:~:text=Over%20a%20quarter%20(27.6%25),to%202020%20(Figure%201; Ortiz-Ospina, E. (2019, December 10). *The rise of living alone: How one-person households are becoming increasingly common around the world.* Our World In Data. https://ourworldindata.org/living-alone; Klinenberg, E. (2012). *Going solo: The extraordinary rise of living alone.* Penguin.

4. Ratner, R. K., & Hamilton, R. W. (2015). Inhibited from bowling alone. *Journal of Consumer Research, 42*(2), 266–283. https://doi.org/10.1093/jcr/ucv012

5. Sun, J., Harris, K., & Vazire, S. (2020). Is well-being associated with the quantity and quality of social interactions? *Journal of Personality and Social Psychology, 119*(6), 1478–1496. https://doi.org/10.1037/pspp0000272

6. U.S. Census Bureau. (n.d.). *Migration/geographic mobility: Percentage of movers to a different residence.* U.S. Department of Commerce. Retrieved July 27, 2023, from https://data.census.gov/ International Organization for Migration. (2021). *World migration report 2022.* Geneva, Switzerland. https://publications.iom.int/books/annual-report-2021

7. Lun, J., Roth, D., Oishi, S., & Kesebir, S. (2013). Residential mobility, social support concerns, and friendship strategy. *Social Psychological and Personality Science, 4* (3), 332–339. https://doi.org/10.1177/1948550612453345

8. Oishi, S., Lun, J., & Sherman, G. D. (2007). Residential mobility, self-concept, and positive affect in social interactions. *Journal of Personality and Social Psychology, 93,* 131–141. https://doi.org/10.1037/0022-3514.93.1.131

9. Holmes, C. (2023). *Happier hour: How to beat distraction, expand your time, and focus on what matters most.* Random House; Mogilner, C. (2010). The pursuit of happiness: Time, money, and social connection. *Psychological Science, 21*(9), 1348–1354. https://doi. org/10.1177/0956797610380696; Whillans, A. V., & Dunn, E. W. (2019). Valuing time over money is associated with greater social connection. *Journal of Social and Personal Relationships, 36*(8), 2549–2565. https://doi.org/10.1177/0265407518791322; Whillans, A. V., Weidman, A. C., & Dunn, E. W. (2016). Valuing time over money is associated with greater happiness. *Social Psychological and Personality Science, 7*(3), 213–222. https://doi. org/ 10.1177/1948550615623842

10. Aknin, L. B., Dunn, E. W., & Whillans, A. V. (2022). The emotional rewards of prosocial spending are robust and replicable in large samples. *Current Directions in Psychological Science, 31*(6), 536–545. https://doi.org/10.1177/09637214221121100; Caprariello, P. A., & Reis, H. T. (2013). To do, to have, or to share? Valuing experiences over material possessions depends on the involvement of others. *Journal of Personality and Social Psychology, 104*(2), 199–215. https://doi.org/10.1037/a0030953; Dunn, E. W., Whillans, A. V., Norton, M. I., & Aknin, L. B. (2020). Prosocial spending and buying time: Money as a tool for increasing subjective well-being. *Advances in Experimental Social Psychology, 61,* 67–126. https://doi. org/10.1016/bs.aesp.2019.09.001

11. Bellezza, S., Paharia, N., & Keinan, A. (2017). Conspicuous consumption of time: When busyness and lack of leisure time become a status symbol. *Journal of Consumer Research, 44* (1), 118–138. https://doi.org/10.1093/jcr/ucw076; Giurge, L. M., Whillans, A. V., & West, C. (2020). Why time poverty matters for individuals, organisations and nations. *Nature Human Behavior, 4,* 993–1003. https://doi.org/10.1038/s41562-020-0920-z; Holmes, C. (2023). *Happier hour.*

12. Dunn, E. W., Whillans, A. V., Norton, M. I., & Aknin, L.B. (2020). Prosocial spending and buying time: Money as a tool for increasing subjective well-being.

13. Mogilner, C., Chance, Z., & Norton, M. I. (2012). Giving time gives you time. *Psychological Science, 23*(10), 1233–1238. https://doi.org/10.1177/0956797612442551; Lanser, I., & Eisenberger, N. I. (2023). Prosocial behavior reliably reduces loneliness: An investigation across two studies. *Emotion, 23*(6), 1781–1790. https://doi.org/10.1037/emo0001179

14. Hsee, C. K., Yang, A. X., & Wang, L. (2010). Idleness aversion and the need for justifiable busyness. *Psychological Science, 21*(7), 926–930. https://doi.org/10.1177/095679761 0374738

15. Kushlev, K., & Leitao, M. R. (2020). The effects of smartphones on well-being: Theoretical integration and research agenda. *Current Opinion in Psychology, 36,* 77–82. https://doi.org/ 10.1016/j.copsyc.2020.05.001

16. McDaniel, B. T., & Coyne, S. M. (2016). "Technoference": The interference of technology in couple relationships and implications for women's personal and relational well-being. *Psychology of Popular Media Culture, 5*(1), 85–98. https://doi.org/10.1037/ppm0000065; Rainie, L., & Zickuhr, K. (2015). Americans' views on mobile etiquette; Perrin, A., & Atske, S. (2021, March 26). *About three-in-ten U.S. adults say they are 'almost constantly' online.*

Pew Research Center. https://www.pewresearch.org/short-reads/2021/03/26/about-three-in-ten-u-s-adults-say-they-are-almost-constantly-online/; Roberts, J. A., & David, M. E. (2016). My life has become a major distraction from my cell phone: Partner phubbing and relationship satisfaction among romantic partners. *Computers in Human Behavior*, *54*, 134–141. https://doi.org/10.1016/j.chb.2015.07.058; Pancani, L., Gerosa, T., Gui, M., & Riva, P. (2021). "Mom, Dad, look at me": The development of the Parental Phubbing Scale. *Journal of Social and Personal Relationships*, *38*(2), 435–458. https://doi.org/10.1177/026540752 0964866. McDaniel, B. T., & Radesky, J. S. (2018). Technoference: Parent distraction with technology and associations with child behavior problems. *Child Development*, *89*(1), 100–109. https://doi.org/10.1111/cdev.12822; David, M. E., & Roberts, J. A. (2017). Phubbed and alone: Phone snubbing, social exclusion, and attachment to social media. *Journal of the Association for Consumer Research*, *2*, 155–163. https://doi.org/10.1086/690940; Barrick, E. M., Barasch, A., & Tamir, D. I. (2022). The unexpected social consequences of diverting attention to our phones. *Journal of Experimental Social Psychology*, *101*, 104344. https://doi. org/10.1016/j.jesp.2022.104344

17. Barrick, E. M., Barasch, A., & Tamir. D. I. (2022). *The unexpected social consequences*; Sanbonmatsu, D. M., Strayer, D. L., Medeiros-Ward, N., & Watson, J. (2013). Who multi-tasks and why? Multi-tasking ability, perceived multi-tasking ability, and sensation seeking. *PLoS One*, *8*(1), Article e54402. https://doi.org/10.1371/journal.pone.0054402

18. Dwyer, R. J., Kushlev, K., & Dunn, E. W. (2018). Smartphone use undermines enjoyment of face-to-face social interactions. *Journal of Experimental Social Psychology*, *78*, 233–239. https://doi.org/10.1016/j.jesp.2017.10.007

19. Kushlev, K., & Dunn, E. W. (2019). Smartphones distract parents from cultivating feelings of connection when spending time with their children. *Journal of Social and Personal Relationships*, *36*(6), 1619–1639. https://doi.org/10.1177/0265407518769387

20. Kushlev, K., Hunter, J. F., Proulx, J., Pressman, S., & Dunn, E. W. (2019). Smartphones reduce smiles between strangers. *Computers in Human Behavior*, *91*, 12–16. https://doi.org/10.1016/j.chb.2018.09.023; Rainie, L., & Zickuhr, K. (2015). Americans' views on mobile etiquette.

21. Orlowski, J. (Director). (2020). *The social dilemma* [Film]. Exposure Labs; Argent Pictures; The Space Program.

22. Hari, J. (2021). *Stolen focus: Why you can't pay attention and how to think deeply again.* Crown.

23. Oulasvirta, A., Rattenbury, T., Ma, L., & Raita, E. (2012). Habits make smartphone use more pervasive. *Personal and Ubiquitous Computing*, *16*, 105–114.

24. Fitz, N., Kushlev, K., Jagannathan, R., Lewis, T., Paliwal, D., & Ariely, D. (2019). Batching smartphone notifications can improve well-being. *Computers in Human Behavior*, *101*, 84–94. https://doi.org/10.1016/j.chb.2019.07.016; Heitmayer, M., & Lahlou, S. (2021). Why are smartphones disruptive? An empirical study of smartphone use in real-life contexts. *Computers in Human Behavior*, *116*, 106637. https://doi.org/10.1016/j.chb.2020.106637

25. Auxier, B., & Anderson, M. (2012, April 7). *Social media use in 2021*. Pew Research Center. https://www.pewresearch.org/internet/2021/04/07/social-media-use-in-2021/; Statista. (2022). *Number of social media users worldwide from 2017 to 2027 (in billions)* [Graph]. Statista. https://www.statista.com/statistics/278414/number-of-worldwide-social-netw ork-users/; Wallace, K. (2015, January 9). Separated at birth, reunited on Facebook. CNN. https://www.cnn.com/2014/11/12/living/separated-at-birth-reunited-on-facebook-pare nts/index.html

26. Clark, J. L., Algoe, S. B., & Green, M. C. (2018). Social network sites and well-being: The role of social connection. *Current Directions in Psychological Science*, *27*(1), 32–37. https://doi.org/10.1177/0963721417730833; Nowland, R., Necka, E. A., & Cacioppo, J. T. (2018). Loneliness and social internet use: Pathways to reconnection in a digital world? *Perspectives on Psychological Science*, *13*(1), 70–87. https://doi.org/10.1177/1745691617713052

27. Reed, H. (2019, February 27). They left me out, and I saw it all. *The New York Times*. https://www.nytimes.com/2019/02/27/style/the-edit-fomo-left-out.html

28. Primack, B. A., Shensa, A., Sidani, J. E., Whaite, E. O., Lin, L. Y., Rosen, D., Colditz, J. B., Radovic, A., & Miller, E. (2017). Social media use and perceived social isolation among young adults in the U.S. *American Journal of Preventive Medicine*, *53*(1), 1–8. https://doi.org/10.1016/j.amepre.2017.01.010

29. Primack, B. A. (2021). *You are what you click: How being selective, positive, and creative can transform your social media experience*. Chronical Prism.

30. Hunt, M. G., Marx, R., Lipson, C., & Young, J. (2018). No more FOMO: Limiting social media decreases loneliness and depression. *Journal of Social and Clinical Psychology*, *37*(10), 751–768. https://doi.org/10.1521/jscp.2018.37.10.751; Hunt, M. G., Xu, E., Fogelson, A., & Rubens, J. (2023). Follow friends one hour a day: Limiting time on social media and muting strangers improves well-being. *Journal of Social and Clinical Psychology*, *42*(3), 187–213. https://doi.org/10.1521/jscp.2023.42.3.187

31. Ishizuka, P. (2019). Social class, gender, and contemporary parenting standards in the United States: Evidence from a national survey experiment. *Social Forces*, *98*(1), 3158, https://doi.org/10.1093/sf/soy107; Mecking, O. (2020, February 26). American parenting styles sweep Europe. BBC. https://www.bbc.com/worklife/article/20200225-the-parenting-style-sweeping-europe.

32. Miller, C. C. (2018, December 25). The relentlessness of modern parenting. *The New York Times*. https://www.nytimes.com/2018/12/25/upshot/the-relentlessness-of-modern-parenting.html; Schiffrin, H. H., Godfrey, H., Liss, M., & Erchull, M. J. (2015). Intensive parenting: Does it have the desired impact on child outcomes? *Journal of Child and Family Studies*, *24*, 2322–2331. https://doi.org/10.1007/s10826-014-0035-0

33. Rizzo, K. M., Schiffrin, H. H., & Liss, M. (2013). Insight into the parenthood paradox: Mental health outcomes of intensive mothering. *Journal of Child and Family Studies*, *22*(5), 614–620. https://doi.org/10.1007/s10826-012-9615-z; Weinshenker, M., & Kim, S. (2023). Concerted cultivation and parental satisfaction: A profile analysis via principal component analysis. *Journal of Family Studies*, *29*(3), 1249–1269. https://doi.org/10.1080/13229400.2022.2040574

34. Coleman, J. (2021, April 18). Parents are sacrificing their social lives on the altar of intensive parenting. *The Atlantic*. https://www.theatlantic.com/family/archive/2021/04/intensive-parenting-bad-parents-social-lives/618629/ Cigna Corporation. (2021). *The loneliness epidemic persists: A post-pandemic look at the state of loneliness among U.S. Adults*. https://newsroom.thecignagroup.com/loneliness-epidemic-persists-post-pandemic-look; Nowland, R., Thomson, G., McNally, L., Smith, T., & Whittaker, K. (2021). Experiencing loneliness in parenthood: A scoping review. *Perspectives in Public Health*, *141*(4), 214–225. https://doi.org/10.1177/17579139211018243

35. Haspel, E. (2022, May 10). How to quit intensive parenting. *The Atlantic*. https://www.theatlantic.com/family/archive/2022/05/intensive-helicopter-parent-anxiety/629813/

36. Blum, R. W., Mmari, K., & Moreau, C. (2017). It begins at 10: How gender expectations shape early adolescence around the world. *Journal of Adolescent Health*, *61*, S3–S4. https://

doi.org/10.1016/j.jadohealth.2017.07.009; Kågesten, A., Gibbs, S., Blum, R. W., Moreau, C., Chandra-Mouli, V., Herbert, A., & Amin, A. (2016). Understanding factors that shape gender attitudes in early adolescence globally: A mixed-methods systematic review. *PloS One*, *11*(6), Article e0157805. https://doi.org/10.1371/journal.pone.0157805; Levant, R. F., & Richmond, K. (2007). A review of research on masculinity ideologies using the Male Role Norms Inventory. *Journal of Men's Studies*, *15*(2), 130–146. https://doi.org/10.3149/jms.1502.130; Levant, R. F., & McDermott, R. (2022, October 6). Clarifying the American Psychological Association's guidelines for boys and men. *Newsweek*. https://www.newsweek.com/clarifying-american-psychological-associations-guidelines-boys-men-opinion-1749228

37. Dhont, L. (Director). (2022). *Close* [Film]. Menuet; Diaphana Films; Topkapi Films; Versus Production.

38. Way, N. (2011). *Deep secrets: Boys' friendships and the crisis of connection*. Harvard University Press. https://www.tedmed.com/talks/show?id=730069

39. Cox, D. A. (2021, June 8). *The state of American friendship: Change, challenges, and loss*. Survey Center of American Life. https://www.americansurveycenter.org/research/the-state-of-american-friendship-change-challenges-and-loss/

40. American Psychological Association. (2018). *APA guidelines for psychological practice with boys and men*. http://www.apa.org/about/policy/psychological-practice-boys-men-guidelines.pdf

41. Moore, P. (2016, May 23). *The decline of the manly man*. YouGov. https://today.yougov.com/topics/society/articles-reports/2016/05/23/decline-manly-man

42. https://www.cbc.ca/player/play/2186126403638

43. Wright, P. H. (1982). Men's friendships, women's friendships and the alleged inferiority of the latter. *Sex Roles*, *8*, 1–20. https://doi.org/10.1007/BF00287670

44. Bastian, B., Koval, P., Erbas, Y., Houben, M., Pe, M., & Kuppens, P. (2015). Sad and alone: Social expectancies for experiencing negative emotions are linked to feelings of loneliness. *Social Psychological and Personality Science*, *6*(5), 496–503. https://doi.org/10.1177/1948550614568682; Bidwell, M., Briscoe, F., Fernandez-Mateo, I., & Sterling, A. (2013). The employee relationship and inequality: How and why changes in employment practices are reshaping rewards in organizations. *Academy of Management Annals*, *7*(1), 61–121. https://doi.org/10.5465/19416520.2013.761403

Chapter 3

1. Hastorf, A. H., & Cantril, H. (1954). They saw a game: A case study. *The Journal of Abnormal and Social Psychology*, *49*(1), 129–134. https://doi.org/10.1037/h0057880

2. Epley, N., Keysar, B., Van Boven, L., & Gilovich, T. (2004). Perspective taking as egocentric anchoring and adjustment. *Journal of Personality and Social Psychology*, *87*(3), 327–339. https://doi.org/10.1037/0022-3514.87.3.327

3. Gilovich, T., Medvec, V. H., & Savitsky, K. (2000). The spotlight effect in social judgment: An egocentric bias in estimates of the salience of one's own actions and appearance. *Journal of Personality and Social Psychology*, *78*(2), 211–222. https://doi.org/10.1037/0022-3514.78.2.211

4. Gilovich, T., et al., (2000). The spotlight effect in social judgment.

5. Savitsky, K., Epley, N., & Gilovich, T. (2001). Do others judge us as harshly as we think? Overestimating the impact of our failures, shortcomings, and mishaps. *Journal of Personality and Social Psychology, 81*(1), 44–56. https://doi.org/10.1037/0022-3514.81.1.44

6. Newton, E. (1990). *The rocky road from action to intentions.* [Unpublished doctoral dissertation]. Stanford University.

7. Gilovich, T., Savitsky, K., & Medvec, V. H. (1998). The illusion of transparency: Biased assessments of others' ability to read one's emotional states. *Journal of Personality and Social Psychology, 75*(2), 332–346. https://doi.org/10.1037/0022-3514.75.2.332

8. Savitsky, K., & Gilovich, T. (2003). The illusion of transparency and the alleviation of speech anxiety. *Journal of Experimental Social Psychology, 39*(6), 618–625. https://doi.org/10.1016/20022-1031(03)00056-8

9. Lyubomirsky, S., & Ross, L. (1997). Hedonic consequences of social comparison: A contrast of happy and unhappy people. *Journal of Personality and Social Psychology, 73*(6), 1141–1157. https://doi.org/10.1037/0022-3514.73.6.1141

10. Deri, S., Davidai, S., & Gilovich, T. (2017). Home alone: Why people believe others' social lives are richer than their own. *Journal of Personality and Social Psychology, 113*(6), 858–877. https://doi.org/10.1037/pspa0000105

11. Baumeister, R. F., Bratslavsky, E., Finkenauer, C., & Vohs, K. D. (2001). Bad is stronger than good. *Review of General Psychology, 5*(4), 323–370. https://doi.org/10.1037/1089-2680.5.4.323

12. https://greatergood.berkeley.edu/article/item/the_neuroscience_of_happiness.

13. Jones, E. E., & Harris, V. A. (1967). The attribution of attitudes. *Journal of Experimental Social Psychology, 3*(1), 1–24. https://doi.org/10.1016/0022-1031(67)90034-0; Krull, D. S., Loy, M. H., Lin, J., Wang, C. F., Chen, S., & Zhao, X. (1999). The fundamental attribution error: Correspondence bias in individualist and collectivist cultures. *Personality and Social Psychology Bulletin, 25*(10), 1208–1219. https://doi.org/10.1177/0146167299258003

14. Snyder, M., Tanke, E. D., & Berscheid, E. (1977). Social perception and interpersonal behavior: On the self-fulfilling nature of social stereotypes. *Journal of Personality and Social Psychology, 35*(9), 656–666. https://doi.org/10.1037/0022-3514.35.9.656

15. Curtis, R. C., & Miller, K. (1986). Believing another likes or dislikes you: Behaviors making the beliefs come true. *Journal of Personality and Social Psychology, 51*(2), 284–290. https://doi.org/10.1037/0022-3514.51.2.284; Stinson, D. A., Cameron, J. J., Wood, J. V., Gaucher, D., & Holmes, J. G. (2009). Deconstructing the "reign of error": Interpersonal warmth explains the self-fulfilling prophecy of anticipated acceptance. *Personality and Social Psychology Bulletin, 35*(9), 1165–1178. https://doi.org/10.1177/0146167209338629

16. Eyal, T., Steffel, M., & Epley, N. (2018). Perspective mistaking: Accurately understanding the mind of another requires getting perspective, not taking perspective. *Journal of Personality and Social Psychology, 114*(4), 547–571. https://doi.org/10.1037/pspa0000115

17. Perlman, D., & Peplau, L. A. (1981). Toward a social psychology of loneliness. In S. W. Duck & R. Gilmore (Eds.), *Personal relationships in disorder* (pp. 31–56). Academic Press; Cacioppo, S. (2022). *Wired for love: A neuroscientist's journey through romance, loss, and the essence of human connection.* Flatiron.

18. Cacioppo, J. T., & Cacioppo, S. (2018). The growing problem of loneliness. *The Lancet, 391*(10119), 426; https://www.ipsos.com/sites/default/files/ct/news/documents/2021-03/global_perceptions_of_the_impact_of_covid-19.pdf, https://doi.org/10.1016/S0140-6736(18)30142-9; Cigna Corporation. (2021). *The loneliness epidemic persists: A postpandemic look at the state of loneliness among U.S. adults.* https://newsroom.thecignagroup.

com/loneliness-epidemic-persists-post-pandemic-look; Witters (2023, April 4). *Loneliness in U.S. subsides from pandemic high*. https://news.gallup.com/poll/473057/loneliness-subsi des-pandemic-high.aspx#:~:text=Loneliness%20Highest%20Among%20Young%20Adu lts,to%20the%20February%202023%20survey

19. Adams, T. (2016, February 28). John Cacioppo: "Loneliness is like an iceberg—it goes deeper than we can see." *The Guardian*. https://www.theguardian.com/science/2016/feb/ 28/loneliness-is-like-an-iceberg-john-cacioppo-social-neuroscience-interview

20. Holt-Lunstad, J., Smith, T. B., & Layton, J. B. (2010). Social relationships and mortality risk: A meta-analytic review. *PLoS Medicine, 7*(7), Article e1000316. https://doi.org/ 10.1371/journal.pmed.1000316

21. Cacioppo, J. T., Cacioppo, S., & Boomsma, D. I. (2014). Evolutionary mechanisms for lone-liness. *Cognition and Emotion, 28*(1), 3–21. https://doi.org/10.1080/02699931.2013.837379

22. Cacioppo, S., Bangee, M., Balogh, S., Cardenas-Iniguez, C., Qualter, P., & Cacioppo, J. T. (2016). Loneliness and implicit attention to social threat: A high-performance electrical neuroimaging study. *Cognitive Neuroscience, 7* (1–4), 138–159. https://doi.org/10.1080/ 17588928.2015.1070136; Layden, E. A., Cacioppo, J. T., & Cacioppo, S. (2018). Loneliness predicts a preference for larger interpersonal distance within intimate space. *PLoS One, 13*(9), e0203491. https://doi.org/10.1371/journal.pone.0203491

23. Spithoven, A. W. M., Bijttebier, P., & Goossens, L. (2017). It is all in their mind: A review on information processing in lonely individuals. *Clinical Psychology Review, 58*, 97–114. https://doi.org/10.1016/j.cpr.2017.10.003

24. Lucas, G. M., Knowles, M. L., Gardner, W. L., Molden, D. C., & Jefferis, V. E. (2010). Increasing social engagement among lonely individuals: The role of acceptance cues and promotion motivations. *Personality & Social Psychology Bulletin, 36*(10), 1346–1359. https://doi.org/10.1177/0146167210382662; Saporta, N., Peled-Avron, L., Scheele, D., Lieberz, J., Hurlemann, R., & Shamay-Tsoory, S. G. (2022). Touched by loneliness: How loneliness impacts the response to observed human touch: A tDCS study. *Social Cognitive and Affective Neuroscience, 17*(1), 142–150. https://doi.org/10.1093/scan/nsab122

25. Knowles, M. L., Lucas, G. M., Baumeister, R. F., & Gardner, W. L. (2015). Choking under so-cial pressure: Social monitoring among the lonely. *Personality & Social Psychology Bulletin, 41*(6), 805–821. https://doi.org/10.1177/0146167215580775; Matthews, T., Fisher, H. L., Bryan, B. T., Danese, A., Moffitt, T. E., Qualter, P., Verity, L., & Arseneault, L. (2022). This is what loneliness looks like: A mixed-methods study of loneliness in adolescence and young adulthood. *International Journal of Behavioral Development, 46*(1), 18–27. https://doi.org/ 10.1177/0165025420979357

26. Cacioppo, S., et al. (2016). Loneliness and implicit attention to social threat. https://doi.org/ 10.1080/17588928.2015.1070136

27. Masi, C. M., Chen, H. Y., Hawkley, L. C., & Cacioppo, J. T. (2011). A meta-analysis of interventions to reduce loneliness. *Personality and Social Psychology Review, 15*(3), 219–266. https://doi.org/10.1177/1088868310377394

28. Cacioppo, J. T., & Patrick, W. (2008). *Loneliness: Human nature and the need for social con-nection*. W. W. Norton & Company.

29. Maguire, S. (Director). (2001). *Bridget Jones's diary* [Film]. Lionsgate.

30. Kerr, N. A., & Stanley, T. B. (2021). Revisiting the social stigma of loneliness. *Personality and Individual Differences, 171*, 110482. https://doi.org/10.1016/j.paid.2020.110482

31. Vanhalst, J., Soenens, B., Luyckx, K., Van Petegem, S., Weeks, M. S., & Asher, S. R. (2015). Why do the lonely stay lonely? Chronically lonely adolescents' attributions and emotions

in situations of social inclusion and exclusion. *Journal of Personality and Social Psychology*, *109*(5), 932–948. https://doi.org/10.1037/pspp0000051

32. Knowles, M. L., et al. (2015). Choking under social pressure, 805–821. https://doi.org/10.1177/0146167215580775

33. Cacioppo, S. (2022). *Wired for love.*

34. Lindsay, E. K., Young, S., Brown, K. W., Smyth, J., & Creswell, J. D. (2019). Mindfulness training reduces loneliness and increases social contact in a randomized controlled trial. *Proceedings of the National Academy of Sciences*, *116*(9), 3488–3493. https://doi.org/10.1073/pnas.1813588116

35. Salzberg, S. (2011). *Real happiness: The power of meditation.* Workman.

36. Cacioppo, J. T., Chen, H. Y., & Cacioppo, S. (2017). Reciprocal influences between loneliness and self-centeredness: A cross-lagged panel analysis in a population-based sample of African American, Hispanic, and Caucasian adults. *Personality and Social Psychology Bulletin, 43* (8), 1125–1135. https://doi.org/10.1177/0146167217705120

37. Fritz, M. M., Walsh, L. C., Cole, S. W., Epel, E., & Lyubomirsky, S. (2020). Kindness and cellular aging: A pre-registered experiment testing the effects of prosocial behavior on telomere length and well-being. *Brain, Behavior, and Immunity—Health, 11*, 100187. https://doi.org/10.1016/j.bbih.2020.100187

Chapter 4

1. Jimmy Fallon blew a chance to date Nicole Kidman. (January 6, 2015) [Video]. YouTube. https://www.youtube.com/watch?v=qtsNbxgPngA

2. Epley, N., Kardas, M., Zhao, X., Atir, S., & Schroeder, J. (2022). Undersociality: Miscalibrated social cognition can inhibit social connection. *Trends in Cognitive Sciences*, *26*(5), 406–618. https://doi.org/10.1016/j.tics.2022.02.007; Mastroianni, A. M., Gilbert, D. T., Cooney, G., & Wilson, T. D. (2021). Do conversations end when people want them to? *Proceedings of the National Academy of Sciences*, *118* (10), Article e2011809118. https://doi.org/10.1073/pnas.2011809118

3. Instructions for the connection condition were: "Please have a conversation with a new person on the train today. Try to make a connection. Find out something interesting about him or her and tell them something about you. The longer the conversation, the better. Your goal is to try to get to know your community neighbor this morning." Epley, N., & Schroeder, J. (2014). Mistakenly seeking solitude. *Journal of Experimental Psychology: General, 143*, 1980–1999. https://doi.org/10.1037/a0037323; Schroeder, J., Lyons, D., & Epley, N. (2022). Hello, stranger? Pleasant conversations are preceded by concerns about starting one. *Journal of Experimental Psychology: General, 151*(5), 1141–1153. https://doi.org/10.1037/xge0001118

4. Epley, N., & Schroeder, J. (2014). Mistakenly seeking solitude.

5. Schroeder, J., et al. (2021). Hello, stranger?

6. Sandstrom, G. M., & Dunn, E. W. (2014). Is efficiency overrated? Minimal social interactions lead to belonging and positive affect. *Social Psychological and Personality Science, 5*, 436–441. https://doi.org/10.1177/1948550613502990

7. Atir, S., Wald, K., & Epley, N. (2022). Talking to strangers is surprisingly informative. *Proceedings of the National Academy of Sciences*, *110*(34), Article e2206992119. https://doi.org/10.1073/pnas.2206992119

8. Dunn, E. W., Biesanz, J. C., Human, L. J., & Finn, S. (2007). Misunderstanding the affective consequences of everyday social interactions: The hidden benefits of putting one's best face forward. *Journal of Personality and Social Psychology*, *92*(6), 990–1005. https://doi.org/10.1037/0022-3514.92.6.990

9. Sandstrom, G. M., Boothby, E. J., & Cooney, G. (2022). Talking to strangers: A week-long intervention reduces fear of rejection and increases conversational ability. *Journal of Experimental Social Psychology*, *102*, 1–12.. https://doi.org/10.1016/j.jesp.2022.104356

10. Eisenberger, N. I., Lieberman, M. D., & Williams, K. D. (2003). Does rejection hurt? An FMRI study of social exclusion. *Science*, *302* (5643), 290–292. https://doi.org/10.1126/science.1089134; Sandstrom, G. M., & Boothby, E. J. (2021). Why do people avoid talking to strangers? A mini meta-analysis of predicted fears and actual experiences talking to a stranger. *Self and Identity*, *20*(1), 47–71. https://doi.org/10.1080/15298868.2020.1816568

11. Mastroianni, A. M., et al. (2021). Do conversations end when people want them to? *Proceedings of the National Academy of Sciences*, *118*, e2011809118.

12. Sandstrom, G. M., & Dunn, E. W. (2014). Is efficiency overrated? Minimal social interactions lead to belonging and positive affect. *Social Psychological and Personality Science*, *5*(4), 437–442.Wesselmann, E., Cardoso, F., Slater, S., & Williams, K. (2012). To be looked at as though air: Civil attention matters. *Psychological Science*, *23*(2), 166–168. https://doi.org/10.1177/0956797611427921.

13. Schroeder, J., et al. (2021). Hello, stranger?

14. Murthy, V. H. (2020). *Together: The healing power of human connection in a sometimes lonely world*. HarperCollins.

15. Boothby, E. J., & Bohns, V. K. (2021). Why a simple act of kindness is not as simple as it seems: Underestimating the positive impact our compliments have on others. *Personality and Social Psychology Bulletin*, *47*(5), 826–840. https://doi.org/10.1177/0146167220949003; Zhao, X., & Epley, N. (2021). Insufficiently complimentary? Underestimating the positive impact of compliments creates a barrier to expressing them. *Journal of Personality and Social Psychology*, *121*, 239–256. https://doi.org/10.1037/pspa0000277

16. Fiske, S. T., Cuddy, A. J., & Glick, P. (2007). Universal dimensions of social cognition: Warmth and competence. *Trends in Cognitive Sciences*, *11*, 77–83. https://doi.org/10.1016/j.tics.2006.11.005

17. Zhao, X., & Epley, N. (2021). Kind words do not become tired words: Undervaluing the positive impact of frequent compliments. *Self and Identity*, *20*, 25–46. https://doi.org/10.1080/15298868.2020.1761438

18. Algoe, S. B., Gable, S. L., & Maisel, N. C. (2010). It's the little things: Everyday gratitude as a booster shot for romantic relationships. *Personal Relationships*, *17*, 217–233. https://doi.org/10.1111/j.1475-6811.2010.01273.x; Wood, A. M., Maltby, J., Gillett, R., Linley, P. A., & Joseph, S. (2008). The role of gratitude in the development of social support, stress, and depression: Two longitudinal studies. *Journal of Research in Personality*, *42*, 854–871. https://doi.org/10.1016/j.jrp.2007.11.003

19. See https://ggia.berkeley.edu/practice/gratitude_letter for detailed instructions. Seligman, M. E., Steen, T. A., Park, N., & Peterson, C. (2005). Positive psychology progress: Empirical validation of interventions. *American Psychologist*, *60*(5), 410–421. https://doi.org/10.1037/0003-066X.60.5.410

20. Kumar, A., & Epley, N. (2018). Undervaluing gratitude: Expressers misunderstand the consequences of showing appreciation. *Psychological Science*, *29*(9), 1423–1435 https://doi.org/10.1177/0956797618772506

21. https://ggia.berkeley.edu/practice/gratitude_letter; Walsh, L. C., Regan, A., Twenge, J. M., & Lyubomirsky, S. (2023). What is the optimal way to give thanks? Comparing the effects of gratitude expressed privately, one-to-one via text, or publicly on social media. *Affective Science, 4*, 82–91. https://doi.org/10.1007/s42761-022-00150-5

22. Brown, S. L., Nesse, R. M., Vinokur, A. D., & Smith, D. M. (2003). Providing social support may be more beneficial than receiving it: Results from a prospective study of mortality. *Psychological Science, 14*(4), 320–327. https://doi.org/10.1111/1467-9280.14461

23. Curry, O. S., Rowland, L. A., Van Lissa, C. J., Zlotowitz, S., McAlaney, J., & Whitehouse, H. (2018). Happy to help? A systematic review and meta-analysis of the effects of performing acts of kindness on the well-being of the actor. *Journal of Experimental Social Psychology, 76*, 320–329. https://doi.org/10.1016/j.jesp.2018.02.014; Varma, M. M., Chen, D., Lin, X., Aknin, L. B., & Hu, X. (2023). Prosocial behavior promotes positive emotion during the COVID-19 pandemic. *Emotion, 23* (2), 538–553. https://doi.org/10.1037/emo0001077

24. Peterson, C., & Seligman, M. E. P. (2004). *Character strengths and virtues: A handbook and classification*. Oxford University Press and American Psychological Association; Weinstein, N., & Ryan, R. M. (2010). When helping helps: Autonomous motivation for prosocial behavior and its influence on well-being for the helper and recipient. *Journal of Personality and Social Psychology, 98*(2), 222–244. https://doi.org/10.1037/a0016984

25. Dungan, J. A., Munguia Gomez, D. M., & Epley, N. (2022). Too reluctant to reach out: Receiving social support is more positive than expressers expect. *Psychological Science, 33*(8), 1300–1312. https://doi.org/10.1177/09567976221082942

26. Cohen, S., & Wills, T. A. (1985). Stress, social support, and the buffering hypothesis. *Psychological Bulletin, 98*(2), 310–357. https://doi.org/10.1037/0033-2909.98.2.310; Semmer, N. K., Elfering, A., Jacobshagen, N., Perrot, T., Beehr, T. A., & Boos, N. (2008). The emotional meaning of instrumental social support. *International Journal of Stress Management, 15*(3), 235–251. https://doi.org/10.1037/1072-5245.15.3.235

27. Small, M. L. (2017). *Someone to talk to*. Oxford University Press.

28. Maisel, N. C., & Gable, S. L. (2009). The paradox of received social support: The importance of responsiveness. *Psychological Science, 20*(8), 928–932. https://doi.org/10.1111/j.1467-9280.2009.02388.x

29. Welker, C., Walker, J., Boothby, E. J., & Gilovich, T. (2023). Pessimistic assessments of ability in informal conversation. *Journal of Applied Social Psychology, 53*, 555–569. https://doi.org/10.1111/jasp.12957

30. Boothby, E. J., Cooney, G., Sandstrom, G. M., & Clark, M. S. (2018). The liking gap in conversations: Do people like us more than we think? *Psychological Science, 29*(11), 1742–1756. https://doi.org/10.1177/0956797618783714

31. Mastroianni, A. M., Cooney, G., Boothby, E. J., & Reece, A. G. (2021). The liking gap in groups and teams. *Organizational Behavior and Human Decision Processes, 162*, 109–122. https://doi.org/10.1016/j.obhdp.2020.10.013

Chapter 5

1. Pompliano, P. (2020, December 23). The profile dossier: Dwayne "The Rock" Johnson, the most likable person in the world. *The Profile*. https://theprofile.substack.com/p/dwayne-the-rock-johnson. Jordan, J. (2016, November 15). Dwayne "The Rock" Johnson is this year's sexist man alive. *People*. https://people.com/celebrity/sexiest-man-alive-2016-dwa

yne-johnson-the-rock/; Dion, K., Berscheid, E., & Walster, E. (1972). What is beautiful is good. *Journal of Personality and Social Psychology, 24*(3), 285–290. https://doi.org/10.1037/h0033731; Tskhay, K. O., Zhu, R., Zou, C., & Rule, N. O. (2018). Charisma in everyday life: Conceptualization and validation of the General Charisma Inventory. *Journal of Personality and Social Psychology, 114*(1), 131–152. https://doi.org/10.1037/pspp0000159.

2. https://wset.com/news/local/the-rock-stuns-fans-at-gym-in-charlottesville

3. Carnegie, D. (2009). *How to win friends and influence people.* Simon & Schuster.

4. Aronson, E. (2018). *The social animal* (12th ed.). Worth Publishers.

5. Note that meeting online was more common in LGBTQ couples and in younger respondents.Brown, A. (2020, August 20). *Nearly half of U.S. adults say dating has gotten harder for most people in the last 10 years.* Pew Research Center. https://www.pewresearch.org/social-trends/2020/08/20/nearly-half-of-u-s-adults-say-dating-has-gotten-harder-for-most-people-in-the-last-10-years/

6. Sommers, S. (2011). *Situations matter: Understanding how context transforms your world.* Riverhead.

7. Festinger, L., Schachter, S., & Back, K. (1950). *Social pressures in informal groups: A study of human factors in housing.* Harper.

8. Goodfriend, W., & Hack, T. (2022). *Proximity and mere exposure.* Routledge. https://doi.org/10.4324/9780367198459-REPRW43-1; Shin, J. E., Suh, E. M., Li, N. P., Eo, K., Chong, S. C., & Tsai, M. H. (2019). Darling, get closer to me: Spatial proximity amplifies interpersonal liking. *Personality and Social Psychology Bulletin, 45*(2), 300–309. https://doi.org/10.1177/0146167218784903

9. Zajonc, R. B. (1968). Attitudinal effects of mere exposure. *Journal of Personality and Social Psychology, 9*(2), 1–27. https://doi.org/10.1037/h0025848

10. Moreland, R. L., & Beach, S. R. (1992). Exposure effects in the classroom: The development of affinity among students. *Journal of Experimental Social Psychology, 28*(3), 255–276. https://doi.org/10.1016/0022-1031(92)90055-O

11. Brooks, A. C. (2023, January 5). How we learned to be lonely. *The Atlantic.* https://www.theatlantic.com/family/archive/2023/01/loneliness-solitude-pandemic-habit/672631/

12. Reis, H. T., Maniaci, M. R., Caprariello, P. A., Eastwick, P. W., & Finkel, E. J. (2011). Familiarity does indeed promote attraction in live interaction. *Journal of Personality and Social Psychology, 101*(3), 557–570. https://doi.org/10.1037/a0022885

13. Forest, A. L., & Wood, J. V. (2012). When social networking is not working: Individuals with low self-esteem recognize but do not reap the benefits of self-disclosure on Facebook. *Psychological Science, 23*(3), 295–302. https://doi.org/10.1177/0956797611429709

14. Byrne, D. (1969). Attitudes and attraction. In L. Berkowitz (Ed.), *Advances in experimental social psychology* (Vol. 4, pp. 35–89). Academic Press.Montoya, R. M., Horton, R. S., & Kirchner, J. (2008). Is actual similarity necessary for attraction? A meta-analysis of actual and perceived similarity. *Journal of Social and Personal Relationships, 25,* 889–922. https://doi.org/10.1177/0265407508096700

15. Fehr, B. (2008). Friendship formation. In S. Sprecher, A. Wenzel, & J. Harvey (Eds.), *Handbook of relationship initiation* (pp. 29–54). Psychology Press. Gouldner, H., & Strong, M. S. (1987). *Speaking of friendship: Middle-class women and their friends.* Greenwood Press.

16. Mallett, R. K., Wilson, T. D., & Gilbert, D. T. (2008). Expect the unexpected: Failure to anticipate similarities leads to an intergroup forecasting error. *Journal of Personality and Social Psychology, 94*(2), 265–277. https://doi.org/10.1037/0022-3514.94.2.94.2.265

17. Dovidio, J. F., Gaertner, S. L., & Validzic, A. (1998). Intergroup bias: Status, differentiation, and a common in-group identity. *Journal of Personality and Social Psychology, 75*(1), 109–120. https://doi.org/10.1037/0022-3514.75.1.109; Gaertner, S. L., & Dovidio, J. F. (2000). *Reducing intergroup bias: The common ingroup identity model.* Psychology Press.

18. Collins, H. K., Hagerty, S. F., Quoidbach, J., Norton, M. I., & Brooks, A. W. (2022). Diversity in social portfolios predicts well-being. *Proceedings of the National Academy of Sciences, 119,* Article e2120668119. https://doi.org/10.1073/pnas.2120668119 Gouldner, H. & Strong, M. S. (1987). *Speaking of friendship.* Denrell, J. (2005). Why most people disapprove of me: Experience sampling in impression formation. *Psychological Review, 112,* 951–978. https://doi.org/10.1037/0033-295X.112.4.951

19. Golle, J., Mast, F. W., & Lobmaier, J. S. (2014). Something to smile about: The interrelationship between attractiveness and emotional expression. *Cognition and Emotion, 28*(2), 298–310. https://doi.org/10.1080/02699931.2013.817383 Lyubomirsky, S., King, L., & Diener, E. (2005). The benefits of frequent positive affect: Does happiness lead to success? *Psychological Bulletin, 131,* 803–855. https://doi.org/10.1037/0033-2909.131.6.803; Martin, J., Rychlowska, M., Wood, A., & Niedenthal, P. (2017). Smiles as multipurpose social signals. *Trends in Cognitive Sciences, 21*(11), 864–877. https://doi.org/10.1016/j.tics.2017.08.007; Tsukiura, T., & Cabeza, R. (2008). Orbitofrontal and hippocampal contributions to memory for face-name associations: the rewarding power of a smile. *Neuropsychologia, 46*(9), 2310–2319. https://doi.org/10.1016/j.neuropsychologia.2008.03.013

20. Kurtz, L. E., & Algoe, S. B. (2017). When sharing a laugh means sharing more: Testing the role of shared laughter on short-term interpersonal consequences. *Journal of Nonverbal Behavior.* https://doi.org/10.1007/s10919-016-0245-9

21. Dunn, E. W., Biesanz, J. C., Human, L. J., & Finn, S. (2007). Misunderstanding the affective consequences of everyday social interactions: The hidden benefits of putting one's best face forward. *Journal of Personality and Social Psychology, 92,* 990–1005. https://doi.org/10.1037/0022-3514.92.6.990; Jones, E. E., & Wortman, C. (1973). *Ingratiation: An attributional approach.* General Learning Press.

22. Vedantam, S. (Host). (2020, August 3). You 2.0: Our pursuit of happiness. [Audio podcast transcript]. In *Hidden brain.* NPR. https://www.npr.org/transcripts/897673162

23. Dunn, E. W., et al., (2007). Misunderstanding the affective consequences of everyday social interactions.

24. Holt-Lunstad, J., & Uchino, B. N. (2019). Social ambivalence and disease (SAD): A theoretical model aimed at understanding the health implications of ambivalent relationships. *Perspectives on Psychological Science, 14*(6), 941–966. https://doi.org/10.1177/1745691619861392

25. Curtis, R. C., & Miller, K. (1986). Believing another likes or dislikes you: Behaviors making the beliefs come true. *Journal of Personality and Social Psychology, 51,* 284–290. https://doi.org/10.1037/0022-3514.51.2.284; Montoya, R. M., & Insko, C. A. (2008). Toward a more complete understanding of the reciprocity of liking effect. *European Journal of Social Psychology, 38,* 477–498. https://doi.org/10.1002/ejsp.431

26. Montoya, R. M., & Insko, C.A. (2008). Toward a more complete understanding.

27. Castel, A. D., Rhodes, M. G., McCabe, D., & Myers, D. G. (2010). Relationship rewards. In *Social Psychology* (10th ed., pp. 418–420). McGraw-Hill. Sprecher, S. (1998). Insiders' perspectives on reasons for attraction to a close other. *Social Psychology Quarterly, 61*(4), 287–300. https://doi.org/10.2307/2787031; Soderstrom, N. C., & Loaiza, V. M. (2012). Rapid communication: The fate of being forgotten: Information that is initially forgotten is

judged as less important. *Quarterly Journal of Experimental Psychology, 65*(12), 2281–2287. https://doi.org/10.1080/17470218.2012.739183; Ray, D. G., Gomillion, S., Pintea, A. I., & Hamlin, I. (2019). On being forgotten: Memory and forgetting serve as signals of interpersonal importance. *Journal of Personality and Social Psychology, 116*(2), 259–276. https://doi.org/10.1037/pspi0000145

28. Willingham, D. (2021, August 22). Tricks for remembering names. *The Washington Post.* https://www.washingtonpost.com/health/tricks-for-remembering-names/2021/08/20/e889beda-f566-11eb-9738-8395ec2a44e7_story.html

29. Gerwig, G. (Director). (2017). *Lady Bird.* [Film]. IAC Films; Scott Rudin Productions; Management 360.

30. Murphy, K. (2020). *You're not listening: What you're missing and why it matters.* Celadon Books.

31. Bryant, A. (2020). How to be a better listener. *The New York Times.* https://www.nytimes.com/guides/smarterliving/be-a-better-listener; Collins, H. (2022). When listening is spoken. *Current Opinion in Psychology, 47.* https://doi.org/10.1016/j.copsyc.2022.101402; Kluger, A. N., & Itzchakov, G. (2022). The power of listening at work. *Annual Review of Organizational Psychology and Organizational Behavior, 9.* https://doi.org/10.1146/annurev-orgpsych-012420-091013

32. Carnegie, D. (1936). *How to win friends..*

33. Jones, W. H., Hobbs, S. A., & Hockenbury, D. (1982). Loneliness and social skill deficits. *Journal of Personality and Social Psychology, 42*(4), 682–689. https://doi.org/10.1037/0022-3514.42.4.682

34. Okabe-Miyamoto, K., Walsh, L. C., Ozer, D. J., & Lyubomirsky, S. (2024). Measuring the experience of social connection within specific social interactions: The Connection During Conversations Scale (CDCS). *PLoS One, 19*(1), Article e0286408. https://doi.org/10.1371/journal.pone.0286408.

35. Murphy, K. (2020). *You're not listening.*

36. Hall, J. A. (2019). How many hours does it take to make a friend? *Journal of Social and Personal Relationships, 36*(4), 1278–1296. https://doi.org/10.1177/0265407518761225; Bureau of Labor Statistics (2023). *American time use survey summary.* https://www.bls.gov/news.release/atus.nr0.htm

37. Reis, H. T., Regan, A., & Lyubomirsky, S. (2022). Interpersonal chemistry: What is it, how does it emerge, and how does it operate? *Perspectives on Psychological Science, 17*(2), 530–558. https://doi.org/10.1177/1745691621994241

Chapter 6

1. Rowe, T. (2018, September 30). So many acquaintances, yet no real friends. *Live. Love. Nashville.* https://www.livelovenashville.org/blog/2018/9/29/so-many-acquaintances-yet-no-real-friends

2. https://www.weforum.org/agenda/2022/11/friendships-less-is-now-more/; https://www.unwomen.org/sites/default/files/Headquarters/Attachments/Sections/Library/Publications/2019/Progress-of-the-worlds-women-2019-2020-Executive-summary-en.pdf; https://ourworldindata.org/marriages-and-divorces

3. Clark, M. S., & Lemay, E. P. (2010). Close relationships. In S. T. Fiske, D. T. Gilbert, & G. Lindzey (Eds.), *Handbook of social psychology* (pp. 898–940). Wiley & Sons.

4. McAdams, D. P. (1995). What do we know when we know a person? *Journal of Personality*, *63*, 365–396. https://doi.org/10.1111/j.1467-6494.1995.tb00500.x

5. Hall, J. A. (2019). How many hours does it take to make a friend? *Journal of Social and Personal Relationships*, *36*(4), 1278–1296. https://doi.org/10.1177/0265407518761225

6. Carpenter, A., & Greene, K. (2015). Social penetration theory. *The International Encyclopedia of Interpersonal Communication*, 1–4. https://doi.org/10.1002/9781118540190.wbeic160; Collins, N. L., & Miller, L. C. (1994). Self-disclosure and liking: A meta-analytic review. *Psychological Bulletin*, *116*(3), 457–475. https://doi.org/10.1037/0033-2909.116.3.457; Sermat, V., & Smyth, M. (1973). Content analysis of verbal communication in the development of relationship: Conditions influencing self-disclosure. *Journal of Personality and Social Psychology*, *26*(3), 332–346. https://doi.org/10.1037/0033-2909.116.3.457; Sprecher, S., Treger, S., Wondra, J. D., Hilaire, N., & Wallpe, K. (2013). Taking turns: Reciprocal self-disclosure promotes liking in initial interactions. *Journal of Experimental Social Psychology*, *49*(5), 860–866. https://doi.org/10.1016/j.jesp.2013.03.017

7. Taylor, D. A., & Altman, I. (1987). Communication in interpersonal relationships: Social penetration processes. In M. E. Roloff & G. R. Miller (Eds.), *Interpersonal processes: New directions in communication research* (pp. 257–277). Sage; Thibaut, J. W., & Kelley, H. H. (1959). *The social psychology of groups*. Wiley.

8. Collins, N. L., & Miller, L. C. (1994). Self-disclosure and liking; Sprecher, S., Treger, S., & Wondra, J. D. (2012). Effects of self-disclosure role on liking, closeness, and other impressions in get-acquainted interactions. *Journal of Social and Personal Relationships*, *30*(4), 497–514.https://doi.org/10.1177/0265407512459033; Sprecher, S., et al. (2013). Taking turns.

9. Brown, B. (2012). *Daring greatly: How the courage to be vulnerable transforms the way we live, love, parent, and lead*. Penguin; Lee, F. (1997). When the going gets tough, do the tough ask for help? Help seeking and power motivation in organizations. *Organizational Behavior and Human Decision Processes*, *72*, 336–363. https://dx.doi.org/10.1006/obhd.1997.2746

10. Bruk, A., Scholl, S. G., & Bless, H. (2018). Beautiful mess effect: Self-other differences in evaluation of showing vulnerability. *Journal of Personality and Social Psychology*, *115*(2), 192–205. https://doi.org/10.1037/pspa0000120

11. Bruk, A., Scholl, S. G., & Bless, H. (2022). You and I both: Self-compassion reduces self–other differences in evaluation of showing vulnerability. *Personality and Social Psychology Bulletin*, *48*(7), 1054–1067.https://doi.org/10.1177/01461672211031080

12. Franco, M. G. (2022). *Platonic: How the science of attachment can help you make—and keep—friends*. Putnam.

13. Forest, A. L., Kille, D. R., Wood, J. V., & Holmes, J. G. (2014). Discount and disengage: How chronic negative expressivity undermines partner responsiveness to negative disclosures. *Journal of Personality and Social Psychology*, *107*(6), 1013–1032. https://doi.org/10.1037/a0038163

14. Mehl, M. R., Vazire, S., Holleran, S. E., & Clark, C. S. (2010). Eavesdropping on happiness: Well-being is related to having less small talk and more substantive conversations. *Psychological Science*, *21*(4), 539–541. https://doi.org/10.1177/0956797610362675

15. Molinsky, A. (27 February, 2013). The big challenge of American small talk. *Harvard Business Review*. https://hbr.org/2013/02/the-big-challenge-with-america; Sandstrom, G. M., & Dunn, E. W. (2014). Is efficiency overrated? Minimal social interactions lead to belonging and positive affect. *Social Psychological and Personality Science*, *5*, 436–441. https://doi.org/10.1177/1948550613502990

16. Kardas, M., Kumar, A., & Epley, N. (2022). Overly shallow? Miscalibrated expectations create a barrier to deeper conversation. *Journal of Personality and Social Psychology, 122*(3), 367–398. https://doi.org/10.1037/pspa0000281; Mehl, M. R., et al. (2010). Eavesdropping on happiness.

17. The researchers do mention that people on the receiving end of these conversations were a part of the research as well, meaning they had consented to engage in conversation. While it's unclear how strangers in the real world would respond to deep conversational topics, previous research on talking to strangers, which we discussed in Chapter 4, suggests that they are more open to it than we might expect!

18. Kashdan, T. B., McKnight, P. E., Fincham, F. D., & Rose, P. (2011). When curiosity breeds intimacy: Taking advantage of intimacy opportunities and transforming boring conversations. *Journal of Personality, 79*(6), 1369–1402. https://doi.org/10.1111/j.1467-6494.2010.00697.x

19. Aron, A., Melinat, E., Aron, E. N., Vallone, R., & Bator, R. (1997). The experimental generation of interpersonal closeness: A procedure and some preliminary findings. *Personality and Social Psychology Bulletin, 23*, 363–377. https://doi.org/10.1177/0146167297234003

20. Catron, M. L. (2015, January 9). To fall in love with anyone, do this. *The New York Times*. https://www.nytimes.com/2015/01/11/style/modern-love-to-fall-in-love-with-anyone-do-this.html The entire list of Aron's questions can be found here—https://ggia.berkeley.edu/practice/36_questions_for_increasing_closeness

21. Bissoy, J. (2018, May 30). How walking and talking allows men to be vulnerable. *On Being*. https://onbeing.org/blog/jeffrey-bissoy-how-walking-and-talking-allows-men-to-be-vulnerable/.

22. Doughty, K. (2013). Walking together: The embodied and mobile production of a therapeutic landscape. *Health & Place, 24*, 140–146. https://doi.org/10.1016/j.healthplace.2013.08.009; Kinney, P. (2017). Walking interviews. *Social Research Update, 67*, 1–4.

23. Aron, A., Norman, C. C., Aron, E. N., McKenna, C., & Heyman, R. (2000). Couples shared participation in novel and arousing activities and experienced relationship quality. *Journal of Personality and Social Psychology, 78*, 273–283. https://doi.org/10.1037//0022-3514.78.2.273; Harasymchuk, C., Lonn, A., Impett, E. A., & Muise, A. (2022). Relational boredom as an obstacle for engaging in exciting shared activities. *Personal Relationships, 29*, 350–365. https://doi.org/10.1111/pere.12421

24. Harasymchuk, C., Walker, D., Muise, A., & Impett, E. A. (2021). Planning date nights that promote closeness: The roles of relationship goals and self-expansion. *Journal of Social and Personal Relationships, 38*, 1692–1709. https://doi.org/10.1177/02654075211000436

25. Reiner, R. (Director). (1989). *When Harry met Sally*. [Film]. Castle Rock Entertainment; Nelson Entertainment.

26. Reis, H. T., Crasta, D., Rogge, R. D., Maniaci, M. R., & Carmichael, C. L. (2018). Perceived Partner Responsiveness Scale (PPRS). In D. L. Worthington & G. D. Bodie (Eds.), *The sourcebook of listening research: Methodology and measures* (pp. 516–521). Wiley Blackwell. https://doi.org/10.1002/9781119102991.ch57

27. Itzchakov, G., Reis, H. T., & Weinstein, N. (2022). How to foster perceived partner responsiveness: High-quality listening is key. *Social and Personality Psychology Compass, 16*(1), Article e12648. https://doi.org/10.1111/spc3.12648; Reis, H. T., & Shaver, P. (1988). Intimacy as an interpersonal process. In S. Duck (Ed.), *Handbook of personal relationships* (pp. 367–389). John Wiley & Sons.

28. Gable, S. L., Reis, H. T., Impett, E. A., & Asher, E. R. (2004). What do you do when things go right? The intrapersonal and interpersonal benefits of sharing positive events. *Journal of Personality and Social Psychology, 87*(2), 228–245.https://doi.org/10.1037/0022-3514.87.2.228

29. Berscheid, E., & Reis, H. T. (1998). Attraction and close relationships. In D. T. Gilbert, S. T. Fiske, & G. Lindzey (Eds.), *The handbook of social psychology* (4th ed., Vol. 2, pp. 193–281). McGraw-Hill; Gable, S. L., et al. (2004). What do you do when things go right? Morelli, S. A., Lieberman, M. D., & Zaki, J. (2015). The emerging study of positive empathy. *Social and Personality Psychology Compass, 9*(2), 57–68. https://doi.org/10.1111/spc3.12157; Pagani, A. F., Parise, M., Donato, S., Gable, S. L., & Schoebi, D. (2020). If you shared my happiness, you are part of me: Capitalization and the experience of couple identity. *Personality and Social Psychology Bulletin, 46,* 258–269. https://doi.org/10.1177/0146167219854449; Peters, B. J., Reis, H. T., & Gable, S. L. (2018). Making the good even better: A review and theoretical model of interpersonal capitalization. *Social and Personality Psychology Compass, 12,* e12407.https://doi.org/10.1111/spc3.12407

30. Reis, H. T., Smith, S. M., Carmichael, C. L., Caprariello, P. A., Tsai, F. F., Rodrigues, A., & Maniaci, M. R. (2010). Are you happy for me? How sharing positive events with others provides personal and interpersonal benefits. *Journal of Personality and Social Psychology, 99*(2), 311–329.https://doi.org/10.1037/a0018344

31. Algoe, S. B. (2012). Find, remind, and bind: The functions of gratitude in everyday relationships. *Social and Personality Psychology Compass, 6*(6), 455–469. https://doi.org/10.1111/j.1751-9004.2012.00439.x; Algoe, S. B., Haidt, J., & Gable, S. L. (2008). Beyond reciprocity: Gratitude and relationships in everyday life. *Emotion, 8*(3), 425–429. https://doi.org/10.1037/1528-3542.8.3.425

32. Brady, A., Baker, L. R., Muise, A., & Impett, E. A. (2021). Gratitude increases the motivation to fulfill partners' sexual needs. *Social Psychological and Personality Science, 12,* 273–281. https://doi.org/10.1177/1948550619898971

33. It's safe to assume that this one-time expression of gratitude in a laboratory was a representation of how they normally respond to each other's good news. As much as it felt good in the moment, it's probably not this one-time experience that affected participants six months later. Algoe, S. B., Fredrickson, B. L., & Gable, S. L. (2013). The social functions of the emotion of gratitude via expression. *Emotion, 13*(4), 605–609. https://doi.org/10.1037/a0032701

34. Arpin, S. N., & Mohr, C. D. (2019). Transient loneliness and the perceived provision and receipt of capitalization support within event-disclosure interactions. *Personality and Social Psychology Bulletin, 45*(2), 240–253. https://doi.org/10.1177/0146167218783193

35. Algoe, S. B., & Zhaoyang, R (2015). Positive psychology in context: Effects of expressing gratitude in ongoing relationships depend on perceptions of enactor responsiveness. *Journal of Positive Psychology, 11*(4), 399–415. https://doi.org/10.1080/17439760.2015.1117131; Tissera, H., Visserman, M. L., Impett, E. A., Muise, A., & Lyon, J. E. (2022). Understanding the links between perceiving a partner's gratitude and romantic relationship satisfaction using an accuracy and bias framework. *Social Psychological and Personality Science, 14*(8). https://doi.org/10.1177/19485506221137958

36. Park, Y., Visserman, M. L., Sisson, N. M., Le, B. M., Stellar, J., & Impett, E. A. (2021). How can I thank you? Highlighting the benefactor's responsiveness or costs when expressing gratitude. *Journal of Social and Personal Relationships, 38,* 504–523. https://doi.org/10.1177/0265407520966049

37. Don, B. P., Fredrickson, B. L., & Algoe, S. B. (2022). Enjoying the sweet moments: Does approach motivation upwardly enhance reactivity to positive interpersonal processes? *Journal of Personality and Social Psychology*, *122*(6), 1022–1055. https://doi.org/10.1037/pspi0000312

38. Crowe, K., & McDowell, E. (2017). *There is no good card for this: What to say and do when life is scary, awful, and unfair to people you love*. Harper One. Dungan, J. A., Munguia Gomez, D. M., & Epley, N. (2022). Too reluctant to reach out: Receiving social support is more positive than expressers expect. *Psychological Science*, *33*(8), 1300–1312. https://doi.org/10.1177/09567976221082942

39. Little, L. M., Kluemper, D., Nelson, D. L., & Ward, A. (2013). More than happy to help? Customer-focused emotion management strategies. *Personnel Psychology*, *66*(1), 261–286. https://doi.org/10.1111/peps.12010; Sahi, R. S., He, Z., Silvers, J. A., & Eisenberger, N. I. (2023). One size does not fit all: Decomposing the implementation and differential benefits of social emotion regulation strategies. *Emotion*, *23*(6), 1522–1535. https://doi.org/10.1037/emo0001194

40. Feng, B. (2009). Testing an integrated model of advice giving in supportive interactions. *Human Communication Research*, *35*, 115–129. https://doi.org/10.1111/j.1468-2958.2008.01340.x

41. Brooks, D. (2023, February 9). How do you serve a friend in despair? *The New York Times*. https://www.nytimes.com/2023/2/09/opinion/despair-friendship-suicide.html?smid=url-share *If you are having thoughts of suicide, call or text 988 to reach the National Suicide Prevention Lifeline or go to* SpeakingOfSuicide.com/resources *for a list of additional resources.*

Chapter 7

1. Brown, B. (2022). *Atlas of the heart*. HBO Max.

2. Nhat Hanh, T. (2021, April 2). *Thich Nhat Hanh on the art of embracing loneliness*. Plum Village. https://plumvillage.app/thich-nhat-hanh-on-the-art-of-embracing-loneliness/

3. Lewandowski, G. W., Nardone, N., & Raines, A. J. (2010). The role of self-concept clarity in relationship quality. *Self and Identity*, *9*, 416–433. https://doi.org/10.1080/15298860903332191; Merdin-Uygur, E., Sarial-Abi, G., Gurhan-Canli, Z., & Hesapci, O. (2019). How does self-concept clarity influence happiness in social settings? The role of strangers versus friends. *Self and Identity*, *18*(4), 443–467. https://doi.org/10.1080/15298868.2018.1470563; Wilson, T. D. (2009). Know thyself. *Perspectives on Psychological Science*, *4*(4), 384–389. https://doi.org/10.1111/j.1745-6924.2009.01143.x

4. Brach, T. (2004). *Radical acceptance: Embracing your life with the heart of a Buddha*. Random House.

5. Yancy, P. (2020, July 17). The surprising gift of solitude. *Patheos*. https://www.patheos.com/blogs/evangelicalpulpit/2020/07/the-surprising-gift-of-solitude/ Nguyen, T. T., Ryan, R. M., & Deci, E. L. (2018). Solitude as an approach to affective self-regulation. *Personality and Social Psychology Bulletin*, *44* (1), 92–106. https://doi.org/10.1177/0146167217733073; Weinstein, N., Hansen, H., & Nguyen, T. V. (2023). Definitions of solitude in everyday life. *Personality & Social Psychology Bulletin*, *49*(12), 1663–1678. https://doi.org/10.1177/01461672221115941

6. Leikas, S., & Ilmarinen, V. J. (2017). Happy now, tired later? Extraverted and conscientious behavior are related to immediate mood gains, but to later fatigue. *Journal of Personality*, *85*(5), 603–615. https://doi.org/10.1111/jopy.12264

7. Weinstein, N., et al., (2022). Definitions of solitude in everyday life.

8. Coplan, R. J., Hipson, W. E., Archbell, K. A., Ooi, L. L., Baldwin, D., & Bowker, J. C. (2019). Seeking more solitude: Conceptualization, assessment, and implications of aloneliness. *Personality and Individual Differences*, *148*, 17–26. https://doi.org/10.1016/j.paid.2019.05.020

9. Wilson, T. D., Reinhard, D., Westgate, E. C., Gilbert, D., Ellerbeck, N., Hahn, C., Brown, C., & Shaked, A. (2014). Just think: The challenges of the disengaged mind. *Science*, *345*, 75–77. https://doi.org/10.1126/science.1250830

10. Rodriguez, M., Bellet, B. W., & McNally, R. J. (2020). Reframing time spent alone: Reappraisal buffers the emotional effects of isolation. *Cognitive Therapy and Research*, *44*(6), 1052–1067. https://doi.org/10.1007/s10608-020-10128-x

11. Holt-Lunstad, J. (2021). The major health implications of social connection. *Current Directions in Psychological Science*, *30*(3), 251–259. https://doi.org/10.1177/0963721421999630; Ren, D., & Evans, A. M. (2021). Leaving the loners alone: Dispositional preference for solitude evokes ostracism. *Personality and Social Psychology Bulletin*, *47*(8), 1294–1308. https://doi.org/10.1177/0146167220968612

12. Neff, K. D. (2023). Self-compassion: Theory, method, research, and intervention. *Annual Review of Psychology*, *74*, 193–218. https://doi.org/10.1146/annurev-psych-032420-031047

13. Neff, K. D., & McGehee, P. (2010). Self-compassion and psychological resilience among adolescents and young adults. *Self and Identity*, *9*(3), 225–240. https://doi.org/10.1080/15298860902979307; Xie, Q., Manova, V., & Khoury, B. (2023). How do dispositional mindfulness and self-compassion alleviate loneliness? The mediating role of rejection sensitivity. *Current Psychology*, *42*, 23712–23721. https://doi.org/10.1007/s12144-022-03549-2

14. Vu, H. A., & Rivera, L. M. (2023) Self-compassion and negative outgroup attitudes: The mediating role of compassion for others. *Self and Identity*, *22*(3), 470–485, https://doi.org/10.1080/15298868.2022.2117241

15. See https://ggia.berkeley.edu/practice/how_would_you_treat_a_friend for a full description of this practice. Neff, K. D., & Germer, C. K. (2013). A pilot study and randomized controlled trial of the mindful self-compassion program. *Journal of Clinical Psychology*, *69*(1), 28–44. https://doi.org/10.1002/jclp.21923

16. For examples and instructions, see Kristin Neff's website, self-compassion.org.

17. Ernst, M., Niederer, D., Werner, A. M., Czaja, S. J., Mikton, C., Ong, A. D., Rosen, T., Brähler, E., & Beutel, M. E. (2022). Loneliness before and during the COVID-19 pandemic: A systematic review with meta-analysis. *American Psychologist*, *77*(5), 660–677. https://doi.org/10.1037/amp0001005

18. Dennis, A., & Ogden, J. (2022). Nostalgia, gratitude, or optimism: The impact of a two-week intervention on well-being during COVID-19. *Journal of Happiness Studies*, *23*, 2613–2634. https://doi.org/10.1007/s10902-022-00513-6; Desrochers, J. E., Bell, A. L., Nisbet, E. K., & Zelenski, J. M. (2022). Does spending time in nature help students cope with the COVID-19 pandemic? *Sustainability*, *14*(4), 2401. https://doi.org/10.3390/su14042401; Humphries, A., Tasnim, N., Rugh, R., Patrick, M., & Basso, J. C. (2023). Acutely enhancing affective state and social connection following an online dance intervention during the COVID-19 social isolation crisis. *BMC Psychology*, *11*(1), 13. https://doi.org/10.1186/s40359-022-01034-w

19. Salzberg, S. (2011). *Real happiness: A 28-day program to realize the power of meditation.* Workman.

20. Salzberg, S. (2011). *Real happiness.*

21. Salzberg, S. (2011). *Real happiness.*

22. Chambers, R., Lo, B. C. Y., & Allen, N. B. (2008). The impact of intensive mindfulness training on attentional control, cognitive style, and affect. *Cognitive Therapy and Research, 32,* 303–322. https://doi.org/10.1007/s10608-007-9119-0; Keng, S. L., Smoski, M. J., & Robins, C. J. (2011). Effects of mindfulness on psychological health: A review of empirical studies. *Clinical Psychology Review, 31*(6), 1041–1056. https://doi.org/10.1016/j.cpr.2011.04.006

23. Lim, D., Condon, P., & DeSteno, D. (2015) Mindfulness and compassion: An examination of mechanism and scalability. *PLoS One, 10,* Article e0118221. https://doi.org/10.1371/journal.pone.0118221

24. Lindsay, E. K., Young, S., Brown, K. W., Smyth, J., & Creswell, J. D. (2019). Mindfulness training reduces loneliness and increases social contact in a randomized controlled trial. *Proceedings of the National Academy of Sciences, 116*(9), 3488–3493. https://doi.org/10.1073/pnas.1813588116

25. Salzberg, S. (2002). *Loving-kindness: The revolutionary art of happiness.* Shambhala.

26. Don, B. P., Algoe, S. B., & Fredrickson, B. L. (2021). Does meditation training influence social approach and avoidance goals? Evidence from a randomized intervention study of midlife adults. *Mindfulness, 12,* 582–593. https://doi.org/10.1007/s12671-020-01517-0

27. Klimecki, O. M., Leiberg, S., Lamm, C., & Singer, T. (2013). Functional neural plasticity and associated changes in positive affect after compassion training. *Cerebral Cortex, 23* (7), 1552–1561. https://doi.org/10.1093/cercor/bhs142; Weng, H. Y., Fox, A. S., Shackman, A. J., Stodola, D. E., Caldwell, J. Z., Olson, M. C., Rogers, G. M., & Davidson, R. J. (2013). Compassion training alters altruism and neural responses to suffering. *Psychological Science, 24*(7), 1171–80. https://doi.org/10.1177/0956797612469537

28. Boellinghaus, I., Jones, F. W., & Hutton, J. (2014). The role of mindfulness and loving-kindness meditation in cultivating self-compassion and other-focused concern in health care professionals. *Mindfulness, 5,* 129–138. https://doi.org/10.1007/s12671-012-0158-6; Hutcherson, C. A., Seppälä, E. M., & Gross, J. J. (2008). Loving-kindness meditation increases social connectedness. *Emotion, 8*(5), 720–724. https://doi.org/10.1037/a0013237; Lutz, A., Brefczynski-Lewis, J., Johnstone, T., Davidson R. J. (2008). Regulation of the neural circuitry of emotion by compassion meditation: Effects of meditative expertise. *PLoS One, 3*(3), Article e1897. https://doi.org/10.1371/journal.pone.0001897

29. Ladwig, J. (2013, May 22). *Brain can be trained in compassion, study shows.* University of Wisconsin-Madison. https://news.wisc.edu/brain-can-be-trained-in-compassion-study-shows/

30. Emmons, R. A., & McCullough, M. E. (2003). Counting blessings versus burdens: An experimental investigation of gratitude and subjective well-being in daily life. *Journal of Personality and Social Psychology, 84*(2), 377–389. https://doi.org/10.1037/0022-3514.84.2.377

31. Bartlett, M. Y., Condon, P., Cruz, J., Baumann, J., & Desteno, D. (2012). Gratitude: Prompting behaviours that build relationships. *Cognition & Emotion, 26*(1), 2–13. https://doi.org/10.1080/02699931.2011.561297

32. Algoe, S. B., Haidt, J., & Gable, S. L. (2008). Beyond reciprocity: Gratitude and relationships in everyday life. *Emotion*, 8, 425–429. https://doi.org/10.1037/1528-3542.8.3.425; Algoe, S. B., & Stanton, A. L. (2012). Gratitude when it is needed most: Social functions of gratitude in women with metastatic breast cancer. *Emotion*, *12*(1), 163–168. https://doi.org/10.1037/a0024024

33. Emmons, R. A. (2016). *Gratitude works! A 21-day program for creating emotional prosperity.* Jossey-Bass; Lyubomirsky, S., & Layous, K. (2013). How do simple positive activities increase well-being? *Current Directions in Psychological Science*, *22*(1), 57–62. https://doi.org/10.1177/09637214124698

34. Koo, M., Algoe, S. B., Wilson, T. D., & Gilbert, D. T. (2008). It's a wonderful life: Mentally subtracting positive events improves people's affective states, contrary to their affective forecasts. *Journal of Personality and Social Psychology*, *95*(5), 1217–1224. https://doi.org/10.1037/a0013316

35. For the Record. (2020, April 14). *Spotify listeners are getting nostalgic: Behavior science writer David DiSalvo and Cyndi Lauper share why.* Spotify. https://newsroom.spotify.com/2020-04-14/spotify-listeners-are-getting-nostalgic-behavioral-science-writer-david-disalvo-and-cyndi-lauper-share-why/; Keveney, B. (2021, March 19). Exclusive: Nielson finds nostalgia fuels interest in classic TV comedies during pandemic. *USA Today*. https://www.usatoday.com/story/entertainment/tv/2021/03/19/nielsen-finds-covid-19-tv-viewing-spikes-classic-sitcoms/4754533001/

36. Dai, Y., Jiang, T., Wildschut, T., & Sedikides, C. (2023). Nostalgia counteracts social anxiety and enhances interpersonal competence. *Social Psychological and Personality Science*, *15*(5). https://doi.org/10.1177/19485506231187680; Wildschut, T., & Sedikides, C. (2023). Water from the lake of memory: The regulatory model of nostalgia. *Current Directions in Psychological Science*, *32*(1), 57–64. https://doi.org/10.1177/09637214221121768

37. Dai Y., et al., (2023). Nostalgia counteracts social anxiety; Stephan, E., Wildschut, T., Sedikides, C., Zhou, X., He, W., Routledge, C., Cheung, W. Y., & Vingerhoets, A. J. (2014). The mnemonic mover: Nostalgia regulates avoidance and approach motivation. *Emotion*, *14*(3), 545–561. https://doi.org/10.1037/a0035673; Wildschut, T., Sedikides, C., Routledge, C., Arndt, J., & Cordaro, F. (2010). Nostalgia as a repository of social connectedness: The role of attachment-related avoidance. *Journal of Personality and Social Psychology*, *98*(4), 573–586. https://doi.org/10.1037/a0017597; Zhou, X., Sedikides, C., Wildschut, T., & Gao, D. G. (2008). Counteracting loneliness: On the restorative function of nostalgia. *Psychological Science*, *19*(10), 1023–1029. https://doi.org/10.1111/j.1467-9280.2008.02194.x

38. Sedikides, C., Leunissen, J., & Wildschut, T. (2022). The psychological benefits of music-evoked nostalgia. *Psychology of Music*, *50*(6), 2044–2062. https://doi.org/10.1177/03057356211064641; Wildschut, T., Sedikides, C., Arndt, J., & Routledge, C. (2006). Nostalgia: Content, triggers, functions. *Journal of Personality and Social Psychology*, *91*(5), 975–993. https://doi.org/10.1037/0022-3514.91.5.975

39. Newman, D. B., & Sachs, M. E. (2020). The negative interactive effects of nostalgia and loneliness on affect in daily life. *Frontiers in Psychology*, *11*, 2185. https://doi.org/10.3389/fpsyg.2020.02185

40. Fredrickson, B. L. (2001). The role of positive emotions in positive psychology: The broaden-and-build theory of positive emotions. *American Psychologist*, *56*(3), 218–226. https://doi.org/10.1037//0003-066x.56.3.218; Weinstein, N., Przybylski, A. K., & Ryan, R. M. (2009). Can nature make us more caring? Effects of immersion in nature on intrinsic aspirations and generosity. *Personality and Social Psychology Bulletin*, *35*(10), 1315–1329.

https://doi.org/10.1177/0146167209341649; Zhang, J. W., Piff, P. K., Iyer, R., Koleva, S., & Keltner, D. (2014). An occasion for unselfing: Beautiful nature leads to prosociality. *Journal of Environmental Psychology, 37*, 61–72. https://doi.org/10.1016/j.jenvp.2013.11.008

41. Passmore, H., & Holder, M. D., (2017). Noticing nature: Individual and social benefits of a two-week intervention. *The Journal of Positive Psychology, 12*(6), 537–546. https://doi.org/10.1080/17439760.2016.1221126

42. Bratman, G. N., Hamilton, J. P., Hahn, K. S., & Gross, J. J. (2015). Nature experience reduced rumination and subgenual prefrontal cortex activation. *Proceedings of the National Academy of Sciences of the United States of America, 112*(28), 8567–8572. https://doi.org/10.1073/pnas.1510459112

43. Piff, P. K., Dietze, P., Feinberg, M., Stancato, D. M., & Keltner, D. (2015). Awe, the small self, and prosocial behavior. *Journal of Personality and Social Psychology, 108*(6), 883–899. https://doi.org/10.1037/pspi0000018

44. Keltner, D., & Haidt, J. (2003). Approaching awe, a moral, spiritual, and aesthetic emotion. *Cognition & Emotion, 17*(2), 297–314. https://doi.org/10.1080/02699930302297

45. Perlin, J. D., & Li, L. (2020). Why does awe have prosocial effects? New perspectives on awe and the small self. *Perspectives on Psychological Science, 15*(2), 291–308. https://doi.org/10.1177/1745691619886006; Piff, P. K., et al. (2015). Awe, the small self, and prosocial behavior.

46. Goldy, S. P., Jones, N. M., & Piff, P. K. (2022). The social effects of an awesome solar eclipse. *Psychological Science, 33*(9), 1452–1462. https://doi.org/10.1177/09567976221085501

47. Yaden, D. B., Iwry, J., Slack, K. J., Eichstaedt, J. C., Zhao, Y., Vaillant, G. E., & Newberg, A. B. (2016). The overview effect: Awe and self-transcendent experience in space flight. *Psychology of Consciousness: Theory, Research, and Practice, 3*(1), 1–11. https://doi.org/10.1037/cns0000086

48. Keltner, D. (2023). *Awe: The new science of everyday wonder and how it can transform your life.* Penguin Press.

49. https://www.youtube.com/watch?v=H9mHJmDZRFU;   https://www.youtube.com/watch?v=T_ox4bfPhlo; https://www.youtube.com/watch?v=RzQ4Eafd-xE&t=1s

50. Gabriel, S., Naidu, E., Paravati, E., Morrison, C. D., & Gainey, K. (2020). Creating the sacred from the profane: Collective effervescence and everyday activities. *Journal of Positive Psychology, 15*(1), 129–154. https://doi.org/10.1080/17439760.2019.1689412

51. https://science.nasa.gov/mission/hubble/science/universe-uncovered/hubble-galaxies/

52. Diebels, K. J., & Leary, M. R. (2019). The psychological implications of believing that everything is one. *Journal of Positive Psychology, 14*(4), 463–473. https://doi.org/10.1080/17439760.2018.1484939

53. Seppälä, E. M., Bradley, C., Moeller, J., Harouni, L., Nandamudi, D., & Brackett, M. A. (2020). Promoting mental health and psychological thriving in university students: A randomized controlled trial of three well-being interventions. *Frontiers in Psychiatry, 11*, 590. https://doi.org/10.3389/fpsyt.2020.00590; Balban, M. Y., Neri, E., Kogon, M. M., Weed, L., Nouriani, B., Jo, B., Holl, G., Zeitzer, J. M., Spiegel, D., & Huberman, A. D. (2023). Brief structured respiration practices enhance mood and reduce physiological arousal. *Cell Reports: Medicine, 4*(1), 100895. https://doi.org/10.1016/j.xcrm.2022.100895

54. https://www.youtube.com/watch?v=ZEl3FAaSrX4

Index